P9-CCQ-032

Please remember that this is a library book,
and that it belongs only temporarily to each
person who uses it. Be considerate. Do
not write in this, or any, library book.

Creative Teaching
of Art
in the
Elementary School

JOHN E. RITSON
JAMES A. SMITH
State University College
Oswego, New York

Allyn and Bacon, Inc.
Boston, London, and Sydney

To Sadie and Dot

Library of Congress Cataloging in Publication Data

Ritson, John E   1919–
    Creative teaching of art in the elementary school.

    Includes bibliographies and index.
    1. Art—Study and teaching (Elementary)—United States. I. Smith, James A., joint author. II. Title
N362.R57   372.5'044   74-23192

ISBN 0-205-04678-9 (paperbound)
ISBN 0-205-04677-0 (hardbound)

CONTENTS

PART ONE: THE FOUR NATURES
OF ART IN THE ELEMENTARY SCHOOL

PART TWO: THE NURTURE AND USE
OF ART IN THE ELEMENTARY SCHOOL

CHAPTER V: Setting Conditions for Teaching Art
in the Elementary School   155

CHAPTER VI: Teaching Art for Art's Sake   182

FOREWORD

In the Foreword of the first editions of the Creative Teaching Series, E. Paul Torrance expressed concern that the fate of the creative movement would be the same as that of many other exciting, meaningful, and potentially important ideas that died because no one translated them into practical methods. Fortunately, this has not been the case. In the past ten years educational literature has been flooded with reports of research studies, theories, and experimental programs that focus on the creative development of each child as a goal of modern education.

Including the developing of creativity in each child as an educational objective is a staggering challenge for all school personnel. It calls for the invention of new materials and tools, the development of new time schedules and new patterns of organization, a new approach to child study, the invention of new testing methods and new instructional materials, the devising of unique evaluation processes, and the creation of new textbooks and teaching procedures. And, most of all, the task calls for a commitment and dedication on the part of many people who must take risks, make choices and decisions, and push their own creative potential to new limits.

This has been done! In the past ten years the creative spark has caught fire. Thousands of people in all walks of life have found in the creative movement self-realization and a challenge to make life meaningful for others. The educational scene in America has become peppered with experimental projects in the development of creative thinking.

No movement in education has swept the world as the creative movement has. The need for creative people across the globe today is tremendous. Developing the creative potential of each child has become an educational objective even in the far corners of the world. The authors of the Creative Teaching

Series hope these volumes will contribute in some bold measure to the changes that must be made in teaching methods in the elementary school in order to realize this objective.

John E. Ritson
James A. Smith
Oswego, New York

PREFACE

There is a myth currently afoot regarding the teaching of art in the elementary schools of America. It centers around the belief that our public schools are staffed with art teachers and support art programs to the extent that every child is receiving a knowledge of art, a background in art appreciation, and a body of experiences in art skills.

This myth has evolved from the fact that art teaching, which was once handled almost entirely by the regular classroom teacher, has been subjected to a historical evolution which has caused it to wander from its original goals and purposes.

In the beginning, young teachers were trained to some extent to integrate and correlate art experiences into the regular school program, and courses in art methodology were required, just as methods courses in all subject areas were required. Art educators and elementary school teachers soon came to feel that the background training of the average teacher did not prepare him adequately to handle the art program in the classroom and pushed for the type of program that would provide an art expert in each school. Schools of art and education began to train art teachers for the elementary schools.

Subsequently, many teachers colleges throughout the land abolished such courses as "Art for the Elementary School Teacher" and "Art for the Young Child." They felt that in hiring an art teacher, each school had made available on its premises an art expert equipped to offer advice and to teach skills in art and art appreciation to the children and the teachers within the school.

At first the plan worked well. Art teachers served as consultants to classroom teachers who still correlated art activities into the classroom program. However, as time passed, history made demands on the public schools. World War II made vast cuts in the number of well-trained art teachers as teachers answered draft calls or were lured away from teaching by higher salaries in industry. The subsequent population explosion flooded the schools with children and the number of art teachers did not increase correspondingly. Classroom teachers, trained under new intensified programs, received less and less background in art and almost no background in art education. More and more responsibility was placed on the art teacher. He was given more classes to visit, heavier and more demanding programs to fulfill, tight, almost impossible schedules to meet, fewer and inadequate supplies and equipment with which to work, and more teachers to contact, although he had less time to do it.

Inevitably, the results have been tragic. The teaching of art has been placed more and more into the hands of the art teacher. In many instances, this has come from pressure on the part of the art teacher himself, who has come to feel that the regular teacher is not trained sufficiently to handle an adequate art program. In other instances, the pressure has come from the classroom teacher, who admits to feeling inadequately trained and is perfectly willing to release all responsibility for art to an art teacher. Still other pressures have stemmed from administrators who see art as a frill and set up schedules where the regular classroom teacher is committed to other obligations (such as cafeteria duty) or is allowed a coffee break when the art teacher is in her classroom. Thus art is severed completely from the total school life experience of the child and does become a frill once or twice a week.

In some places, schedules for art teachers who must travel from school to school have become so demanding that art instruction per se has been withdrawn from the classroom (either the primary grades or the intermediate grades depending on the whims of the administrators and teachers) and the classroom teachers have been left to shift for themselves. This situation could be a good one except that classroom teachers, it must be remembered, are receiving less and less training in art, yet are expected to take more and more responsibility for teaching it.

Thus the original plan for art teaching in the elementary schools of America has been aborted. The reality of the early plans has not been realized; only a myth remains.

After a recent study by the national art educators, a statement was made to the effect that only a small number of the nation's children are receiving art instruction and that only about ten percent of the nation's schools are manned by a skilled art teacher or have a planned art program (see p. 107).

Because of the recent emphasis on creativity and the need for its development in contemporary man, and because art is the most natural means by which man expresses that creativity, the authors have felt a pressing need to add this volume to the current series of books on creativity in order to fully explore the place of art in modern elementary education.

Their purpose is a simple one: they believe that art is not a frill. They believe that art forms a natural way of living and that it cannot be commissioned to any one person or any one period of time if it is to play an effective part in the life of the child. They believe that art is made up of a body of skills that, when experienced, change human behavior. They believe that creativity is naturally and normally developed in children through their art expression. They believe that the regular classroom teacher and the art teacher must work as a team to fulfill the objectives of an art program in a school and that art must be taught as part of all school experience rather than as an isolated "subject." Finally, they believe that activities can become meaningful only when the interdependence of creativity, art, and child growth is understood.

Simply stated, the main purpose of this book is to help in planning the art program of the elementary school so that art becomes a way of life in school and so that creativity is developed in children. The authors hope to clarify the concept of creativity, the objectives of art teaching in relation to creative development, and the normal needs of the child to express himself creatively (particularly through art products), and they hope to provide many practical and tried examples demonstrating creative development through the teaching and/or use of art.

They feel strongly that the elementary school teacher must take an active part in the art program of his classroom and that training colleges must strive to prepare the teacher better for his job. They believe that art can be taught effectively by those who lack fine art training, if they keep in mind the philosophy contained in this book.

This book is geared to five audiences: the practicing classroom teacher, the practicing art teacher, the classroom teacher in training, the art teacher in training, and the curriculum coordinator.

The authors feel qualified to utilize the above approach. One is an art educator who for many years has taught art to children in the elementary school, and then to college students in teacher education. The other has been an elementary education specialist. He has taught elementary school, has been an elementary school principal, and has taught college students in preparation to teach elementary school.

The problems that confront the administrator, the art teacher, and the classroom teacher are very much a part of the authors' background. Varying points of view, conflicts, and problems that school personnel face in planning an art program were also faced by the authors in compiling this volume. The discussions that led to the method of presentation of the materials gave each better insights into the problems confronted by the other in his unique role as classroom teacher, art teacher, or administrator. It is hoped that similar dialogues within the schools may help to establish a richer, more meaningful art program and will contribute to dissolving the myth of art teaching as it exists today.

In this volume, reference to the teacher is made in most instances in the feminine gender. Some readers may object to this. It was done because in the experiences related, a majority of the teachers observed were women. Consequently, use of "she" or "her" was easier because of the particular situation that the authors had in mind.

Special acknowledgments must be made to a few people without whose help this work would not have been realized. First the authors would like to thank the many teachers and children who supplied them with illustrations and allowed them to observe their classrooms. Some teachers were kind enough to allow them to teach in their classrooms. Many parents gave their permission for the use of the pictures in this book. The authors are personally grateful to Mrs. Wilma Baitsell, art teacher, Campus School, State University College at Oswego, New York; Mr. Joseph Pittarelli and his colleagues Mrs. Maureen Davison and Mrs. Kathleen Brown of Brewerton Elementary School; Mrs. Mary Dixon; Mrs. Holly Weller; Mrs. Kathy King; and all the boys and girls of the Palmer Central School in Baldwinsville for their invaluable material and assistance.

The authors extend a special thanks to their wives, who contributed encouragement and patience and who became the sounding boards against which they refined their ideas.

John E. Ritson
James A. Smith
Oswego, New York

PART 1

The Four Natures of Art
in the Elementary School

The joy of art alone.

CHAPTER I

The Nature of Creative Teaching

"Art is man's nature: nature is God's art."

PHILIP JAMES BAILEY[1]

As man crosses the threshold of the space age, he does so with the realization that he can no longer dip into his past experiences to seek the answers to his problems. Never before in his history has he been forced to live with nuclear power; never before has he been *forced* to get along with his neighbor regardless of color or creed; never before has he been obliged to live with the pollution he has created. Cures are needed for diseases that did not formerly exist, substitutes are needed for dwindling resources, and solutions are needed for problems concerning housing, education, traffic, and urban renewal that are unique to his world.

The answers to these problems do not lie in the history of books; they lie in the creative mind of man. The need for creative thinking and living has grown in proportion to the growth of the problems that twentieth-century man faces. There is competition in our times for the creative mind of man.

The development of the creative aspects of human growth has been neglected in the American schools. This is probably due to the fact that, until recently, little was known about creativity and how to develop it.

In this chapter, the authors lay a foundation for the

1. Philip James Bailey, in *Festus*.

philosophy of this book by exploring the studies of creativity conducted in the last ten years and by relating these studies to teaching.   It is our contention that all human beings are born with the power to create and that this power can become a dynamic force in the behavior of youngsters when it is released through creative teaching.   We believe that art is the most natural form of creative expression in children and that the development of the child's total creativity is essential to the realization of his creative expression in art.

WHAT IS CREATIVITY?

Creativity, in this volume, is defined as the ability to tap past experiences and come up with something new.   This product need not be new to the world, but it must be new to the individual.   The most creative acts are those that result in something new to the world.

We begin our explorations of this theme by looking in on a creative teacher in a middle-school classroom.

"Miss Larkin, how can we make a lot of programs for our play?" asked Gerry.   "Do we have to paint a separate cover for each one?"

"Good question," said Miss Larkin.   "Let's gather around and discuss this—maybe we can come up with something."

The children brought their chairs to the discussion circle. They planned to present an original puppet play entitled *Fractured Fairy Tales* to the other children in the fourth, fifth, and sixth grades and to their parents.   They wanted to be able to give a program to each person who came to the performance, which meant they would need two hundred programs.   Miss Larkin asked Gerry to restate the problem, which he did.

"The time has come," said Miss Larkin, "to learn something about printing and prints.   Now, can anyone tell me the difference between a painting and a print, or between painting and printing?"

After some deep thinking, Marcia said, "I think a painting is made when you put paint on a surface directly, but a print is made when you put paint on something else and then press it onto a surface."

"Very good," said Miss Larkin.   "I'd like to add another idea.   It doesn't have to be paint, does it?   Couldn't it be ink or dye or some other pigment?"

The children agreed that it could. "Now, let's see if you know any ways to print, or if you know about any special kinds of printing," said Miss Larkin.

"We went to the newspaper office last year," Bill volunteered, "and saw a newspaper printed."

"That's one kind of printing, isn't it?" said Miss Larkin. "In this case the ink is applied to type set on metal rollers, and then they are pushed against the paper. Any more ideas?"

"Books," said Georgiana.

"Yes, same principle," said Miss Larkin.

"I know how to make a block print," said Beth.

"Good," said Miss Larkin. "You can teach the rest of us how. Let's examine all the ways of printing that we can think of and then we'll select one or two ways to make our programs. I think we can see that there are advantages to printing rather than painting two hundred programs separately, right? All right then, let's brainstorm all the ways we can think of to apply a design to paper by putting ink, dye, or paint to the design first. Let's see how many ideas we can get in five minutes."

The resulting list included:

Glue string to a piece of heavy cardboard.
Cut a design in a potato or turnip.
Make a block print.
Cut a design in corrugated cardboard.
Use vegetables (or fruits) to make designs.
Crush tin foil.
Use corrugated cardboard glued to wood.
Glue innertubing or sponge rubber to a block of wood.
Press paper on fingerpaints.
Press designs into styrofoam with a pencil and then print the
    high part.
Use natural designs on the bottom of pill boxes, fruit baskets, etc.
Use leaves, pine needles, or sticks.
Cut designs in dowels.
Make sponge designs.
Use utensils like potato mashers.
Glue felt designs onto wood.

After much discussion, the children decided to divide the class into three groups and to make three different programs. Each group was to print seventy programs.

The three techniques chosen were block printing (which Beth demonstrated), string painting, and styrofoam printing, for which they used meat trays from the supermarket. Some of the results are shown in Fig. 1–1.

FIGURE 1–1. Experimentation with printmaking resulted in a wall full of prints.

This situation is an example of creative teaching. On the following pages we will see why.

BASIC PRINCIPLES OF CREATIVITY

Research in the area of creativity over the past decade has been extensive. It has guided the authors in compiling a set of principles which were fully developed in another book in this series, *Setting Conditions for Creative Teaching in the Elementary School.*[2] The following review of this list forms a foundation for the present volume.

1. *All children are born with creative talent.* Creativity is not a special talent doled out to a chosen few. It is present in every individual, although it varies in degree. Its development depends largely on both environment and intelligence.

2. *There is a relationship between creativity and intelli-*

2. James A. Smith, *Setting Conditions for Creative Teaching in the Elementary School* (Boston: Allyn and Bacon, Inc., 1966).

gence. Highly intelligent people are not always creative. Although creativity is a form of giftedness inherent to some degree in each individual, intelligence determines the quality of the creative product. Even slow-learning children are creative, however.

3. *Creativity is a form of giftedness that is not measured by current intelligence tests.* J. P. Guilford explains that our creative powers are developed through the exercise of our divergent thinking abilities and that this component of the intellect has been grossly neglected in our elementary schools.[3] Almost all teaching has been designed to develop the convergent thinking processes. Convergent thinking processes are those in which the child comes up with one correct answer, whereas in divergent thinking processes many answers are possible, and the uniqueness of one's answer may be the important factor in solving a problem. All intelligence tests up to this time measure only convergent thinking processes and therefore do not measure creativity.

Our current definition of intelligence (as set by intelligence tests) excludes a wide range of the thinking abilities that are known to mankind and that are necessary for his survival. Among these is the whole area of creative thinking. Skills needed for divergent thinking include many that are not, as such, "taught" in the elementary school: the ability to see relationships, to imagine, to question, to make decisions, to pass judgment, to find form and order, to think intuitively, to rethink and restructure, and to develop perceptions—in short, to think divergently.

4. *All areas of the curriculum can be used to develop creativity.* The development of creativity is not limited to a program in the creative arts. Creativity, as this series of books shows, can be developed through all areas of the curriculum. It is not something to be added to the heavy schedules of teachers, or something that should be taught during a given period once or twice a week; it is a quality, a characteristic, and a *way* of learning. Research has shown that the results of creative learning are superior to those of more traditional methods both in quantity and quality, and that creative learning calls for creative teaching.

Inasmuch as the elementary school teacher is concerned with the development of creativity in children, and inasmuch as creative thinking can be developed through all areas of the

3. J. P. Guilford, "Three Faces of Intellect," *American Psychologist,* 14 (1959), 469–479.

curriculum, she should be guided in her selection of art experiences by two basic criteria: (1) Will the experience develop the child's overall creative powers? and (2) Will it contribute specifically in some unique manner to developing his art appreciation and/or art ability?

5. *Creativity is a process and a product.* Although research has not been conclusive in this area, the following steps have been identified as those that human beings include in the creative process:

a. *Period of preparation:* the creator becomes involved with and identifies with the problem at hand.
b. *Period of incubation:* the creator lives with and is even tormented by the problem.
c. *Period of insight:* all parts of the problem seem to become clear.
d. *Period of illumination or inspiration:* ideas or answers seem to come (this may also be classified as a moment of discovery).
e. *Period of verification, elaboration, perfection, and evaluation:* the product is tested for its worth and tension is relieved.[4]

More recent studies of creative processes stress creativity as a thinking ability. It is also considered as attitude development.

6. *All creative processes cannot be developed at one time or in one lesson.* The total personality of the creative person is made up of many characteristics, skills, and qualities, each of which can be developed when teaching is directed toward it. Just as all skills in reading cannot be developed in one lesson, all the components of creativity cannot be developed at once. Each must be a separate target for instruction, contributing to the development of those qualities, skills, and characteristics that make the creative individual. Therefore, the development of creativity, affected by the environment in which it is taking place, requires a long period of time.

7. *Creativity cannot be taught.* Although some of the components of the creative character (such as visual acuity, evaluation skills, and comprehension skills) can be taught, total creativity, as such, is not taught. We can only set conditions for it and insure its reappearance through reinforcement. Chapter 5 deals with the conditions necessary to develop creativity in the teaching of the creative arts.

4. Mary Lee Marksberry, *Foundation of Creativity* (New York: Harper & Row, Publishers, 1963).

8. *Knowledge, skills, and facts are required in order for a person to be creative.* The more the individual has to work with and the more knowledge, skills, and facts he has to tap, the greater is his potential for creative production.

9. *Theories of creative development lead us to believe that the unconscious plays a role in creative development.* Children must be free to consider all of life's experiences in order to become truly creative. Unnecessary rules and actions may force many experiences into the subconscious, where they are not available to the child. He is afraid of losing social status if he taps this resource for the purpose of creating.

If a child has difficulty in drawing, for instance, it means he has not had or does not remember having had a highly personal reaction to the object he is trying to draw and its environment. It is better to help him recall or enter again into his past experience with the object, or to give him a new experience with the object, than it is to give him stereotyped patterns to copy.

10. *Excessive conformity and rigidity are true enemies of creativity.* Conformity is necessary to maintain a society, but conformity is the greatest known killer of creative development.

11. *Children go through definite steps in the creative process.* These steps were outlined above in item 5.

12. *Children who have lost much of their creativity can be helped to regain it by special methods of teaching.* This, of course, means the employment of methods of creative teaching in the classroom. These methods are derived from a set of basic principles culled from research on creativity.

WHAT IS CREATIVE TEACHING?

Creativity cannot be taught. We can only set conditions for it to happen. Because it is a quality deeply imbedded in the human personality, it can be developed by reinforcement when it does appear, but the main function of the creative teacher is to maintain within her classroom the physical, psychological, social-emotional, and intellectual conditions that allow creativity to rise freely to the surface, where she can reach it to develop it. Thus the conditions set for developing creativity become very important in the regular classroom. Under proper conditions, every child may come to possess it.

FIGURE 1–2.   A creative project: a puppet show entitled Fractured Fairy Tales.

BASIC PRINCIPLES OF CREATIVE TEACHING

The following is a discussion of the basic principles of creative teaching as they were developed in *Setting Conditions for Creative Teaching in the Elementary School.*[5]

1. *Something new, different, or unique results from creative teaching.* In the creative teaching of art, every piece of sculpture, every painting, and every print must be different from all others. Because children tap their own experiences, and because these experiences are each different in perception and form, every interpretation is unique. No two people can *create* the same thing.

Miss Larkin and her students created a puppet show that was unique and different from all others. The script was original, the children designed and made the puppet stage from a discarded television box, a group of girls tie-dyed the curtains,

5. Smith, *op. cit.*

10

various groups painted scenery using such media as tempera paint, polymer and tissue, construction paper, spray paint and sponges, and colored lights to produce various effects. The session on programs alone resulted in three creative group projects. Many of Miss Larkin's objectives were met in the puppet project. Some of her general objectives read as follows.

As a result of this experience, the children will:

a. Explore and use new media, as evidenced by their application of these media to the final puppet show.
b. Learn many facts about art to be used in divergent thinking situations, as evidenced by their discussions and brainstorming sessions.
c. Learn new skills and techniques, as evidenced by their work in the final project.
d. Develop the technique of brainstorming, as evidenced in the brainstorming sessions.
e. Have "discovery" experiences with line, form, texture, color, shapes, and values, as evidenced by individual and group artwork during the project.

Under these general objectives, Miss Larkin spelled out her specific objectives and the behavior changes she hoped to effect. The new media explored under objective 1 included colored lights, printing ink, papier mâché, polymer and tissue, and enamel paint. Facts that she hoped the children would "discover" under her guidance or within the environment she had planned included: (1) paint is pigment applied to a surface with a tool; (2) linear movement is the base for all drawings; and (3) tints are made by adding various amounts of white to a basic color. New skills and techniques Miss Larkin hoped to develop included various forms of printing, spray painting, painting with sponges, block-print carving, clay modeling, and tie-dyeing. Brainstorming was taught in one brief session and used a great deal throughout the unit. For objective 5 she planned a series of art lessons in which the children experimented with some specific art problems. One was a lesson in perspective. The children wanted to paint one scene of the puppet show in the woods but had difficulty in getting the look of depth they needed. Because this was one of the experiences Miss Larkin had planned on developing, she seized this opportunity to capitalize on the children's interest. One thing she had the children do was to paint a row of trees on a large rectangle of foam rubber. Then the children pulled the foam rubber away from them and observed what happened to the painting of the trees. They were fatter, but smaller. Through discussion, the children discovered some valuable concepts about traditional perspective. The lesson did not end at that point, however. The children became so interested in the effect of the designs made by twisting and stretching the foam rubber (Fig. 1–3) that every child experimented with it.

The entire puppet show project was riddled with new group experiences; it was also valuable to many individuals as an art experience, for it provided the stimulation and sensory (especially visual) motivation some students needed to produce real art products. On the days immediately following the experimentation with painting on foam rubber, for instance, every child painted new and exciting designs on art paper that were inspired by the designs that appeared on the stretched foam rubber.

2. *In creative teaching, divergent thinking processes are stressed.* Divergent thinking processes do not produce an absolute or correct answer. In divergent thinking, knowledge, facts, concepts, understandings, and skills gained through convergent thinking are put to new uses that result in new answers rather

FIGURE 1–3.   *Designs are created by painting on foam rubber and stretching it.*

than in one correct answer. Divergent thinking processes develop such qualities as flexibility, fluency, spontaneity, and originality. These are the bases of creative thinking.

In teaching art, the teacher is provided with innumerable opportunities to develop the divergent functions of the intellect. Learning how to mix a powder paint is both an exercise in the memorization of facts and an illustration of convergent thinking processes. The actual free-form painting made with the paint is an example of the divergent thinking process. All paintings are unique; all are acceptable.

In Miss Larkin's classroom the children listed all the ways they had ever seen to create puppets. This was convergent thinking used to solve a problem: How can we make puppets? Then Miss Larkin posed an open-ended question: "Think of the actions your particular puppet character must make. Then consider other ways you can construct your puppet so it can easily carry out the actions you feel it must perform." Each child chose a technique from the resulting list. This is convergent thinking put to divergent use.

3. *Motivational tensions are a prerequisite to creative teaching; the creative process serves as a tension-relieving agent.* When a child engages in an art activity he is trying to solve a problem. He is trying to transform an idea, an image, or a feeling into some material. He is engaged in a tension-filled, intellectual process made up of many intellectual components.

Motivation of some sort is essential to all learning; this is particularly true of creative learning. Rugg implies that the motivation for creating can best be described as a "passion for learning."[6] A problem confronting a creative person appears to plague him and, at times, even to torment him—the drive to use the right word in the right place, the right color in the right place, the right note in the right place. Although a great deal of creative motivation is intrinsic, introductory lessons for children (especially children who are not highly creative or easily motivated) must be planned with great care to set the mood and fire the imagination.

Miss Hill felt her class was very conventional in their approach to using color. She had suggested many ways the children might experiment with color rather than using the conventional tempera paint jars in the room, but without much success.

6. Harold Rugg, *Imagination: An Inquiry into the Sources and Conditions That Stimulate Creativity* (New York: Harper & Row, Publishers, 1965).

One day Miss Hill planned a lesson around a new use of color, hoping to motivate the children and to teach some specific facts as well.

She played recordings of a variety of rhythms, including a march, a waltz, a foxtrot, and a tango, and encouraged the children to interpret these rhythms on the walls of the classroom. A box of varicolored cellophane squares was placed before the children. By covering flashlights with the various pieces of cellophane, they created exotic light patterns on the walls (Fig. 1–4). Soon groups of children were experimenting with creating designs and exploring ideas, such as what happens when a yellow and blue light are blended. This led to other group experiments with light and music. Some children were looking through music books; others were using flashlights to experiment with different colors. Transferral of many of their learnings to paper was a simple step Miss Hill took when she asked, "I wonder if we can tell any of these stories or gain any of these effects by using colors on paper as we have on the walls?"

Other lessons in linear movement followed, and collections of pictures showing linear movement appeared on the bulletin board: a time exposure film of automobile lights, a

FIGURE 1–4. An experience with color: colored lights tell a story.

skywriter in a dome of blue, a railroad track taken from an airplane, etc.[7]

When children are led to discover learnings in challenging, exciting experiences, their motivation runs high.

4. *In creative teaching, open-ended situations are utilized.* Open-endedness in teaching means presenting children with situations where they put their knowledge, understandings, and skills to work. The one great difference between lessons that develop convergent thinking processes and those that develop divergent thinking processes is that in the former the lesson ends when knowledge is gained, whereas in the latter a situation is provided in which newly acquired knowledge is put to work to solve a problem. The acquisition of knowledge *begins* the divergent thought process.

This principle is demonstrated several times in the puppet show project in Miss Larkin's class. The brainstorming session conducted by Miss Larkin to list kinds of prints and ways prints could be made was open-ended. "Open-ended" means that several answers are acceptable and worthy of trial rather than one particular answer. Miss Hill's lesson with the colored lights was open-ended: first, there were many possible interpretations of the rhythms, and secondly, the designs inspired by the moving flashlight spots were all different because the directions set minimal boundaries on experimentation and discovery.

5. *In creative teaching, there comes a time when the teacher withdraws and the children face the unknown themselves.* At that moment, the teacher and the children change roles. The teacher, in building high motivational tensions, is the planner, the guide, and the producer. At one point in the lesson she withdraws from this role and the children, spurred on by the tensions she has created, become the planners, the guides, and the producers. Each leads himself to the fulfillment of the creative act. It is an essential part of the creative act that each individual solve the problem in his own way, arriving at his own unique solution or product.

This moment of role reversal was demonstrated clearly by Miss Hill. At first Miss Hill talked, guided, used materials, presented facts, provided experiences, made decisions, passed judgments, and manipulated the environment. Then, at a certain point in her lesson, she stopped talking and became a helper and listener. The children did the talking. They used the

7. Dorothy Hickock and James A. Smith, *The Creative Teaching of Music* (Boston: Allyn and Bacon, Inc., 1974), pp. 79–86.

materials, shared known facts, created experiences, made decisions, passed judgments, and manipulated their environment. In so doing, they developed many of the characteristics unique to creative children.

6. *In creative teaching, the outcomes are unpredictable.* Another unique quality of the creative teaching process is that the teacher cannot know exactly what the product will be. The process of teaching an arithmetic lesson may be very creative, but the teacher knows at the onset of the lesson that the children (with the possible exception of a few slow ones) will learn the correct answers and how to obtain them by the end of the lesson. The teacher who is teaching for creative production cannot know what the products will be. She must possess the power to motivate children to produce and the faith that their creative products will be worthy of the time spent.

"We are going to make program covers," said Gerry. At that point Miss Larkin had no idea *how* the covers would be made or *what* they would look like. "Create a *light* story," Miss Hill's assignment card said, and at that point no one knew *what* the story would be or *how* it would be presented. If the product can be predicted before the process has begun, the chances are great that it will not be creative.

Because creative products are unpredictable, many problems arise when teachers try to write objectives in behavioral terms. There are many educators who believe that objectives for creative development cannot realistically be written as behavioral objectives.

7. *In creative teaching, conditions must be set that make possible preconscious thinking.* Children must be constantly encouraged to draw from their experiences. Ideas should not be considered silly or impossible; each one should be evaluated. Conformity to preconceived rules must be discouraged. If a child decides he would like to try to fingerpaint with his knuckles or the palm of his hand, he should be encouraged to do so even if a previous teacher has told him to use only his fingers. The rigid, conforming rules under which children often labor for status or approval need to be relaxed.

The artist learns to draw heavily on his reserve of images and feelings. With him, art is a way of life. All his experiences are stored in his subconscious or conscious mind, and he must be able to tap them for use in his creative work. His ability to perceive, to make transferences, to make analogies, to reorder, and to restructure depends on his ability to utilize *all* his experiences.

Children often come to school heavily prejudiced against certain social acts and unable to discuss many problems or experiences they have had because of stigmas they have already learned. The inability to draw on all resources of the mind limits the creator. The ability to face all experiences, "good" and "bad," not only makes a person healthy mentally, but it enhances his chances for creative development. Although teachers need not violate the trust placed in them by parents in discussing certain topics in school, they can help children search their subconscious by relieving children of guilt feelings they may have in discussing certain topics, such as sex, love, and violence. Preconscious thinking is that which results when hidden feelings, experiences, and ideas are pulled from the subconscious and put to use in the conscious mind. A question like "How did you feel when you hit your sister?" or a statement like "Paint the way you felt when you hit your sister" helps a child explore new ways of communication and releases many of his guilt feelings and his tensions. Often the products of such assignments are very creative.

8. *In creative teaching, students are encouraged to generate and develop their own ideas.* Research in identifying the creative personality indicates that creative children are often treated along punitive lines by their teachers; they are considered to have silly and senseless ideas. Yet many of the world's greatest inventions and discoveries have come from such silly ideas. Unusual and even silly ideas are the threshold of creative discovery and must be encouraged if creativity is to be developed.

Miss Larkin stimulated the children to explore their own ideas in the brainstorming sessions described in this chapter. Miss Hill encouraged the children to show ways of making rhythms, then she asked each child to interpret the music with his flashlight, choosing his own color and doing it in his own way. Each of the group assignments that followed was a logical sequel to the lesson the children had had together, yet each placed the children in a situation where they were motivated to use their own ideas.

No art expression is possible unless a child is able to identify with himself, with the experience he is about to express, and with the material or medium he is about to use in his expression. Creative expression is a true expression of the self.

Self-expression is simply the process by which an individual uses his emotions, thoughts, feelings, experiences, and skills at a given point in his development to communicate in constructive forms. The mode of expression is the art form.

9. *In creative teaching, the process is as important as the*

FIGURE 1–5.   *The process of creating is as important as the product.*

product. The process of creative production as defined at the beginning of this chapter occurs more frequently among children when practice is afforded them in creative thinking.   In some instances creativity is fostered more readily by the process than by the product, as would be the case in the creative teaching of arithmetic.

The processes employed by Miss Larkin and Miss Hill are obviously as important to the children's creative development as the products they create.   In planning for creative production, strategies should be employed that put children in open-ended situations where their thoughts are challenged, where an incubation period is allowed, and where insight is respected.

10. *In creative teaching, certain conditions must be set to permit creativity to appear.* The unique conditions necessary to develop creative production in the creative arts will be developed in Chapter 5.   However, there are some general conditions necessary for all creative production.   Most obvious among these are certain *physical conditions.*   The classroom must be a learning laboratory where readily available material is arranged so that the task at hand can be accomplished.

Certain *psychological* conditions are also necessary. Good rapport must exist between the teacher and the children and among the children themselves; they must be comfortable with and accept each other. An "air of expectancy" must pervade; children must feel that they are expected to create. The atmosphere must be permissive to the degree that children feel comfortable experimenting, manipulating, and exploring. They must feel free to make mistakes. A great deal of uncertainty is present when children face the unknown in the creative act, and they will be more secure if their creative behavior is rooted in the psychological securities mentioned above.

Certain *intellectual* conditions must also prevail if creative development is to take place. Children must be motivated to think; their imagination must be teased by problems posed to keep them thinking most of the time. A great many facts and skills must be available to each child; some of them will be taught by convergent thinking processes and put to divergent uses. The more knowledge, skills, and facts a child has, the more there is available for his use when he taps his experiences in order to create.

Sound *social* and *emotional* conditions must prevail among the children. Children who are emotionally upset often find outlets for their pent-up emotions in creative products if the proper social climate, one of acceptance and understanding, exists. Under such circumstances, creative energy is dispelled in creative, constructive acts rather than uncreative, destructive acts.

Jerome Hausman says:

> A key factor in the teaching of art, at any level, involves creating conditions in which students can learn the joy and excitement in the search for and discovery of visual ideas, in the investment of their own ideas and feelings toward realizing new forms. Necessarily such teaching would have to help students to court mystery, deal with ambiguity, and on occasion suffer the pain and disappointment of failure.[8]

11. *Creative teaching is oriented toward success rather than failure.* Disapproval, sarcasm, and other forms of verbal punishment are often interpreted by the child as failure. Nega-

8. Jerome J. Hausman, "Teacher as Artist and Artist as Teacher," in George Pappas, ed., *Concepts in Art and Education* (New York: Macmillan Publishing Co., Inc., 1970), pp. 333–340.

tive criticism is dangerous unless a creative relationship has been established between the teacher and the student.   Once this rapport has been established, constructive criticism and disapproval may be useful.

Even at the onset of the creative act, excessive evaluation may be construed by children as disapproval and thus may check their flow of creative ideas.   The work of many researchers recommends that evaluation and criticism of ideas be postponed until all ideas are out.   This is called "the principle of deferred judgment."

The creative child must be willing to make mistakes, but he needs to develop skills for finding out when he makes a mistake and how to correct it.   A set of criteria should be worked out with the child for evaluating ideas so the child understands that criticism, disapproval, or rejection of his ideas is due to the fact that they are not the best; it is not because they are unworthy of consideration.   The ability of the teacher to turn failures into successes keeps her teaching success-oriented, because failures are utilized as a base for a more appropriate solution to the problem.

12. *In creative teaching, self-initiated learning is encouraged.*   The release of tension and the aesthetic satisfaction that come with the creation of a new product or with the working through of a problem make the creative process cyclic.   Release and satisfaction become a part of the high motivation required for successive creative acts.   Children become truly creative when they constantly occupy themselves with self-imposed problems, producing poems, paintings, dances, songs, and other creative products without the continual motivation of the teacher.

The brainstorming session in Miss Larkin's room exposed the children to many ideas for making prints.   Only three of the ideas were put to use in making programs for the puppet show, but many of the children, who had had their curiosity aroused, proceeded in their free time to try making fruit prints, string prints, and other prints suggested on the list.   They came to school with materials to try out their ideas.   Creative children are rarely bored or unoccupied.   By developing self-initiating learning skills in the children, the teacher is helping them become more creative.

13. *In creative teaching, provision is made to learn many concepts and skills, but provision is also made to apply these concepts and skills to new problem-solving situations.*   Learning to read music is a skill that can be learned by convergent thought

processes, but the skill is best retained when children create and record their own music.

In Miss Larkin's room, Beth passed along her knowledge of the process of making a block print. The creative aspect of the situation came when the children designed their program covers, cut a block of their own design, and printed the covers.

14. *In creative teaching, skill in constructive criticism and evaluation is developed.* Many convergent thought processes are essential to the full development of creative thinking. For example, the application of evaluation skills is an aid to the creative process if it is practiced at the conclusion of the creative act. A set of criteria worked out with the child to measure the effectiveness or the usefulness of his creative products will help him to be constructively critical and to evaluate effectively.

In the puppet show project in Miss Larkin's room, each idea offered by a child was immediately evaluated—it was put to use. If the idea worked, it was kept; if not, it was discarded and the child saw immediately why it was not a good idea. In many instances an idea proposed by one child was topped by another child's idea. For instance, in one scene of *Fractured Fairy Tales,* the children were working with colored lights to create the illusion of a fire on stage. One child suggested that they tie red silk (which had been shredded) to the top of an electric fan and hold it horizontally below the front of the proscenium arch so the flames leaped up on the stage. Something seemed to be lacking until another child suggested they flicker a red light on the stage to give the illusion of licking flames. The exclamations of delight at the effect when the idea was put to a test were sufficient evaluation of the value of the idea.

At the end of the total project, group or individual, the teacher can hold a more formal evaluation where she asks such questions as "Did you learn any things that will help you next time we do a puppet show?" "What other material could we have used for our stage?" and "Can you show me the excitement you felt on the day of the show with paint, chalk, or crayon on paper?"

15. *In creative teaching, ideas and objects are manipulated and explored.* The more children are allowed to discover, manipulate, explore, experiment with, and resolve their own failures, the more creative they become.

Certainly the examples given above show this to be a fact. In Miss Hill's lesson the groups of children manipulated music, flashlights, their own bodies, cardboard notes, and many other materials.

16. *Creative teaching employs democratic processes.* Because creativity is a form of individualism and because a principle basic to democratic ideology is that individuals are important, democratic procedures in the classroom develop creativity in children.   No person ever became great or famous by copying that which other individuals had already accomplished. In order to become self-realized as a democratic citizen, each person must remain an individual, helping the total culture to move forward by contributing his own unique ideas.   This goal is synonymous with that of creative development, and true democratic living in the classroom calls for the development of the individual powers of each student—all the creative power he can muster.   Creative people are needed in our country today more than ever before.

17. *In creative teaching, methods are used that are unique to the development of creativity.*   Among these special methods are the following ones, suggested by Sidney Parnes in his courses on creative problem solving at the University of Buffalo.[9]

Brainstorming.   The brainstorming technique was used in Miss Larkin's room in developing ideas for making prints. Following are some basic considerations that help to make brainstorming sessions successful.

In brainstorming, a moderator (usually the teacher) poses the problem very specifically and generally sets a time limit for the session.   A recorder (usually a child who is deft at note-taking) is appointed to list the ideas as they are given by members of the group.   All ideas, no matter how inadequate or how foolish they may seem at the moment, are recorded.   No judgment is passed on any idea until the end of the session (deferred judgment).   The moderator can encourage the flow of ideas (creative ideation) by stopping the session and asking the recorder how many ideas have been recorded in the first ten minutes of brainstorming.   He then says, "Let's see if we can double the number of ideas in the next ten minutes" (ideational fluency).

In order to keep similar ideas together on the recorder's list, the hitchhiking technique is used.   If one person presents an idea that sets off a related idea in another person's mind, the latter snaps his fingers and the moderator calls on him next so his

9. Sidney J. Parnes, *Instructor's Manual for Semester Courses in Creative Problem Solving,* rev. ed. (Buffalo, N.Y.: The Creative Foundation, 1963), pp. 32–66.

"hitchhiking" idea will come on the recorder's list immediately after the idea that prompted it.

After the session, a committee chosen from the group meets and leisurely evaluates the ideas that resulted from the large-group brainstorming session. All ideas are considered carefully. Some are discarded as impractical: too expensive, too time-consuming, too involved, or too difficult to carry out. The reduced list is often brought back to the large group for further discussion and decision making.

Deferred judgment. See p. 20.

Creative ideation. This process has been mentioned under brainstorming above. In creative ideation, various criteria are applied to a product in an attempt to make the creative thinker see new uses for the product or to create in his mind a new solution to a problem. Examples of these criteria are: How can I put it to new uses? How can it be adapted to new purposes? Can it be modified to suit a new cause? Can it be magnified to change its use? Can it be "minimized," rearranged, reversed, or combined with something else? Can something be substituted for it? Some of these criteria are demonstrated in the following sample situations.

New uses. An uncreative person will see a paper clip as a paper clip—an item used to fasten papers together for temporary use. A creative person will see many other uses for a paper clip: making delicate chains, doing wire sculpture, fastening pieces of styrofoam together, making hooks, making mobiles, etc. Fingerpaint was invented to give children a medium with which they could work directly on paper without the use of brushes and paint, but creative people have found many new uses for it. It can be used in a simple silk screen process, it can be used in making prints, and it can be squeezed onto surfaces with a cake decorating tool.

Modification. In the puppet play *Fractured Fairy Tales* described at the onset of this chapter, Miss Larkin's students had no puppet theater, but one of the boys in the room had a father who ran an appliance store. He donated a TV box. The box was studied, adapted, and modified for the class's use. Christmas tree lights were used on the inner side as stage lights. Two of the boys rigged a curtain that would roll up and down with the pulling of a string. The box was painted to resemble a small theater, and curtains (rolls of white butcher paper) were hung on the sides to hide the actors from the view of the audience. These are all modifications of a TV box to change it into a workable puppet stage.

FIGURE 1–6. Adaptation and modification: a child uses a branch from a tree and modifies it by adding papier mâché and paint.

Adaptation.   The TV box alterations also fit under the category of adaptation.   Adaptation is changing one tool or medium to fit a new situation or use.   Old wax crayons can be melted down in cupcake tins and used as a medium for painting beautiful pictures which closely resemble oils.   This is an adaptation of the cupcake tin and the wax crayon.

Magnification.   Some of the children in Miss Larkin's room experimented with tiny pieces of cut sponge to make prints for cards.   Then one day when the children were laboriously painting large areas of scenery with brushes and tempera paint, one child suggested that the children dab the paint on with a large sponge to cover the grass and sky area in a faster and more efficient way.   This was done with handsome effects.   A child had magnified his idea to develop a more efficient, effective, and creative way of working.   Samples of magnification are all around us: packaging our detergents in larger boxes to promote sales, widening our roads into double-lane highways with an intervening mall to make them safer, making loaves of bread longer for bigger families, etc.

Minification.   The opposite of magnification is minification.   How can we minify objects to solve some of our problems creatively? Everywhere around us we see this principle applied with great effect: mini-buses, mini-skirts, mini-bikes, mini-cars, mini-courses, etc. An excellent example of minification in the art field is the invention of the watercolor set or the painter's kit. It is difficult for the mobile artist who likes to paint outdoors to carry large cans of paint and big brushes in the quantities needed, so watercolors have been packaged in little cakes, oils and dacron paints have been put in small tubes, and both have been assembled in kits that are easy for the artist to transport.

The principle of minification was used by the students in Miss Larkin's class when they had to plan ways to make everything smaller for their puppet show. This presented many problems. One scene took place in a bedroom and an old-fashioned bedstead was needed. Through the process of minification and substitution (see the discussion below of substitution) one child came up with the idea of using clothes pins for the posts on the bedstead. They worked very effectively. In another scene, tiny dishes were needed, so pill-bottle tops were collected and painted.

Rearrangement. Sometimes a more creative motivation or solution comes about if the order or position of the usual elements in a process is simply rearranged. Instead of teaching the children in her room to play the piano, Miss Hill allowed them to have a rather sophisticated and meaningful experience with the piano first; they created a musical light show of George the Bullfrog and Airsy the Dragon Fly. This experience inspired a great interest in the piano, in rhythms, and in color. Putting the children through the tedious drills of piano lessons or note-reading lessons would not have resulted in the enthusiastic love of music and experimentation Miss Hill developed in her children after a year of meaningful experiences. Children interested in playing the piano were still free to do so with the instrumental teacher, but all children learned some of the possibilities of the use of the piano. It is interesting to note that more children from Miss Hill's room studied piano (and other instruments) than from any other group in the school.

Reversal. It is a common practice to teach note values, scales, etc. by introducing the written symbols for the notes and then explaining to the children what they mean. Miss Hill reversed the process in her effective lesson on note values: the children experienced the beat (value) of the note first by seeing and feeling it before they were introduced to the symbol. The result was a very creative and highly motivating experience, merely because the teacher dared to try a technique in reverse of the usual pattern.

An excellent example of the use of reversals in teaching art is the introduction of the negative-positive concept to children (see Chapter 2). As in photography, sometimes the reverse of the design is as effective and as interesting as the original design.

Combination. When one thing does not work well, can I combine it with something else to salvage it, to make it work better, or to create a new tool? The Orientals combined the concept of the smoking pipe with the purpose of a brush to create a tool that, more efficiently than either, makes possible the application of hot wax to cloth in order to create batik.

In the above examples of teachers working with children, notice how many ways teachers combined ideas to create a new product. Miss Hill first combined music with colored lights, then she combined music, light, movement, and voice. Miss Larkin urged the children to combine the sponge painting technique with tempera paint to make efficient and effective progress on their scenery. One of the children combined string painting and potato printing to produce highly dramatic designs on tissue wrapping paper.

Substitution. In Miss Larkin's class the children chose block prints as a technique for making their programs for the puppet plays. If Miss Larkin had not had linoleum blocks or tools, the children could have brainstormed other media they could have substituted to get a result similar to a block print. A potato print might have sufficed, or a styrofoam print. Sometimes a substitute for a material turns out to be more effective than the material itself. One of the authors of this book once taught in a rural school where supplies were at a minimum. Wishing his students to have art experiences, he looked around for substitutes for regular art materials. In many instances these materials were excellent and much more meaningful than the store-ordered materials. He took the children on field trips to the river bed where they dug clay, brought it back to the school in buckets, and learned to cure it. For drawing paper, he had the students write letters home for old wallpaper rolls that were hiding in farm attics. The wallpaper that came to the school as a result of this venture was beautiful and varied: figures, flowers, and plain colors of beautiful hues. That which was unsuitable for use on the front side was excellent for painting on the reverse side, for the paper came in multiple textures and shades. Finding substitutes for common materials can, in and of itself, become a very creative exercise.

Forcing relationships. We have seen this principle illus-
trated above under combinations.   In forced relationships, two
apparently unrelated objects are suddenly glorified because someone has placed them in a new relationship and has, as a result,
created a new product or a new process.

A rose and a bar of soap are placed before a group of
people. "Create a relationship between these two products," they
are told.   The result might be scented soap shaped like tiny pink
rosebuds for milady's boudoir.

A chair and a telephone are set before a group. They are
told to force relationships between the two. The result might be
the modern telephone stand equipped with note paper, pencils,
telephone books, lights, and even a loudspeaker system for conference telephoning.

A teacher places colored felt-tipped pens and pieces of
cloth before the children and tells them to put them together
somehow.   Results include placemats, wall hangings, napkins,
pillow covers, and a multitude of products made by putting the
dye from the felt-tipped pens onto the cloth, rather than dipping
the cloth into the dye.

One teacher gave a group of children a box of fluorescent
chalk, a blue light, and the book *Where the Wild Things Are* by

FIGURE 1–7.   Where the Wild Things Are.

Maurice Sendak. She told them that the book was a mysterious story, and from the other materials she wanted to know if they could create a mysterious play or puppet show.

The results were fascinating. The children painted a bedroom scene for their puppet show from tempera paint and over it they drew a forest scene with the white chalk, which was invisible on the paper while the stage lights were on. At the point where the little boy puppet got into bed, the stage lights went out and the blue light was turned on. All the strange trees and flowers broke into weird, glowing colors. To add to the effect, each of the "wild things" was painted with colored fluorescent paint.

SUMMARY

There is a decided difference in the methodology of creative teaching and that of traditional teaching. In the area of art more than in any other area, homage has been paid to these differences. But even the art curriculum has not been free from violations and abuses of the creative powers of children. Research in the past decade has provided us with a fuller understanding of creativity and the manner in which it develops. The job of the elementary school has always been to develop those components of the intellect that are necessary for life in a democratic society, and today creative powers are needed more than ever before.

Strategies in art teaching must be based on the known principles of creative teaching developed in this chapter and the known principles of art developed in the next chapter. Some special strategies have already been identified and defined here. These include brainstorming, deferred judgment, creative ideation, and forcing relationships.

The basic principles of creativity and creative teaching as summarized in this chapter provide the framework for creative teaching. Now that we know a great deal about creativity and how it is developed, we can wed it to our knowledge of art.

Art experiences provide an unsurpassed opportunity to reinforce creative thinking. They provide a means by which children can explore their ideas without too much censorship. Art, because it has a history in American education, offers the most accessible avenue to creative development in the elementary school program at this time.

ACTIVITIES

1. Identify five great artists and/or artist-teachers and decide which ones were creative in their approach to teaching. Write a description of a great teacher under whom you have studied.

2. Do some research on the Montessori method of teaching and determine its creative and noncreative aspects as it relates to the teaching of art.

3. Discuss ways you could measure the creative teaching abilities of a teacher. Devise some items to fit your plans.

4. Can you think of other forms of giftedness besides creativity that might not be measured by intelligence tests? List them.

5. Check your own creativity with some of the following exercises:
   a. Think of all the ways you can use a motion picture in the classroom.
   b. Think of all the ways that audiovisual aids can be used to develop creativity.
   c. Think of all the ways that textbooks and workbooks can be used to develop creativity.
   d. Can arithmetic be taught creatively? How?

6. Brainstorm all the ways you can use colored lights to teach a unit on pollution.

7. Find products in your environment that have been produced because some clever person applied the principles of creative ideation. Try each of these criteria:
   a. *New uses.* Example: a penny—making a print, a mold, or a rubbing.
   b. *Modification.* Example: soap—making soap powder, soap chips, soap flakes, scented soap, sculpted soap, molded soap, floating soap, or "pure" soap.
   c. *Minification.* Examples: tires—removing the tube to create tubeless tires; TV—removing excess materials and new inventions to make portable TV sets.
   d. *Rearrangement.* Example: light—throwing light up instead of down to create indirect lighting, or throwing light at a white surface to get reflected light.

8. Now find evidence of the application of these criteria strictly in the art field.
   a. *New uses.* Example: using a block print to make prints on paper for cards or programs, on cloth for dresses or curtains, on tissue for wrapping paper, on glass for church and club windows.

b. *Modification.* Example: tie-dyeing—using rubber bands instead of string; folding the cloth before dyeing; tying in bolts, nuts, or odd-shaped chunks of wood; tying knots in cloth; twisting cloth before dyeing.

9. Think of all the things you are now doing that help in the development of creativity, such as building visual acuity and comprehension skills in your reading program or developing evaluation skills in social studies. Make a list of the characteristics described in this chapter that develop creativity. Indicate which ones you are already working on in your instructional program.

10. Which statement in each of the following sets is likely to produce strong motivational tensions in children?

a. "Listen carefully while I explain each step of the dance. Once you know the pattern we will listen to the music."
"I have a very exciting dance record here. Listen and show me what it tells you to do."

b. "Now that we have read the story, let's make a play from it. I will have each of you read some parts. The best ones will be chosen for the play."
"Now that we have read the story, can you work in groups and tell it in some new and different way?"

c. "When I nod my head all of you hit your instruments to the beat in the music."
"Now that each of you has chosen an instrument, let's let each person show us what he can do with it."

d. "Here is a new kind of paint. See what you can do with it."
"Take the brush I gave you. Now dip it in water. Place a drop of water on the cake of paint I gave you. Rub the brush on the wet paint. Now make a mark on the paper like this."

11. In the above sets of quotations, which ones are apt to produce creative results?

12. Teachers can set conditions for developing creativity simply by the things they say. An example of this is in Manuel Barkan's book, *Through Art to Creativity* (Boston: Allyn and Bacon, 1960). Read it and observe carefully how creative teachers employ this skill.

13. In light of the discussion in this chapter, do you think that creative products in the elementary classroom can be graded with letter or number grades? Discuss this.

14. Place a colored plastic ball before you on a table. Make a list of all the uses to which it could be put. After you have made such a list see if you can stretch it by considering Parnes's suggestions for creative ideation:

a. To what *new uses* could I put it? (Perhaps you could use it as a Christmas tree ornament or a party decoration.)

    b. How can I *adapt* it to other purposes? (Tape ribbons to it and suspend it from the ceiling as a decoration.)

    c. Can I *modify* it so it can be used differently? (Fasten it to a tray and garnish it to resemble a pudding for a prop in *The Christmas Carol.*)

    d. Can I *magnify* it? (Add other balls to it to make a cluster of grapes to decorate a large ballroom.)

    e. Can I *minify* it? (Perhaps use it as the base of a puppet head by pasting on hair, eyes, and lips and putting it on a stick.)

    f. Can I *combine* it with something else? (How about adding a wastepaper basket to it to invent a new version of a basketball game?)

    g. Can I *substitute* something else for it? (You could substitute a balloon, a styrofoam ball, or a round bowl.)

15. If you have not tried the brainstorming technique with children, do so with one of the following topics.

    a. Make a list of all the uses to which you can put a paint brush.

    b. List all the uses you can think of to which you can put a light bulb, a coat hanger, or a brick.

    c. List all the ways you can think of to make the study of ecology interesting.

16. Can you identify the creative teachers on your faculty? What do you look for in doing so?

17. There is a belief among many art educators that art, like creativity in general, cannot really be taught. The teacher's main job is to provide a working, stimulating environment and to help children to relate to it. In this process should be included the privilege of the child to choose options, to form his own decisions and pass judgments, to select or reject, and to plan new directions for himself.

    Discuss this concept. What other processes should be included in the list above to help the child to develop his creativity in art?

SELECTED BIBLIOGRAPHY

Anderson, Harold H., ed. *Creativity and Its Cultivation.* New York: Harper & Row, Publishers, 1959.

————, ed. *Creativity in Childhood and Adolescence.* Cupertino, Calif.: Science and Behavior Books Inc., 1962.

Art Directors Club of New York. *Creativity: An Examination of the Creative Process.* Paul Smith, ed. New York: Hastings House, Publishers, Inc., 1959.

Bryson, L. "Training for Creativity," *School Arts*, 60 (September 1960), 5–8.

Burkhart, Robert C. "The Relation of Intelligence to Art Ability." *Explorations in Creativity.* Ross Mooney and Taher Razik, eds. New York: Harper & Row, Publishers, 1969.

Burton, William. *The Step Beyond: Creativity.* Washington, D.C.: American Association of Elementary-Kindergarten-Nursery Education, 1964.

Cobb, Stanwood. *The Importance of Creativity.* New York: Scarecrow Press, Inc., 1968.

Eisner, Elliot. *Think with Me about Creativity: Ten Essays on Creativity.* Dansville, N.Y.: F. A. Owen Publishing Co., 1964.

Fabun, Dan. *The Dynamics of Change.* Englewood Cliffs, N.J.: Prentice-Hall, Inc., 1967.

———. *You and Creativity.* Beverly Hills, Calif.: Glencoe Press, 1968.

Frye, Northrup. *The Educated Imagination.* Bloomington, Ind.: Indiana University Press, 1964.

Gardner, John. *Self-Renewal: The Individual and the Innovative Society.* New York: Harper & Row, Publishers, 1962.

Getzels, Jacob W., and Phillip W. Jackson. *Creativity and Intelligence.* New York: John Wiley & Sons, Inc., 1962.

Ghiselin, Brewster, ed. *The Creative Process.* New York: Mentor Books, 1955.

Gowan, John Curtis, George D. Demas, and E. Paul Torrance, eds. *Creativity: Its Educational Implications.* New York: John Wiley & Sons, Inc., 1967.

Gruber, Howard, Glenn Terrel, and Michael Wertheimer, eds. *Contemporary Approaches to Creative Thinking.* New York: Lieber-Atherton, Inc., 1962.

Guilford, J. P. "Factors That Aid and Hinder Creativity," *Teachers College Record*, 63 (February 1962), 380–392.

———. *Intelligence, Creativity and Their Educational Implications.* San Diego, Calif.: R. R. Knapp, 1968.

Halprin, Lawrence. *Creative Processes in the Human Environment.* New York: George Braziller, Inc., 1969.

Heist, Paul, ed. *The Creative College Student.* San Francisco: Jossey-Bass, Inc., Publishers, 1968.

Kagan, Jerome. *Creativity and Learning.* Boston: Houghton Mifflin Co., 1967.

Karagulla, Shafica. *Breakthrough to Creativity: Your Higher Sense Perception.* Los Angeles: DeVorss & Co., 1967.

Kneller, George. *The Art and Science of Creativity.* New York: Holt, Rinehart and Winston, Inc., 1965.

Kornbluth, Frances S. *Creativity and the Teacher.* Chicago: American Federation of Teachers, 1966.

MacKinnon, Donald W. "What Makes a Person Creative?" *Saturday Review,* February 10, 1962.

Marksberry, Mary Lee. *Foundation of Creativity.* New York: Harper & Row, Publishers, 1963.

Martin, Warren Bryan. *Conformity.* San Francisco: Jossey-Bass, Inc., Publishers, 1971.

Massialas, B. G., and Jack Zevin. *Creative Encounters in the Classroom: Teaching and Learning through Discovery.* New York: John Wiley & Sons, Inc., 1967

McKeller, P. *Imagination and Thinking.* New York: Basic Books, Inc., Publishers, 1957.

Mearns, Hughes. *Creative Power: The Education of Youth in the Creative Arts.* New York: Dover Publications, Inc., 1958.

Michael, William, ed. *Teaching for Creative Endeavor: Bold New Venture.* Bloomington, Ind.: Indiana University Press, 1968.

Miel, Alice. *Creativity in Teaching: Invitations and Instances.* Belmont, Calif.: Wadsworth Publishing Co., Inc., 1961.

Miller, James G. *The Human Mind.* New York: Golden Press (Western Publishing Co., Inc.), 1965.

Moustakes, Carl E., ed. *The Self: Explorations in Personal Growth.* New York: Harper & Row, Publishers, 1964.

Muenzinger, Karl F. *Contemporary Approaches to Creative Thinking.* New York: Lieber-Atherton, Inc., 1967.

Murphy, Gardner. *Human Potentialities.* New York: Basic Books, Inc., Publishers, 1958.

Osborn, Alex F. *Applied Imagination.* New York: Charles Scribner's Sons, 1963.

Patrick, Catherine. *What Is Creative Thinking?* New York: Philosophical Library, 1955.

Reed, E. G. *Developing Creative Talent.* New York: Vantage Press, Inc., 1962.

Rugg, Harold. *Imagination: An Inquiry into the Sources and Conditions That Stimulate Creativity.* New York: Harper & Row, Publishers, 1963.

Shumsky, Abraham. *Creative Teaching.* New York: Appleton-Century-Crofts, 1965.

Sigel, Irving E., and Frank Hooper, eds. *Logical Thinking in Children: Research Based on Piaget's Theory.* New York: Holt, Rinehart and Winston, 1968.

Smith, James A. *Setting Conditions for Creative Teaching in the Elementary School.* Boston: Allyn and Bacon, Inc., 1966.

Taylor, Calvin W. *Creativity: Progress and Potential.* New York: McGraw-Hill Book Co., 1964.

————. *Widening Horizons in Creativity.* New York: John Wiley & Sons, Inc., 1964.

————, and Frank Barron. *Scientific Creativity: Its Recognition and Development.* New York: John Wiley & Sons, Inc., 1959.

Torrance, E. P. *Creativity: What Research Says to the Teacher.* Washington, D.C.: National Education Association, 1963.

————. *Encouraging Creativity in the Classroom.* Dubuque, Iowa: William C. Brown Co., Publishers, 1970.

————. *Guiding Creative Talent.* Englewood Cliffs, N.J.: Prentice-Hall, Inc., 1962.

————. *Rewarding Creative Behavior.* Englewood Cliffs, N.J.: Prentice-Hall, Inc., 1965.

————, and R. E. Myers. *Creative Learning and Teaching.* New York: Dodd, Mead & Co., 1970.

Werthermer, M. *Productive Thinking.* New York: Harper & Row, Publishers, 1959.

Williams, F. E. *Foundations of Creative Problem Solving.* Ann Arbor, Mich.: J. W. Edwards, Publisher, Inc., 1960.

Wilt, Marion. *Creativity in the Elementary School.* New York: Appleton-Century-Crofts, 1959.

CHAPTER II

The Nature of Art Teaching

Creative and innovative thought must become the life blood of art education methodology if it is to have a future. Teachers who have developed a secure confidence in the guaranteed traditional methods and materials of the past must begin to extend their thinking to include the impact of the new image in art and the knowledge gained through experimental educational research.

GEORGE PAPPAS[1]

Art educators often talk of creativity and art as separate things, but they are not. Art is an intense expression of creativity. If the public school is to develop creativity in children and if teachers are to encourage art expression as a form of creative drive, the principles for creative development mentioned in Chapter 1 need to be wedded to principles of art education in order to create change. Art can be taught without violating creative development. In this chapter the authors come to grips with some of the problems of teaching art in this context.

THE STATUS OF ART EDUCATION

All too often when schools are faced with the necessity of economizing, they start by cutting off funds for the so-called frills. The frills more often than not turn out to be art and

1. George Pappas, *Concepts in Art and Education* (New York: Macmillan Publishing Co., Inc., 1970), p. viii.

— music. If the athletic department has failed to produce a winning streak, it too may be placed in this category.

To regard art and music as frills is to misinterpret their natures and their fundamental importance in the development of the human being. All races in all ages have produced their own distinctive art and music. It is to such sources that we turn in evaluating their cultures. The rise and fall of a culture are reflected accurately and eloquently in the artifacts that it leaves.

When we thoughtlessly eliminate the arts from our schools, there has to be some compelling, underlying social reason. It is a comment on the value that we place on creative self-expression within our society. If we perceive art as the means by which the individual can state his claim to individuality and his rejection of regimentation, then for a society to reject art has a dangerous significance.

Art in Historical Context

Art has always reflected the strengths and weaknesses of a culture. Repression becomes evident not so much in the subject matter, but in the general debility that erodes art as an expressive language. One of the more recent examples of this was the empty posturing of art under the Nazi dictatorship in Germany. The vital, expressive art of the previous decade completely disappeared.

It has been said that creative expression is only possible when it is carried out with no other intention than the desire to create. When art is made the handmaiden of the state it loses its vitality and integrity.

In this context, contemporary American art can tell us a great deal about ourselves. It is a visible commentary on our values and our sense of purpose—where we are and where we wish to go.

The Process and Product

Our free enterprise system with its mass production has made us the envy of much of the world. Our success has led us to confuse the values that we place on creativity and on productivity. We have come to value the product more than the process. For us it is more important to arrive somewhere than to enjoy the wonders of the journey. We are always seeking ways to circumvent the process: faster planes that get us there more quickly, food mixes that reduce the pleasures of cooking, and kits of all types that reduce the need for personal involvement and skills and guarantee a product identical to the one in the advertisment.

All of this has had the inevitable effect of speeding up the pace of our lives and leaving us less time than we had before. It is an odd commentary that while the rest of the world envies our wealth, we desperately try to revert back to a kinder, more leisurely age. We reject modern houses in favor of colonial houses. We are forced to manufacture antiques to fill the demand for reminders of a kinder age. We even disguise our modern gadgetry in French Provincial or Early American wrappings. To a great extent our art reflects the "cult of the latest model"; everything else is left in a state of obsolescence. We confuse cuteness with significance and differentness with creative originality. We fail too often to perceive the true nature of art.

The highly regarded art teacher is often the one who is able to send home with her students clever pieces of art that fit into the expectations that we have set up for art. It matters little that innumerable children are taking home similar offerings. It matters even less that the process involved has produced little in the way of significant learning. The product is all important, and the child is producing an acceptable product.

Art and Affluence

A steady dose of cute projects inevitably produces the same sense of disillusionment that we feel with the rest of our frenetic lives. Even while we are admiring piggy banks fashioned from bleach bottles and planters from popsicle sticks, there is a sneaking feeling that such a program is nice, but not vital.

Reading, writing, and arithmetic are work. Work is what being a student is all about. Art is not work; it is a nice symbol of our affluence. We are rich and can afford to allow time for culture. It is no wonder that when the budget shows signs of strain and something has to go, art stands indefensible and ready for the axe.

Justifying the Teaching of Art

New demands are being made for accountability in education. It is no longer enough to believe that the subject has value. It is now necessary to demonstrate the effectiveness of the instructional procedures.

It is comparatively easy to justify the teaching of core

subjects in our schools.   The advantages the individual derives from the study of reading, writing, and arithmetic are fairly obvious.   Long usage and acquaintance have left them unchallenged.

The philosophies that underlie art education are much more obscure.   As long as art is seen merely as the production of products, it is easy to dismiss art as a frill.   Many of the objectives of art education in recent history have been completely subjective.   Even if one agrees that aesthetic perception is a valuable attribute to develop in the individual, how does one prove that it has been imparted or that it is being practiced?   The same could be said about the ability to compare and contrast qualities within the student's environment.   It is somewhat akin to demanding that we state the strength of a mother's love for her child on a percentile basis.   It sounds ridiculous to say that John's love for Nancy ranks in the 82nd percentile, whereas Nancy's love for John scores in the 95th percentile.   No one doubts love's imperative value simply because degrees of love cannot be measured.   Art education, if it is to survive in our schools, must be seen in a similar light: its value is demonstrable in its ultimate, vital effect upon the well-being of the individual and society.

If those who teach art education are to justify it, they must clearly understand the philosophical base upon which it is founded. They must, in addition, be able to articulate their objectives and methods to parents, school boards, and all who support education.

The fact that there is no single, universal philosophy is not important.   This is true of all complex human activities. What is important is that each individual have an awareness of the many possibilities and a reasonable adherence to a single philosophy that can be advanced to and accepted by teachers, students, and administration.

The fact that little provision is made for the teaching and funding of art programs must, in large part, result from the fact that art has been seen as little more than busywork, a cultural nicety.

THE VALUE OF ART EDUCATION

In forming a philosophy, the first order of business is to decide exactly what we mean by art.   Art produced by the elementary school child is not the same thing as art produced by adults.

It is a fatal mistake to apply the same criteria and evaluations to both. If there were another word that would adequately describe the pre-adolescent activity that we call art, we would do well to use it in this connection. It would help us to clarify in our own minds the things that we might accomplish in this area.

A child learns to scribble and form symbols as naturally as he learns to walk. Long before he has developed a written language that is complex enough to carry his emerging concepts and ideas, he develops a pictorial language (see Chapter 3). With this language he is able to explore his relationship with his environment. He is able to state his emotions, his fears, his frustrations, and his love for his family. With the manipulation of materials he develops physically. He learns to control and coordinate his bodily movements. He talks about concepts that he knows, and he discovers what he still needs to know. Art for the child is an extension of that most vital period of learning that we call play.

We have come to understand that play is vital to the healthy development of humans and animals. We have always felt this, but now we have the reassurance of the experts that this is indeed true. Play is a time of complex learning situations. It is a time of discovery and concept formation. It is probably more vital to the child's development than any other activity. We need to consider our injunction to the young student to quit playing and get down to work. We might more profitably say, "Quit work and get down to play; you are too young to be stuffed with vicarious experiences and trivial facts. Find out who you are and what you need to know."

With this concept of children's art as a starting point, we need to examine each art project for the components that will contribute to the total development of the child. We must ask ourselves if the activity in some way helps him to develop physically, emotionally, and intellectually. Is the project open-ended in the sense that it opens doors to new experiences and concepts?

It is reasonable to propose that unless an art project produces some worthwhile learning, it should not be introduced. The following are qualities that one can hope to develop within the art program.

The Ability to Visualize

The child must discover the multitude of possibilities in the ways that parts and sub-wholes can be combined and reordered. The ability to visualize is the ability to answer such questions as, "What would be the effect if the image were presented in a different color scheme? a different size? in reverse? (See pp. 23–28.) Given a map, can you picture in your mind the natural appearance of the landscape? Given a set of plans, can you see the building? When you read a story do you have a clear mental image of the characters that the author has drawn?" To visualize is to be able to foretell the results of our actions without the necessity of first committing them. Playing with simple building blocks and visualizing the effect of form and mass in space is not as far removed from architectural engineering as might be imagined.

Perceptual Skills

It is a mistake to think that because we all look at the same thing, we see the same thing. Our perception is based upon our experiences, and our experiences form us. Education should be the business of undergoing experiences, coming to grips with them, internalizing them, and adjusting concepts.

When a child draws countless stereotyped lollipop trees, it is not enough to show him how to draw a tree. The concept and the symbol used to carry it must become the teacher's concern.

Children's art is essentially conceptual. They produce on the basis of what they know and not what they see. Concepts have a nasty habit of becoming fixed and generalized. When this happens, the individual's development is arrested. Art projects need to be open-ended enough to allow room for the continued development of conceptual skills. It is all too easy to provide projects that produce successful products and a temporary feeling of success, but that at the same time inhibit new perceptions (see pp. 207–219.)

Physical Coordination of Both Large and Small Muscles

We learn to use the large muscles before the small ones. As we grow older, we grapple with the problem of coordinating the small movements of the fingers to permit us to write. We expend a great deal of time and energy on the project at a time when we are developing lifetime habits and patterns of behavior. During this period there is a real need to involve ourselves in activities that require the continued development of the large muscles. In order to achieve breadth and fluency, the child should draw and paint with the whole body. The action of the fingers on a brush or pencil is too limiting. The conditions under which the child attempts to draw and paint must be designed to give free rein to this total bodily involvement.

It is possible to judge the child's readiness for reading and writing with considerable accuracy by the degree of coordination that he exhibits in his artwork. The child who is unable to draw a reasonably straight line in any direction or is unable to complete a circle would be quite unable to complete the more complex task of putting these shapes together to form letters. Working with clay or other three-dimensional materials develops the ability to apply controlled force. There is a direct relationship between the handling of the natural environment and the handling of writing utensils.

One often-overlooked benefit of a program rich in coordinative skills is the fact that people with these skills tend to be less accident-prone and more self-confident. It is possible that children would develop these skills through their art if they were left to their own devices. We must accept the fact, however, that children are not left alone; we tend to plan their lives and formative years with such dedication and thoroughness that we are apt to plan out some of the necessary ingredients. The art program can become like the white bread on the grocer's shelves—it needs to be enriched with the good things that we have removed in the name of progress.

Divergent Thinking

We have already discussed divergent thinking in Chapter 1. Art projects are based on divergent thinking. Divergent thinking follows convergent thinking, the process by which we converge on the facts. Facts are useless information unless something is done with them. The game of trivia is played by seeing who can assemble the largest body of useless knowledge. A fact only escapes from the category of useless trivia when it is put to good use. Putting facts to good uses requires the ability to think divergently. A wax crayon will melt at about one hundred degrees Fahrenheit. Who cares, unless divergent thinking is brought to bear and ways are found to make use of the fact? Encaustic painting makes use of this fact; images are produced by painting with pigment suspended in molten wax. Most of what passes as education today is devoted to convergent thinking. With the aid of a textbook the teacher lays out all the correct facts for her students, then administers tests in which the students with the best recall are rewarded. Intelligence tests make no pretense of measuring the ability to think divergently. Creative activity is impossible without this type of thinking; it is what differentiates the inventor from the people who are merely content to use his ideas.

Learning from Experience

It is impossible to avoid experiences; they are built into the act of living. Unfortunately, it is all too easy to fail to understand them and come to grips with them. Art, to be worth the name, must consist of practical experiences. Personal involvement, assimilation, and understanding are necessary if experiences are to be meaningful. It is not enough to produce a successful painting; if the success is to be repeated, it is necessary to know what the key factors in that success were. Failure is only an unpleasant experience if one is unable to understand what has happened and to learn from it. Art should provide the opportunity for large and glorious failures. The professional artist in any medium may reject as much as thirty percent of all that he produces as failures. If it were not for these failures, it is doubtful if any significant work would be produced.

People are only free to learn from their experiences and their failures when what they do is completely accepted. If evaluation and grading are always in the offing there is a tendency to play it safe and not to explore the unknown.

Evaluation Skills

When we say that all artwork must be accepted, that should not be taken to mean an abdication of all critical faculties. Evaluation begins the minute creative work is undertaken and continues until the work is complete. When the statement is complete and the child acknowledges it as such, he should mean just that and we should accept his statement. The point is that evaluation is the business of the artist-student. It can only be carried out successfully by him, for only he knows his full intention. There may come a time when he can no longer see the wood for the trees and needs a second opinion. Be flattered if he asks you for one. The opinion requires all the careful thought that a surgeon might give to the question of whether or not to take out your appendix. You need to know who the child is in the most profound sense and how he perceives himself. You need to know what it is that he is trying to say and how it relates to his most pressing experiences. You need to be sensitive enough to know what and how he is feeling and what it is about his work that disturbs him and makes him turn to you for help. You have to decide if you are looking at what he has done in terms of your own concepts or his. Is what he is doing important to you because it reflects on your teaching? The ideal way out of the dilemma is to have the child resolve the matter for himself from the questions that you ask. This technique of leading the student to his own conclusions is discussed in Chapter 10.

Social Organization

One of the essential qualities of a citizen of a highly organized society is the ability to work with others and to respect individual and corporate rights. A picnic spot continues to exist only if the users clean up their litter and leave the table and grill intact. A class can only continue to enjoy art materials if there is a strong sense of social responsibility. Paints must be kept clean and in place for the benefit of the student who is to follow, not because the teacher has mandated that it be that way. Art is a great way to discover the necessity for such concern. The child who habitually leaves materials in a messy state is soon set straight by his fellows (see Chapter 8). Group activities help the child to find and accept his place in the group. He quickly sees that everyone contributes to the final outcome. He needs to recognize what his unique contribution is. If he finds that he is being relegated to a position within the group that he finds unworthy, there are always other groups and he should always have the option of working on his own. One has to decide on an individual basis how necessary it is to have a child participate in group activities. The child who is shy of such activities is usually the one who needs them the most. To force the issue may make him even more reluctant to participate. The key is to provide those activities that help him develop self-confidence and self-identity. Thus equipped, the secure person does not perceive the group situation as a threat.

Work Habits and Responsibility

The younger the child, the more gratification he expects for a given effort. Children, like drums, produce lots of noise with a minimum of effort. Stamping in puddles produces huge splashes. Art for the young needs to be immediate. Projects that are only successful if the successive stages are visualized are for the more mature. The ability to handle more mature concepts requires encouragement and training. The older child who is unable to see a multi-stage project through to its conclusion is suffering from a disability that will seriously affect all that he does. Art education is an area in which the problem can be faced and dealt with. Most people never reach their full potential because they are unable to maintain their interest or drive long enough to arrive at successful conclusions. Art presents the opportunity to develop an understanding of the need for and the characteristics of good work habits. Some activities succeed best when handled with short bursts of intense energy and activity. Others require the ability to sustain the interest and delay the gratification. It is wonderful to plant seeds and have summer flowers in the garden. One needs faith to plant trees that will only mature in the next generation. Art is a way of perceiving the difference between work and play and the ideal situations that arise when the two become synonymous. It is a way of discovering what makes for efficient creative living. It is a way of achieving the essential elements of self-discipline and self-motivation. Handling one's tools becomes an extension of handling oneself. Both require efficient work habits.

Audrey points out in *The Social Contract* that tree-living apes have no fleas and no problem with their excretions. Apes simply keep on the move, so clutter does not become a problem. The human being has trouble with both. Unless he develops good habits, the artist may spend a great deal of time scratching and searching for his brushes. Creative people are often thought of as living in a state of cluttered untidiness. Very often the so-called clutter is the visual stimulation that the individual needs, and it may, in fact, have its own type of order. Good work habits do not mean the creation of a sterile, tidy environment. Human beings with all their complexity have a wide variety of conditions under which they work best. They should be given the opportunity to develop their own conditions; if they do not interfere with other members of the class, we should accept them.

Transferability

The underlying objectives and values discussed thus far make it clear that what we call art is really a way of life. The creative aspect of our being is enhanced, and we perceive ways of becoming all that we are capable of being. We develop the ability to define not only problems, but ways of dealing with them. We develop ways of thinking not only with the conscious rational mind, but with the subconscious and the intuitive mind. Art provides training in the ability to think in analogies, the ability to perceive things in a variety of contexts, the ability to reorder and restructure, and the ability to communicate on levels where normal language is inadequate. Art is the process through which a being becomes an individual. The survival of any species is ultimately determined by the strength of the genetic pool and the useful divergence of its members. The benefits of a well-planned and well-executed art program are not only transferable to other disciplines—they are indispensable to them. If education is ever to be a coherent, related process, it must be based on a strong understanding of the nature and destiny of man.

To teach art as a once-a-week affair with a special teacher in a room divorced from any other activity is to miss the whole point. Such a concept of art education can do more harm than good. To think of the vital natural process that we call art as a frill added on to the real purpose of education calls into question the validity of the whole concept.

All who teach should be accountable not only for their actions as professionals, but also for the curricula that they handle. It is only when one can justify the teaching of art in a realistic, humanitarian way that one is ready to start teaching art.

PLANNING OBJECTIVES IN ART EDUCATION

To formulate a philosophical base for the teaching of art is one thing; to find a practical way to implement it is another. It becomes necessary to set up clear-cut objectives for each of the projects that we wish to offer children.

It is pointless for a teacher to offer an art project to children unless she has some clear-cut objectives in mind. It is necessary to examine these objectives constantly to make sure that they are valid and rational.

In the case of monoprinting with fingerpaints, the main objective might be the stimulation of intuitive thinking. Another objective might be to help the child who still thinks in base line concepts (see p. 79) and stereotyped images to see his images in new relationships. Yet another objective might be to help the child to understand the concept of reversal as a creative problem-solving technique. If one cannot move an object by pulling on it, try pushing it. Flexibility is a good indicator of creative ability. If nothing else derives from the project but the idea that there is more than one way to do something, it has still been worthwhile.

If these objectives are clear in your mind, then you are in a better position to teach art. Teaching is helping the child to discover the things that you have laid at his doorstep. Without valid objectives, the project simply becomes busywork.

The successful art session is one in which these objectives are realized by the children even though they may not be able to verbalize them. Each project should provide the opportunity for the student to formulate some objectives of his own. "I am going to do fifty of these this period," "Can we make a musical story with flashlights?" and "I want to paint designs like those on my styrofoam" are indications of the children's expression of their objectives.

The following are important considerations in formulating these objectives.

Level of Maturity

Many art educators have systematized the teaching of art. The subject has been divided into sequential units that form a continuum. It has been the authors' experience that there is no particular order in which art education can be structured to go from simple to more complex. The academic art schools used to insist that the student master simple skills before he was allowed to move on to the more complicated skills. Proficiency in drawing was required before the student could enter the painting class. Art was seen as a developing skill, and under this system much of what was produced merely reflected these skills.

Generally speaking, all art projects can be offered to all age levels. The only thing that needs to be adjusted is the level of expectation. There are, however, some obvious exceptions.

One does not offer a project involving sharp tools that require a fair amount of coordination to kindergarteners. It is not as obvious that watercolors are a poor choice at this age. Five-year-olds need materials that they can manipulate successfully. Watercolors demand a certain amount of technique and control. Young children may become very frustrated with the medium and may develop very negative attitudes if the material is constantly offered. Projects should be planned that fit the attention span of the child. Projects that require several sequences, even if they can be carried out with a good deal of supervision, are not good for the young child. Activities he can work out in one long, highly motivated sitting are better for his level of maturity. When he receives too much help, he rightfully concludes that the work is not really his own. During early childhood years art expression needs to be direct and simple. Projects that must be continued in the next art period seldom work. A young child does not remember what was started last week. It is important to understand the concept level necessary to carry out the project and achieve any real learning.

Third and fourth graders will happily become involved in design projects involving the concept of positive and negative spaces, although they may not call it that in so many words. Younger children are not capable of handling this concept. They have few ideas about the relationship, or at least the visual relationship, of their symbols. The wise teacher decides how many choices and ideas the child can handle and limits him to areas in which he will not suffer a harmful degree of frustration.

Simply because the child is able to produce a project with supervision does not mean that the project is a suitable one for him. He may merely have been successful in following directions and never have been able to internalize the experience. Unfortunately, too much of what passes for art falls into this category. To plan an art program it is first of all necessary to be aware of the stages of development of the child and how art becomes a manifestation of this growth (see Chapter 3).

Motivation

If a child were able to develop without the pressures of society and a surfeit of parental guidance, it is entirely possible that he would not need any outside stimulation for his creative work. But the fact is that all too often parental and societal pressures dominate him. When one considers the efforts that were made on his behalf to toilet-train him, why should he not expect similar efforts to be made to teach him to work creatively?

Providing children with the freedom, the means, and the environment for creative expression sounds like a wonderful credo. Unfortunately, it is not. It is a good beginning, but it is not enough. It might work well if the child had a great deal of self-motivation and self-discipline. Then he might respond well to the injunction "Here is the art room, children. Why don't we all create?" It is a pity that this has sometimes become the teacher's interpretation of the philosophy of the open classroom. The result is invariably noisy, nonproductive, and disastrous.

Young children are always demanding of parents and grandparents "What can I do now?" The child is eager for new experiences, but with his limited point of view he is unable to see new directions to take. "Go play with Spot" or "See what Jimmy is doing" or "Look at all the toys you have" is the same as saying "Here is the art room." There are no new ideas involved. The child needs a clue to guide him in a new direction. He does not need to be told exactly what that direction should be. He would like the satisfaction of thinking that he had determined that for himself.

The answer to what can we do now requires very careful consideration. This is the point at which the child can be motivated to explore fresh fields and pastures, or he can be inhibited. Providing motivation requires arousing interest and providing the skills and information that will allow the child to proceed on his own.

Motivation can be derived from two sources: the material on hand and experiences. Some materials may prove to be so exciting to the child that motivational tensions build so quickly the child cannot wait for the second half of the procedure—he wants to have it as quickly as possible.

An example of this type of project might be monoprinting. (See the discussion of crafts in Chapter 8.)

Johnny had used fingerpaints in kindergarten and first grade. Then in second grade Miss Love trotted out the same old jars and paper again. Johnny felt that he had exhausted the possibilities of the medium. He had already discovered most of the possible effects, and they did not really satisfy his growing interest in his environment and his exploration of it through his art.

However, Miss Love, who was a down-to-earth, practical,

creative woman whose favorite aphorism was "There is more than one way to skin a cat," immediately challenged Johnny's creative potential.

"We have always used fingerpaints by putting the paint on the paper. I wonder what would happen if we could find a way to put the paper on the paint."

Johnny was initially confused by the words; reversal is a creative ability and he needed time to work at the concept. A completely new relationship between the paper and the paint was called for. "What's the paint going to be doing while it is waiting for the paper?" was Johnny's first thought.

Johnny had been taught ever since he could remember that good boys did not draw on walls or smear things on tables. So strong was the inhibition against smearing things on the table that he never even considered the possibility. Miss Love had anticipated the problem.

"Use that table over there—that's the one that we use as our work table. It doesn't matter how messy it gets. We can easily wipe it clean."

Johnny was interested, challenged, and persistent. If Miss Love did not object to having paint smeared on her table, he had no objection to doing a really good job of smearing it. This became such a fascinating and revolutionary occupation that his original intent became dim. It was only when Miss Love handed him a sheet of paper that a new relationship became clear. Johnny dropped the paper onto the paint, patted it firmly into place, then peeled it off in a moment charged with expectancy.

"Wow. Hey look."

Miss Love looked and said, "I can see a monster in there. What can you see?"

Johnny, who frankly had not expected to see anything, suddenly found that he was looking at a rabbit in a vegetable patch. He was sold. "I am going to do fifty."

Miss Love sat back and resigned herself to the task of verifying the presence of all sorts of unlikely things in each print.

Without knowing it, Johnny and his classmates were off on a voyage of intuitive thinking. A child can find many connections between past experiences and the new and exciting images that are appearing as magically as the passing clouds. In this case the material provided the motivation. Once Johnny had solved the problem of handling the material he was ready to go, and anything else that could have been said or done with the aim of motivating him would have been superfluous and delaying.

Where the material does not provide the excitement, the motivation must come from the desire to examine past experience in visual form.

The answer to what can we paint may well be "See what beautiful grays I can make from orange, blue, and white. Doesn't it remind you of the fog that we had last week?" If the experience of fog was strong enough for the child and if he now perceives ways to express it, that may be motivation enough.

From this example it can be seen that the teacher not only needs to be acutely aware of the child's experiences, but she also needs a thorough understanding of materials and their possibilties.

Motivational tension can be read on the faces of children as clearly as sorrow or rage. Once the signs are there, it is time to back gracefully out of the picture. If every child in the class makes a reasonable facsimile of whatever you used as a demonstration, beware. You are saying too much, doing too much, and trying too hard.

Materials and Equipment

In planning and organizing materials and equipment it pays to run a checklist with all the dedication of an airline pilot and the skepticism of a police desk sergeant.

Miss Crawford had decided that a creative activity that she could tie in with an upcoming birthday party would be the making of placemats by the crayon resist technique. (The design produced by the wax crayon resists a wash of diluted tempera color to produce a design on a rich background.)

Miss Crawford prepared the diluted tempera colors, provided enough containers for the whole class, cleared space for the activity, and covered the tables with newspapers to absorb spills and to facilitate clean-up. She borrowed large wash brushes from the art supervisor. She carefully explained the procedure, being sure not to do anything that might fix in the students' minds her concept of what the results might be. She enthusiastically motivated the class and sat back to await results, confident that she had done all that could possibly be asked of her. But there was an item missing from her checklist, and pretty soon it made itself known.

"Miss Crawford, the black paint covered mine all up!" Sure enough, James displayed a solid black sheet of paper.

Too late Miss Crawford realized that the crayons that the

children had were pressed crayons of an inferior quality and they did not contain enough wax to resist the tempera.

A missing item can cause many a project to end in disaster and frustration. It is necessary to plan for an art project as carefully as for any other project in the curriculum. Trying it yourself sometimes presents some unexpected difficulties that make it unsuitable for the age group that you intend it for.

The creative teacher will not be deterred by lack of money or equipment. It is possible to substitute all kinds of unlikely things for standard supplies. A bobby pin makes an excellent weaving needle; meat packaging trays make the ideal material from which to make prints. No art room or classroom should be without its scrap box. The range of materials that can be used is amazing, so one should never hesitate to include something because there does not seem to be an apparent use for it. Much of the equipment that is sold commercially for children's use is ineffective or unnecessary. If you are going to buy tools it is much better to buy a good grade of adult equipment, perhaps in a small size. Children's carpentry boxes are notorious for being stuffed with feeble tools, many of which are useless (see Chapter 8).

Procedures

Some of the most exciting art projects require several stages for their completion. Unless you are very familiar with the activity, it is a good idea to have the procedures listed, either on a paper for your own reference or on a chart for the class. Simple information such as the fact that wallpaper paste must be added to water and not the other way around can make or break a lesson. You may remember that fact, but did you mention it to the busy little helper-of-the-day who is wondering where all the lumps came from? If there are procedures that the child must know about, then it pays to list them and make sure that the topics are covered.

Pitfalls

We have already mentioned one of the most important pitfalls—neglecting to make sure that your well-planned motivation does not have the unexpected effect of locking the students into your concepts. But you must also check on the skills involved. It is not obvious when you start a simple unit on weaving that half the class cannot tie a knot.   The other half cannot thread a needle, so you spend an entire sewing period with eye strain and an endless succession of "Thread mine, please."   Then there are still unbelievers who will not admit the existence of left-handed scissors.   When a project depends upon being able to cut with a certain precision, the whole thing is wasted on the unfortunate lefty with the right-handed scissors.

Pitfalls can be avoided by careful planning and by trying the procedure yourself.   It is a good rule of thumb that if any activity is physically difficult for you, it will be more difficult or even impossible for the young child.

Creative Possibilities

If a project does not clearly offer creative possibilities, reject it. To be useful it must be open-ended and allow the student to perceive other avenues that he might explore.   Sometimes it is not the project that is at fault, but the way in which it has been presented.

String makes a most interesting way to apply tempera paint.   It is simple and direct and overcomes the notion that the only way to apply paint is with a brush.   One way of presenting it would be to demonstrate the technique: dipping the string in the paint, stretching it out, and applying it to the paper to make patterns of straight lines.   Then one might show how loops printed in succession make very handsome flower forms.   Once the demonstration is over, everyone becomes busy duplicating the very handsome flower forms which were the most exciting part of the demonstration.   If string and paint are offered again, the response will almost certainly be "We have done that."   The truth is that they have indeed done that; there is nothing else to do.

The same project could be handled in an entirely different way, like the way Miss Larkin introduced prints in Chapter 1. In this case, the demonstration might be based on a statement by the teacher like "Everyone paints with brushes.   I wonder how many other ways there are to put paint on paper?   The chances are that if we could find some, they might make paintings very different from the ones we usually make."

If the children are familiar with the brainstorming technique of creative problem solving, they will immediately go to work.   In Chapter 1 there is a discussion of the use of this technique.   All the ideas are first collected for future use: dragging pieces of cardboard on the paint and then printing out lines, using steel wool to cover large areas with a texture remarkably like a field of grass, etc.   Every idea should eventually be tried. If and when the idea of string is raised, you are ready to go to work.   If a child rejects the idea in favor of another that he has thought up, then he should be allowed to try his idea.   He should not be thought of as the disruptive child who is never content to do what everyone else is doing.   The children should be encouraged to discover for themselves all the possibilities of the medium.   If all they have done is straight lines, then feel free to drop the hint that there are also curved ones.   If a piece of string is set down on a photograph in the newspaper on the table, make a comment such as "That's interesting.   I wonder if we could put things like that on the paper first before we use the string."   If the topic is presented in this fashion, the chances are that the child will not have exhausted all his ideas with the end of the class period.   When it is offered again, the response may well be an enthusiastic "Good, can I make some tissue wrapping paper?" Ideas that have been germinating can now be put to use.

Art can only be open-ended if we see the process as being as important as the product.   As long as we see the product as all important there will always be the temptation to do too much for the child and a reluctance to accept his work.   Whatever he produces on his own is always of greater value than something that he has only been able to accomplish through a great deal of help from his teacher.

Imposing on a child a demand that has no meaning to him serves no purpose.   About all that comes of it is that the child surrenders more and more of his own responsibility for decision making and becomes more and more dependent on the adults who make such demands on him.   Eventually he may even look to them to make all his decisions for him or to approve all that he does.   Risk-taking is reduced to a minimum.   He becomes more insecure and less creative.

Integration with Other Disciplines

On the following pages we will discuss some of the more important philosophies that underlie the teaching of art.   Each of the four connects with the total curriculum in a particular fashion. The problem with integration is that it tends to debase art in the service of another area in the same way that other disciplines can be debased to serve the ends of art.

We are all familiar with the complaints that follow the viewing of a new, much-heralded film based on a well-loved literary work. The literary qualities of the book are debased to fit the perceived needs of the film. This does not have to be, but it often happens. The writer and the filmmaker need to be responsive to each other's problems and understand where each can make a unique contribution.

To integrate art with other disciplines it is necessary to make sure that art is given the opportunity to make its unique contribution. Art is capable of making concrete not only the history of man, but also his emotions and feelings. It is capable of forging a link between past cultures and our own. We recognize, however, that the art form that helps one individual to expand his understanding of another discipline may not help the next person.

Fred constructed a model shadoof (a sweep used for raising irrigation water) for a unit on Egypt. He gained insights into man's dependency upon water and the extent to which he had to labor to bring it to his crops in times past. He also discovered much about the nature of balance that he will be able to relate to physics or the construction of mobile sculpture. All of this was lost on Sue, who produced the model faithfully from the book at the teacher's insistence. Sue reached her understandings through the creation of visual images based on feelings that she had gathered from a number of sources: the text, a film, standing in the heat of the boiler room, dressing in a burnous and fez. For Sue, painting was a means of drawing all together so that she could better understand the experience.

PHILOSOPHIES OF ART EDUCATION

The philosophical basis of art education is undergoing rapid and, in some cases, radical changes. Many of these changes have been brought about by the emergence of the open classroom and the humanistic approach to primary education. Periods of change are generally times of confusion. Proponents of changes tend to claim dogmatically that theirs is the sole pathway to success. Philosophies tend to overlap and become blurred. Contemporary art education philosophy can be reduced roughly into four major types.

These four philosophies encompass most of what is happening in art education today. Much depends upon the personality and background of the teacher who implements them.   An overlapping of these separate points of view often occurs.   The result may be a continuing and ongoing approach to art, or it may be that at different times art is seen to have different functions and places in the curriculum.

Structured Art Education

Art educators like Manuel Barkin[2] believe that the content and components of art can be classified into units and taught as such.

Accepting this assumption, Elliot Eisner has prepared a set of sequentially ordered lessons accompanied by specially designed instructional material.[3]   He says of the project: "What we see in this sequence of lessons is a gradual widening and deepening of the child's appreciation. . . ."[4]

His approach has as its main object values that are unique to the visual arts.   Of his aims he says:

We recognized the fact that art activities can be used to achieve a wide variety of purposes—mental health, vocational training, the development of general creative abilities, concrete examples of ideas and artifacts for social studies; we considered the qualities that *only* the visual arts can provide to be its most prized contribution to the education of children.

Second, we believe that artistic action is the product of a complex form of learning and is not an automatic consequence of maturation.[5]

It is reasonable to assume that many elementary teachers do not have sufficient background to achieve these objectives without the help of material similar to that used by Eisner.

The Kettering project report states as one of its beliefs that art education has no monopoly on the development of creativity, but that it does develop the child's ability to see the

2. Manuel Barkan, *Through Art to Creativity* (Boston: Allyn and Bacon, Inc., 1960).
3. Elliot Eisner et al., *Teaching Art to the Young.   A Curriculum Development Project* (Stanford, Calif.: Stanford University School of Education, 1969).
4. Elliot Eisner, "Stanford's Kettering Project," in Al Hurwitz, ed., *Programs of Promise: Art in the Schools* (New York: Harcourt Brace Jovanovich, Inc., 1972), p. 14.
5. *Ibid.*, p. 6.

visual world aesthetically, his visual imagination, and the skills necessary for expressing his imaginative insights in some public, material form.

The Kettering project bases its practices on the belief that sensitive teaching does not hamper children and that art should teach specific content and a specific array of skills.

Art as an Aid to General Learning

According to the general learning philosophy, values unique to the visual arts are less important than the opening up of learning in other areas of the curriculum.   Art is no longer an end in itself; it is a valuable tool which has the potential to facilitate learning and understanding.

Two major influences on the form of this type of philosophy have been the Montessori school and the British primary school with its activity-centered learning.

Jean Piaget, the Swiss psychologist, has concluded from his studies of children that no two people adapt or learn information at the same rate or in the same way and that thinking skills develop only when we work with and organize concrete objects for ourselves.[6] The key to this type of learning is activity and involvement.   The arts are well suited to play this role.

So far this concept is clear-cut and workable.   There are, however, some questions that have to be resolved if such a philosophy is to be profitably developed: Will the child's artistic ability and production expand as he matures in other ways, or does his artistic ability depend upon sensitive and knowledgable teaching?   Is it in fact necessary to *teach* art in order to use art as a tool to employ in other learning?

Art as a Means of Developing the
Fully Functioning Individual

There is little disagreement about the fact that few people make use of their total potential.   This includes physical, mental, and emotional attributes.   So many of us have a book inside of us that we are one day going to write.   We can visualize powerful canvases that will speak to all mankind, but we never learn to

6. Hans G. Furth, *Piaget for Teachers* (Englewood Cliffs, N.J.: Prentice-Hall, Inc., 1970).

paint. We live vicariously through films and books the powerful emotions that have lifted individuals to great heights, yet in our practical lives we inhibit and hide our emotions until they take their revenge in the form of ulcers.

This philosophy views art not so much in the context of the visual arts, but as an expression of life itself. It is a way of doing and thinking that depends upon the well-being of the total individual. In recent years education has tended to place more emphasis on what the child learns than on the child himself. The fragmentation of the curriculum has been accompanied by a fragmentation of the individual. As schooling proceeds, the child tends to conform more and be less creative. He sacrifices his individuality for a place in his peer group.

Sensory and perceptive skills become isolated and wither for want of use.

This philosophy says basically that "too often the visual experiences of adolescents are superficial and do not truly reflect a deeper consciousness because for one reason or another that layer of awareness has not been tapped."[7]

If the sources of the creative experience and art are in the subconscious areas of dreams, myths, and fantasies or in the emotional, sensory, and physical make-up of the individual, then we have to plan a program of greater awareness.

Visual arts are not an end in themselves in this philosophy. The process becomes more important than the product. The visual arts become integrated with all the other arts and learning to become one cohesive activity. This is basically a different approach from the first philosophy in which art is regarded as a tool to other learning. Here art is regarded as inseparable from total learning in much the same way that breathing as an activity is inseparable from living.

Synaesthetic Education

Synaesthetic education, a current movement which had its base in art education, emphasizes the total development of the individual through his senses. It is an expanded version of the third philosophy mentioned above. It is bound to have an impact on art education theories in the next decade and on education in general.

7. Al Hurwitz, *Programs of Promise: Art in the Schools* (New York: Harcourt Brace Jovanovich, Inc., 1972), p. 89.

Synaesthetic education is a discipline based on self-discovery and self-actualization as a result of inner thoughts and psychological transactions between the individual's sensory experiences and his environment.   Subjective and personal relationships enhance the student's feelings and allow him to function in accordance with his needs and capabilities.[8]

Synaesthetic education has grown out of a reaction to the biases, prejudices, and academic expectancies in effect in art education today, which have come about because people tended to lose sight of the real purpose of art education while they attempted to defend various theories.

In synaesthetic education the greatest concern is to permit all that is present in the activity to the learner. He should be permitted to participate in the fullest and most vivid manner.   The experience must be above all an individual-centered experience.   The moment action is extrinsically directed in such a way that the directions eliminate the need for encounter between the person and the environment it ceases to be creative.   It should, therefore, be born in mind that the effectiveness lies in empathizing, in the need for encounter and the whole-hearted enlistment of the learner in developing rapport.   Synaesthetic education is a matter of intimate participation, that is, the satisfying of the need to resolve conflict between man and his environment.[9]

Andrews states that "Synaesthetic education is not an adjustment *to;* but an engagement *with* all that exists."[10]

In a statement of the philosophy of synaesthetic education much of the method for its accomplishment is implied.   It is a broad statement and one that is suitable to the development of all creativity.

Concerning the relationship between the humanities and synaesthetic education, Dr. Ridlon says:

8. James A. Ridlon, "The Dialectics of Synaesthetic Education," in M. Andrews, ed., *Synaesthetic Education* (Syracuse, N.Y.: Syracuse University School of Art and Division of Summer Sessions, 1971), p. 41.

9. Michael Andrews, "The Nature of Synaesthetic Education," in M. Andrews, ed., *Synaesthetic Education* (Syracuse, N.Y.: Syracuse University School of Art and Division of Summer Sessions, 1971), p. 14.

10. *Ibid.*, p. 10.

As disciplines synaesthetic education and the humanities have similar goals to hopefully bring out the best and unique characteristics of each individual through self-discovery and self-actualization. Here the similarity ends. The humanities are a group of disciplines usually consisting of art, music, history, and English or any combination of these courses. During the course of instruction the individual disciplines tend to keep their identity and total integration is never actually realized. In synaesthetic education the opposite should happen. Art should be a vehicle for the other disciplines to work into, forming a totally integrated learning experience of mind, body and "subject matter."[11]

An Emerging Philosophy

The four basic philosophies popular in art education today have tended to create conflict and confusion in the minds of classroom teachers and art teachers. Art teachers sense a contradiction that cannot be resolved between two theories. One states that art teaching should grow from life experiences rich in sensory activities. The other, which says that art should be taught as a planned set of lessons, advocates giving little or no consideration to the school life of the child, making no attempt to integrate the art program and the normal sensory experiences of every school activity, and allowing no time for visual expression in the schedule of a school day.

Classroom teachers who have many subjects to teach find it impractical and time-consuming to set aside special periods to motivate children for a half-hour activity in art. When the children are already enthusiastically and emotionally involved in a social studies activity in an area such as civil rights, these teachers use the ongoing activity to form a basis for lessons in visual expression. Miss Hill and Miss Larkin represent teachers of this type. Only by planning prolonged, meaningful experiences do they see any possibility of engaging the child emotionally and synaesthetically in school activities that result in real art objects.

This book does not support any particular one of the philosophies presented here. In some respects it supports them all, gleaning from each those aspects of art teaching that seem to support its basic premise best. In other respects it rejects parts of some of these philosophies as being functionally unrealistic for today's changing classroom or as being opposed to the basic goal

11. Ridlon, *op. cit.*, p. 42.

of developing each child's creative power. This text rejects the concept that an objective of the elementary school is to develop artists and endorses the concept that an objective of the elementary school is to develop each child's creativity in such a way that he is able to choose his own manner of expressing that creativity, be it art, architecture, music, poetry, fiction, crafts, dance, drama, or whatever.

To that end, art "experiences" included in this text are based on the principles of creativity development that were mentioned in Chapter 1 and those objectives unique to the development of art skills and art appreciation. The authors see this as a realistic way to sustain an art program worthy of the many new organizational plans, such as the open school. It is their sincere contention that art procedures must not violate the principles of creativity if art is to fulfill its function of developing creativity.

Each of the philosophies places emphasis on sensory learnings and a total, sensitive encounter of the child with his environment rather than a lopsided, intellectual–verbal experience with it. The creative-teaching/creative-learning philosophy stresses the planning of sensory experiences in all areas of the curriculum so that children discover that the unity of subject matter lies in these sensory experiences and that they can be expressed aesthetically in verbal and visual forms. Integration is planned deliberately, so creativity is developed through all aspects of the curriculum and the creative teaching philosophy permeates the total school day. This unity supplies the content for the child's visual expression.

This book is peppered with illustrations edited from tape recordings or from classroom observation reports that illustrate the philosophy of creative teaching in action. Hausman says:

> Teachers must be aware that creative activity in art (as in any other field) does not involve the creation of a form from "nothing." Creativity in art is not creativity in a nuptial or biblical sense. The forms that are created grow out of already existing facts, ideas, and skills. To be sure, each student is unique: to some extent his drawings, paintings and sculpture can reflect this uniqueness. . . . Good teaching in art introduces a flux of ideas and images and then helps students to uncover, select, rearrange, combine and synthesize ideas and images drawn from this flux.[12]

12. Jerome J. Hausman, "Teacher as Artist and Artist as Teacher," in George Pappas, ed., *Concepts in Art and Education* (New York: Macmillan Publishing Co., Inc., 1970), pp. 333–340.

The primary purpose of including art in the curriculum of the elementary school is to facilitate the artistic development of human beings, which emerges from general creative development. In conjunction with this philosophy, teachers should consider the following guidelines in planning the creative teaching program:

1. Art education programs should truly free children to create.

2. Art education programs should be planned for individual growth and development rather than for the growth of "the children" as a group.

3. Programs should grow out of the environment of the child and be an expression of his relationship to that environment. Consequently, they should utilize the subject matter of the child's school life as content and be integrated into his full life experiences.

4. They should develop the child's ability to see the visual world aesthetically.

5. Art programs should develop the child's visual imagination and the skills necessary to express his visual images in some material form.

6. Programs should strive to teach through creative methods the knowledge necessary to refine art expression.

7. Programs should develop in each child a nomenclature of art.

8. Programs should provide each child with an understanding of the historical function of art.

9. Art programs should be aimed at developing specific components of creativity, such as visual acuity, perception, understanding of relationships, decision making, and judgment formation.

10. Art programs should free the classroom teacher to become more and more independent and, consequently, more and more creative in planning and executing her own art program.

11. The classroom teacher and the art teacher should work as a team in planning lessons, in setting objectives, in using normal classroom and life experiences for art content, in contriving special experiences, in developing art skills and techniques in the children, and in evaluating their progress (see Chapter 4).

12. Art periods as such should give way to a more flexible program where the art teacher plays the greater role of guide, consultant, and teacher and where her knowledge and skills are accessible to the other teachers through planned in-service programs.

13. Art programs should be concerned with the critical aspect of art, that is, the development of taste.

14. Art programs should be concerned with aesthetic development.

15. Art should be used effectively in the modern school in three roles: as a means of self-expression, as a tool for fulfilling other creative acts, and as an experience in itself.

CREATIVITY AND ART

Are the development of creativity and the development of art the same?   From the foregoing discussion it would almost seem as if art were creativity and as if developing art expression within a child would be the same as developing his creativity.

This is true to a degree.   A true artist is creative in every sense of the word.   But a highly creative person may not necessarily be an artist.   Creative people tend to select one specialized area through which they express their creativity: poetry, art, cooking, music, architecture, fabric designing, etc.   Consequently, these people may all possess many of the same qualities, traits, and characteristics, but they express them differently.

The person who chooses to express his creativity through art forms must seek out and learn many ideas, skills, techniques, and facts in his pursuit of his main love—art.   In the process he develops many qualities, understandings, concepts, and characteristics that make him different from other creative people.

This is as it should be, but it creates many conflicts in the mind of the classroom teacher and often places her in a position where she must make split-second decisions that subject her to criticism by the art teacher or artists among the school patrons.

The teacher's goal is to develop creativity in all children. She hopes, in her daily work, to keep creativity alive so that, when children mature, they have the freedom to select that area in which they want to develop their own creativity.   Even though the principles of teaching art appear to be very similar to the principles of developing creativity, close scrutiny reveals great differences which can create major problems in decision making.

An artist, for instance, walked into a classroom and found an exhibit in one part of the room over which hung a sign which said "The Day of the Oogle Boogle."   On the table beneath were many weird and wonderful creations made by the children. Among them was a beautiful piece of sculpture Bobby had made of junk collected from his father's garage. One child had written a poem about the Oogle Boogle. Another had written a story. Marcia had constructed a weird-looking animal from an old bleach bottle, bits of felt, and other pieces of junk. Freddy too had constructed an animal; his was from pieces of candy, marshmallows, and frosting, all held together with toothpicks. Buddy had transformed a wastebasket into a grotesque and unusual face. Linda had made a queer, Martian-looking animal from folded paper. Fred had made an underwater scene in a large box; in the middle he had hung an octopus-shaped creature with wires attached to his many legs so that he moved and wiggled with a slight shaking of the box.

This exhibit was the result of an open-ended assignment the children had inflicted on themselves. This came about as follows.

Miss Henry, their teacher, was discussing word structure in language arts class one day and the entire class, working in groups, began constructing words. Through an idea of Buddy's, the class got interested in applying the principles they had learned to creating "nonsense" words. Miss Henry had an anthology of children's literature on her desk and she read the children about the Jabberwocky from *Alice in Wonderland.* Soon the children were combining roots with blends, prefixes, suffixes, and endings to create Jabberwocky.

Some of the words amused the children, and before long Miss Henry said, "I wonder what an Oogle Boogle looks like."

That did it! Pete suggested they make one. Miss Henry proposed options. Four words were selected and the children formed committees. Each one was to bring in its ideas on a certain day. The artist arrived on the day of the Oogle Boogle.

Now, the artist visiting the classroom was appalled at Marcia's adaptation of the bleach bottle and at Freddie's marshmallow animal. The teacher herself did not see these as "art," but she accepted them as creative productions: Oogle Boogles. Some of the things the children had brought in for the exhibit were obviously true, visual expressions of their selves and their life experiences; by adult standards they were very beautiful. Others were not; they showed that the children were lacking to some degree in identification with the assignment, that they did not express their personalities, or that they were influenced by or copied things they had seen in their environments, which, to some degree, was dishonest. These projects did not contribute to the children's aesthetic development.

On the other hand, Miss Henry's long-range objectives for

developing creativity had been met, and she was not at all sorry that she had encouraged the fulfillment of the assignment. She did not intend the assignment to be an art lesson. She did learn a great deal about the ability of her children to express themselves through art media and she planned to do something about this on an individual basis at a later time.

What were some of the creativity-developing objectives Miss Henry had in mind when she promoted this activity?

1. The children should be afforded the opportunity to explore and manipulate shapes, materials, and forms.

2. The assignment should be open-ended and allow for personal interpretation on the part of each child. The children should be enthusiastic about the assignment and identify closely with it.

3. The teacher should be able to utilize in a very natural manner some of the basic techniques for developing creativity [mentioned in Chapter 1]. Specifically, various children should develop skill in:

finding new uses for ideas and materials

forcing relationships—putting materials, colors, shapes, and textures together in new ways to create new images.

brainstorming—creating nonsense words.

magnification, minification, modification, adaptation, rearrangement, combination, and *reversals* in creating Oogle Boogles.

4. The assignment should provide the children with the opportunity to apply knowledge, skills, and techniques in a new setting. From this assignment, new and different products should result.

5. The principles of creativity should be respected—each child should have the opportunity to be unique and individual. Each child should be highly motivated for the experience. [This was evident in the enthusiastic manner in which they went along with *Buddy's* idea that they accept the assignment.] Miss Henry had faith in the children, so she withdrew and allowed them to go it alone. Students were encouraged to generate their own ideas. The outcomes were unpredictable.

6. Practice should be obtained in divergent thinking processes. The open-ended assignment should, in a democratic manner, afford the children an opportunity to apply their newly learned skills of word structure.

Miss Henry felt that she could not openly criticize any of the products and spoil or negate the experience. She preferred to defer judgment on the products and handle the "artistic" growth of the children later.

This is an example of a teacher with clear objectives in her mind about creativity and how it is developed. It shows how a conflict can arise between the objectives of the artist or the art teacher and the classroom teacher. It points up the need for the art teacher and the classroom teacher to work together so each knows exactly what the other's objectives are and misconceptions are not developed. Miss Henry's objectives are clear and logical. She, in the long run, is probably helping the children to develop their art as much as anyone else, but she is doing it through the development of the total creativity of the child.

SUMMARY

The teaching of art in the elementary school is basic to the development of a humane personality. Taught with the emphasis on processes rather than products, art education can do more for the individual's personal growth and development than any area of the curriculum. From the beginning of life, art grows out of play patterns and emphasizes the development of the ability to visualize, to perceive, to coordinate, to think divergently, to live experiences with sensitivity, to organize, to develop work habits, to develop responsibility, to develop transferability, and to use evaluative skills.

All teachers are teachers of art, and the effective development of art-teaching processes requires that each teacher be able to identify her objectives clearly and be able to help children form their own objectives. The choice of materials and the integration of art into the total class program require special attention on the part of all teachers of art.

Art education philosophies at the present time can be classified under four categories:

1. Art is an end in itself, taught for the contributions, unique to the subject, that it can make to learning.

2. Art is a tool, a means of opening up learning and expanding horizons in other curriculum areas.

3. Art is a means of developing the fully functioning individual. The end product is no longer as important as the process; art is an integral part of the whole.

4. Art is a visual expression of man's encounter *with* his environment, especially through his senses (the synaesthetic movement). It is based on self-discovery and self-actualization; it is based on the principle of empathy.

This book draws from each of these philosophies in presenting a creative-teaching/creative-learning philosophy. This philosophy stresses, as a major goal of the elementary school, the development of the creativity of its students and the visual expression that is one facet of that creativity. Specific guidelines can be formed for planning projects based on this philosophy, but the basis for the philosophy is mainly the principles of creative teaching discussed in Chapter 1. The philosophy promotes the concept that *sensory* experiences are the unifying agent in all curriculum experiences.

ACTIVITIES

1. Discuss or consider the art periods to which you were exposed when you were a child in elementary school. Can you identify any of the goals of the people who taught you art? In your opinion, how effectively were these goals accomplished?

2. Problem for discussion: The authors contend that teachers do not have to take professional courses in art in order to teach it. How do you react to this? If they do not need professional art courses, what do they need in order to be able to teach art? What role do professional art courses play in the modern concept of art teaching?

3. How does each of the following statements violate a principle of creativity?
   a. "Children, I will show you how to make a wreath from egg cartons."
   b. "When we are finished with our paintings, let's select the best ones to put on the bulletin board."
   c. "Today we are going to learn how to make puppets."
   d. "John, you didn't cut your paper to the edge as I told you to!"
   e. "Your pumpkin doesn't look at all like the ones we described, Arnold. Turn your paper over and do it over on the other side."
   f. "Put away your arithmetic books and get out your crayons."

4. See if you can change each statement so that it fosters creative development.

5. Select a process you have never tried before and work at it for awhile. Try to make something. Note your own reactions. Did you enjoy the process or the product more? How do you

evaluate your product?   What did you learn from the experi-
ence?   Some suggestions to try are:
Polymer and tissue—see p. 287.
Papier mâché—see pp. 294–295.
String painting—see pp. 199 and 220.
Printmaking—see pp. 304–312.
Magic light paint—see pp. 285–287.

6. Invite your school or college psychologist to talk to you about
   the development of perception.   Perhaps he will administer
   some of the current perception tests to you.   It is interesting
   to note how individuals see the same things differently.

7. Place an object before your class or faculty group and ask
   each person to make a simple sketch of it.   Put the products
   before the group and try to answer each of these questions:
   a. How is it possible that each of you saw it differently?
   b. How do you account for the differences in technique used
      by individuals: type of line, shading, materials, place-
      ment, size, and use of space on the page?
   c. Did some people try to symbolize the object or were all the
      sketches representative?
   d. What can you conclude about perception, conceptualiza-
      tion, skill, and organization among individuals from this
      simple exercise?

8. Brainstorm all the ways you can obtain real art products from
   a birthday party in the classroom.

9. Make a list of all the situations where the art teacher and the
   classroom teacher may not see eye to eye, such as the one
   described at the end of the chapter.   If one is not already
   present, invite an art teacher to your group and see if you
   can resolve these problems in light of the creative-teaching/
   creative-learning philosophy.

10. Do you feel the philosophy of synaesthetic education is ap-
    plicable to the rest of education as well as to art education?
    Can children have striking encounters with their environ-
    ment in the language arts?   Plan a lesson that applies the
    principles of synaesthetic education to the language arts.

SELECTED BIBLIOGRAPHY

Andrews, Michael.   "Restatement of Synaesthetic Principles,"
   Journal of Creative Behavior, 6, 2 (1972), 104.
———, and Maud Ellsworth. *Growing with Art*.   Books 1-6.
   Syracuse, N.Y.: The L. W. Singer Company, Inc., 1960.
Association for Childhood Education. *Art for Children's Growing*.
   Washington, D.C.: Association for Childhood Education.

Barkan, Manuel. *A Foundation for Art Education.* New York: The Ronald Press Co., 1955.

———. *Through Art to Creativity.* Boston: Allyn and Bacon, Inc., 1960.

Bingham, Margaret. "Learning Dimensions: A Change Model for the Elementary School." *Programs of Promise: Art in the Schools.* Al Hurwitz, ed. New York: Harcourt Brace Jovanovich, Inc., 1972.

Brigham, Don L. "Visual Art in Interdisciplinary Learning." *Programs of Promise: Art in the Schools.* Al Hurwitz, ed. New York: Harcourt Brace Jovanovich, Inc., 1972.

Brittain, W. Lambert, ed. *Creativity and Art Education.* Washington, D.C.: The National Art Education Association, 1964.

Broudy, Harry. "The Case for Art Education," *Art Education,* January 1960, 708, 719.

Conant, Howard, and Arne Randall. *Art in Education.* Peoria, Ill.: Chas. A. Bennett Co., Inc., 1959.

Conrad, George. *The Process of Art Education in the Elementary School.* Englewood Cliffs, N.J.: Prentice-Hall, Inc., 1964.

Covington, Martin V. "Teaching for Creativity; Some Implications for Art Education," *Journal Creative Education,* 9, 1 (1967), 18.

D'Amico, V. *Creative Teaching in Art,* rev. ed. Scranton, Pa.: Intext Educational Publishers, 1953.

Davis, Donald Jack, and E. Paul Torrance. "How Favorable Are the Values of Art Educators to the Creative Person?" *Studies in Art Education,* 6, 2 (1965), 42.

de Francesco, Italo L. *Art Education: Its Means and Ends.* New York: Harper & Row, Publishers, 1958.

Dewey, John. *Art as Experience.* New York: Capricorn Books, 1958.

Dunkel, H. B. "Creativity and Education," *Education Theory,* 11 (1960), 209–216.

Eisner, Elliot. *Educating Artistic Vision.* New York: Macmillan Publishing Co., Inc., 1972.

———. "Stanford's Kettering Project: An Appraisal of Two Years' Work," *Art Education,* 23, 8 (November 1970), 4–7.

———. "Stanford's Kettering Project: A Radical Alternative in Art Education." *Programs of Promise: Art in the Schools.* Al Hurwitz, ed. New York: Harcourt Brace Jovanovich, Inc., 1972.

———. *Think with Me about Creativity: Ten Essays on Creativity.* Dansville, N.Y.: F. A. Owen Publishing Co., 1964.

————, and David W. Ecker, eds. *Readings in Art Education.* Waltham, Mass.: Blaisdell Publishing Co., Inc. (Xerox), 1966.

Erdt, Margaret Hamilton. *Teaching Art in the Elementary School,* rev. ed. New York: Holt, Rinehart and Winston, Inc., 1962.

Gordon, William J. J. *Synectics: The Development of Creative Capacity.* New York: Harper & Row, Publishers, 1961.

Grombich, Ernest. "Visual Discovery through Art." *Psychology and the Visual Arts.* James Hogg, ed. Baltimore: Penguin Books, 1969.

Hurwitz, Al, ed. *Programs of Promise: Art in the Schools.* New York: Harcourt Brace Jovanovich, Inc., 1972.

Kaufman, Irving. *Art and Education in Contemporary Culture.* New York: Macmillan Publishing Co., Inc., 1966.

————. "The Contexts of Teaching Art." *Concepts in Art Education.* George Pappas, ed. New York: Macmillan Publishing Co., Inc., 1970.

————. *Report on the Commission on Art Education.* Jerome J. Hausman, ed. Washington, D.C.: National Art Education Association, 1965.

Kranyik, Robert D. *Stimulating Creative Learning in the Elementary School.* Englewood Cliffs, N.J.: Prentice-Hall, Inc., 1968.

Lansing, Kenneth. *Art, Artists, and Art Education.* New York: McGraw-Hill Book Co., 1969.

Lowenfeld, Viktor. *The Nature of Creative Activity,* rev. ed. New York: Harcourt Brace Jovanovich, Inc., 1952.

————, and W. Lambert Brittain. *Creative and Mental Growth,* 5th ed. New York: Macmillan Publishing Co., Inc., 1970.

Luca, Mark, and Robert Kent. *Art Education: Strategies of Teaching.* Englewood Cliffs, N.J.: Prentice-Hall, Inc., 1968.

Madjea, Stanley. "A Systems Approach to Teaching the Arts." *Programs of Promise: Art in the Schools.* Al Hurwitz, ed. New York: Harcourt Brace Jovanovich, Inc., 1972.

Merritt, Helen. *Guiding Free Expression in Children's Art.* New York: Holt, Rinehart and Winston, Inc., 1964.

Montgomery, Chandler. *Art for Teachers of Children.* Columbus, Ohio: Charles E. Merrill Publishing Co., 1968.

National Education Association. *Art Education in the Elementary School.* Washington, D.C.: NEA, 1962.

Packwood, Mary M., ed. *Art Education in the Elementary School.* Washington, D.C.: National Art Education Association, 1967.

Read, Herbert. *Education through Art.* New York: Pantheon Books, Inc., 1943.

Reed, E. G. *Developing Creative Talent.* New York: Vantage Press, Inc., 1962.

Schinneller, James A. *Art: Search and Self-Discovery.* Scranton, Pa.: Intext Educational Publishers, 1961.

Taylor, Harold. *Art and the Future.* Blauvelt, N.Y.: Art Education, Inc., 1969.

Tissinger, Betty. "In Search of a Model," *Art Education,* 24 (April 1971), 27.

Trucksess, Fran. *Creative Art: Elementary Grades.* Boulder, Colo.: Pruett Publishing Co., 1962.

Wachowiak, Frank, and Theodore Ramsay. *Emphasis: Art.* Scranton, Pa.: Intext Educational Publishers, 1967.

Weitz, Morris. "The Nature of Art." *Readings in Art Education.* Elliot W. Eisner and David W. Ecker, eds. Waltham, Mass.: Blaisdell Publishing Co., Inc. (Xerox), 1966.

Wickiser, Ralph L. *An Introduction to Art Education.* Yonkers-on-Hudson, N.Y.: World Book Co., 1957.

CHAPTER III

The Nature of Children

Deep in the canyon all gray and green,
With a soft blue tint to the tops of the redwoods
I would like so much to spread my wings,
And fly over you and listen to the roaring of the water
Who took away my wings?

> a child's poem from FLORA J. ARNSTEIN,
> *Poetry in the Elementary Classroom*[1]

Did you ever stop to think that children scribble on paper with a crayon or pencil long before they can talk in complete sentences? Expression by "drawing" is a nonverbal means of communication used, apparently, by children throughout the world. To teach art to children, it is not enough to know the nature of creativity and art; one must know the nature of children. This is the most important phase of the teaching process.

If scribbling comes naturally to children, what else does? In this chapter the authors pull together some of the research available to enlighten us as to the natural ways children develop artistically and creatively.

Each child is an individual who expresses himself uniquely. Each child is different from all other children. Yet each child has many things in common with all other children—and with all other humans. In order to teach art effectively and creatively, teachers must blend the nature of creativity and the

1. Flora J. Arnstein, *Poetry in the Elementary Classroom* (Reading, Mass.: Appleton-Century-Crofts, 1962), p. 120.

nature of art with the nature of all children in general and the nature of each child specifically.

Years ago a great deal of attention was devoted to studies of child growth and development. Normal growth patterns in children were identified. Knowledge of these growth patterns helped teachers a great deal in understanding the behaviors to be expected and accepted at various ages as normal. These studies constituted a breakthrough in understanding; people realized that children were not small adults, but were a unique breed with their own natural ways of growing and developing. Even though the results of these studies have been greatly abused in their application, especially with children who did not comply with the average norms, this body of knowledge is still useful and important when properly applied.

Among the pioneers in the study of children, particularly the relationship of children to normal art processes (that is, art as a means of expression for a child) was Viktor Lowenfeld.[2] Lowenfeld, in his studies of children working with art media, particularly with drawings, discovered certain consistencies and similarities in the techniques and processes they employed. These "stages" he eventually classified and labeled, thus providing a common form of communication and a common terminology for scientific investigation. Recent studies in this area have brought Lowenfeld's work up to date.[3]

Lowenfeld's work threw new light on the creative process and created a revolution in the teaching of art to children. The "drawing" and "tracing" techniques of teaching art, popular at that time, became obsolete; the whole meaning and technique of art education changed. Teachers came to respect children's normal growth in art; the scribbles, the experimentation, the incomplete human figure, and other modes of expression were recognized as important stages of art development. Products became less important than processes.

The work of Lowenfeld and his followers still provides the richest source of material for studying and understanding the characteristics and growth patterns most common to all children, provided, of course, that we remember the opening statement in this chapter: each child is an individual who expresses himself

2. Viktor Lowenfeld, *Creative and Mental Growth* (New York: Macmillan Publishing Co., Inc., 1947).

3. Viktor Lowenfeld and W. Lambert Brittain, *Creative and Mental Growth*, 5th ed. (New York: Macmillan Publishing Co., Inc., 1970), Copyright © 1970, the Macmillan Co. Portions of this text have been adapted and reprinted on the following pages with permission of Macmillan, Inc.

uniquely. Children who deviate from the norms described by the researchers of child development are not necessarily abnormal, queer, or unusual. In fact, they may be the most creative, as the next part of this chapter indicates (see p. 91). Norms are not to be used in this case as norms are used on tests; they are not a measure of a child's achievement at any given age level. Rather, they help a teacher to recognize and understand various behavior patterns in children so she can better help them in their struggle to obtain their own answers to problems they encounter in their environment, instead of imposing her answers on them. It is the *child's* learning that is important. The teacher's job is that of helping each child find his own answers by understanding and recognizing as well as possible those signals that he sends out indicating that a creative problem-solving process is underway.

Although Lowenfeld's studies dealt largely with stages or processes of growth, they were accomplished by focusing attention on the *products* of children—their drawings. Lowenfeld and Brittain say:

> As children change, so does their art. Children draw in predictable ways, going through fairly definite stages starting with the first marks on paper and progressing through adolescence. Although we think of these stages as being different steps in the development of art, it is sometimes difficult to tell where one stage of development stops and another begins. That is, growth in art is continuous and stages are typical midpoints in the course of development.[4]

Lowenfeld categorized the developmental levels of children's art into the following stages: the scribbling stage, the preschematic stage, the schematic stage, the stage of dawning realism, and the pseudo-naturalistic stage.[5]

Lowenfeld's work has not gone undisputed.

Some art educators feel that the growth children show as they move through their maturational stages can be modified by sensitive teaching. Eisner calls them "uncultivated levels of performance."[6] These educators feel that a planned program in art is necessary to help children reach a more sophisticated level of performance. They feel that the art program in the public school should extend far beyond its current limits. They feel that a complete program in art education in the elementary

---

4. *Ibid.*, pp. 36–37.
5. *Ibid.*, pp. 36–42.
6. Elliot W. Eisner, "Stanford's Kettering Project: A Radical Alternative in Art Education" in Al Hurwitz, ed., *Programs of Promise: Art in the Schools* (New York: Harcourt Brace Jovanovich, Inc., 1972), p. 6.

school attends to the critical and historical domains as well as the productive domain.   The critical domain is defined as those experiences that aim at the development of the child's ability to perceive the aesthetic qualities of the world.   The historical domain attempts to help children understand the fact that art is part and parcel of human culture and is affected by human culture.[7]

Some studies in art education,[8] psychology, and general education indicate that the perception and production of art is not an automatic consequence of maturation.   These studies have shown that artistic activity is a complex activity that might be influenced by teaching.   Eisner states that it is not the responsibility of teachers to observe development, but to foster it.[9]

THE YOUNG CHILD: DEVELOPMENTAL STAGES

The Scribbling Stage

Drawing begins very early in life (age 2) when the child makes random marks on paper.   This is also the beginning of handwriting.   The child's manipulation of the instruments that make the random marks is often identified as scribbling, and thus this step in the child's art development is referred to as the scribbling stage.[10]

At first the marks on the paper bear little meaning to a child in terms of pictorial representation.   Adults often try to see recognizable shapes and images in these markings, but the child attributes very little meaning to them.

There is a correlation between the type of scribbles the child makes and his personality.   Children who are gentle, delicate, or quiet generally have scribbles that are gentle, delicate, or quiet.

7. *Ibid.,* p. 6.
8. Brent O. Wilson, "An Experimental Study Designed to Alter Fifth and Sixth Grade Students' Perception of Paintings," *Studies in Art Education,* 8, 1 (1966), 33–42.   R. A. Salome, "The Effects of Perceptual Training upon the Two-Dimensional Drawings of Children," *Studies in Art Education,* 7, 1 (1965), 18–33.
9. Elliot Eisner, *Educating Artistic Vision* (New York: Macmillan Publishing Co., Inc., 1972), p. 117.
10. Lowenfeld and Brittain, *op. cit.*

Careful observation of a child's scribbles over a period of time clearly shows that changes are taking place. These changes reflect certain psychological and physical changes in the child. The scribblings become more plentiful, more sophisticated, and more detailed. The changes may indicate normal growth, or they may reveal a child's fears, insecurity, and/or immaturity.

Lowenfeld and Brittain have charted a summary of the stages of creative growth as they relate to a child's general development.[11] The authors feel it is a valuable reference for teachers of all age groups. Portions of the chart are summarized below.

The characteristics of the child in the scribbling stage (ages two to four) are as follows:

1. *Scribbles are disordered.* Scribbling is a kinesthetic experience; the child has no control over his motions.
2. *Scribbles become more controlled.* Motions are repeated. Coordination between visual and motor activity is established. Motions become controlled and self-assurance of control is reflected in deviations in type of motions.
3. *Scribbles are named.* There is a change from kinesthetic to imaginative thinking. Motions are mixed with frequent interruptions.

The only reference to the human figure at this time is in the last scribbling stage, where a child labels a group of scribbles as a person. His relationship to space is only kinesthetic and imaginative.

The scribbling child makes no conscious approach to color; he uses color for mere enjoyment without any intentions. In the third stage of scribbling, color is used to ascribe different meanings to different scribbles.

At the scribbling stage there is no apparent awareness of design.

It is suggested that the teacher or parent encourage scribbling by not interrupting, discouraging, or diverting the child. In the advanced stage, one should allow him to talk about his scribbles; encouraging him and continuing his stories will help.

11. *Ibid.*, pp. 341–347. [This material appears in chart form in Viktor Lowenfeld and W. Lambert Brittain, "Summary of All Ages" in George Pappas, ed., *Concepts in Art and Education* (New York: Macmillan Publishing Co., Inc., 1970), pp. 341–348.]

The Preschematic Stage

The very young child comes to a peak point in creative expression at about the age of four or five. *The preschematic stage* is the label the researchers have given to this level where the child makes his first representational attempts. At this time, the young child often tries to use art as a means of communication, mainly because people will recognize his forms and will converse with him about them. At this level of growth, the child draws objects in his environment with which he has had experience.

The child's art products at this age indicate that he abstracts easily, or else that he sees simply. The idea he wishes to express fits his attention span, which is short, and his muscular coordination, which is mostly large.

Ideas come to children in the preschematic stage in a completely spontaneous fashion. They may originate from within the child—a chip or a synthesis of his experiences, his emotions, or his imagination—or they may be influenced in part at least by the medium and the skill with which the child uses it. Thus there is an integration of medium and idea. Much intuitive power is displayed: the child's innate feeling for aesthetic form, his remarkable sense of balance, his love for shape and color, and his sensitivity to variety. All combine in a progression of refinements toward drawings that become recognizable about the age of four. Even scribbles are developmental, for they move from the random scribbles mentioned above to organized scribbles and on into objects that are recognizable to others.

The young child is sensitive, eager, and curious. He loves to explore and manipulate, and he feels no restrictions about taking risks unless he has already been conditioned otherwise ("No, John, don't get in that nasty paint. You'll get your clothes dirty"). His lack of concern for the end product has a great deal to do with his willingness to take risks. Because he does not care much about the permanency of his work, he is willing to make mistakes to see how ideas turn out. In like manner, because a young child has little awareness of the standards or values of society (especially standards of art), his paintings are fresh, spontaneous expressions of color, of form, and, later, of representational or imaginative ideas.

Because the child experiments a great deal as he paints or draws and because he learns to manipulate his medium in the process of experimenting, this time in the child's life is referred to as a manipulative–exploratory stage.

The representational ideas he expresses during these years frequently require more muscular control, a greater knowledge of media, and a longer attention span than he is sometimes able to give them. He often becomes involved in detail and therefore becomes less concerned about the total form of the product. At first his objects are often placed randomly on the paper. In time, they become more of an intellectual statement, requiring eye–hand coordination and appearing less distorted than formerly. The child becomes more concerned over the end product. He also becomes concerned about the opinion of his peers, his teacher, his parents, and other adults.

According to Lowenfeld and Brittain, the four- to seven-year-old child in the preschematic stage is discovering a relationship between drawing, thinking, and his environment. He changes the form of his symbols because he is constantly searching for definite concepts.[12]

The human figure is represented with a circular form for the head and longitudinal lines for legs and arms. Head–feet representations develop into a more complex form concept. Symbols used during the art of drawing are dependent on active knowledge.

The youngster at this stage sees himself as the center of a universe where there is no orderly arrangement of objects in space. He identifies objects and emotionalizes relationships: "This is *my* doll."

The use of color at this time shows no relationship to nature. Color is selected according to emotional appeal.

The preschematic child has no conscious approach to design.

Preschool children automatically make play a multi sensory experience. A preschool child can feel, smell, taste, and see paint. He approaches his experiences with full sensations. He relates to his environment in a complete and natural manner without conditioning.

"Daddy," said my four-year-old in disgust, "do you know what Tommy Burns did in nursery school today?"

"No," I said. "I can't imagine!"

"Well," she went on, eyes wide with gossip, "the teacher gave each of us a little paste on a piece of paper for art and Tommy *ate* his!"

I curled my lip down and my nose up. "Ugh," I said. "That must have tasted terrible!"

12. *Ibid.*

Her face lit up. "Well, no," she said. "Actually it tastes pretty good!"

The Schematic Stage

The schematic stage is the next level of growth; it falls between seven and nine years of age. During this stage the child develops a definite *form* concept; he economizes his drawings by using standard symbols that he himself has invented or that he has seen somewhere else (the lollipop-shaped tree, a standard figure of a man). His drawings symbolize experiences with his environment.

One reason why children can express a common experience in a multitude of ways is that they each perceive the experience differently. Perception requires stimuli, and a teacher can develop or change perceptions through stimulating sensory experiences and discussion (see p. 209).

A painting can accurately be called a manifestation of a child's meaningful sensory experiences. It need not be seen, however, as an end product. Paintings at this stage are often merely a point in the child's expression of an experience, a part of the total process of painting a visual expression, and a step in the process of self-realization.

Common characteristics have been observed in drawings of children at this stage whether or not they have associated with other children in classrooms: rays extending from a sun, a common base line with objects lined up across the page, lollipop trees, etc.

According to Lowenfeld and Brittain, it is during this stage of growth that the child forms a definite concept of man and environment. He acquires a great deal of self-assurance through repetition of form symbols as schema.[13] In pure schema no intentional experience is expressed, only the thing itself—the man, the tree, etc. Experiences are expressed by deviations from schema. There is an abundant use of geometric lines.

At this time, the concept of the human figure becomes definite, depending on active knowledge and personality. Deviations expressing experiences can be seen in exaggeration of important parts, neglect or omission of unimportant parts, and change of symbols.

13. *Ibid.*

The child's concepts of space develop at this time. The first space concept to appear in his drawings is a base line suggesting base and/or terrain. The child sees himself now as a part of the universe and relates to others and to his environment. The deviations from the base line express his experiences. Space experiences commonly depicted in the paintings of this age group are folding over (egocentricity), mixed forms of plane and elevation, x-ray pictures, and space-time representations.

The child in the schematic stage discovers the relationship between color and object. Through repetition he develops a color schema; his paintings often use the same color for the same object, and deviations from his color schema show an emotional experience.

Still the child shows no conscious approach to design.

The child is now highly motivated by action, characterized by *we, action, where*. He enjoys topics involving time sequences and x-ray pictures (inside and outside).

Children often focus on one aspect of the visual world at a time and frequently do not recognize the relationship that form has to a visual field. In 1963 Harris indicated that the more a child knows about his environment, the more he is actively aware of and can utilize the components of it, the more intelligently developed he is. Harris points out that it is obvious that the child who has not developed concepts of his environment by the age of five is retarded.[14]

The Stage of Dawning Realism

The stage of dawning realism comes about the age of nine and lasts, with most children, until age eleven. Psychologists often refer to this stage as the gang stage because of the tremendous importance peer prestige has among children of this age. The physical changes that take place in children show in their drawings; they become more aware of self. Their drawings still indicate a generous use of symbolism, and detail is more carefully employed. Their drawings are more restricted and much less free than in earlier stages.

Biological development appears to produce emotional conflicts that greatly affect the child's spontaneity—the socializa-

14. D. B. Harris, *Children's Drawings as Measures of Intellectual Maturity* (New York: Harcourt Brace Jovanovich, Inc., 1963).

tion process often restricts his true creativity. He often hides his drawings and chooses not to share them with others. He often develops a distrust of personal kinds of expression.

As he becomes more and more accurate in his representational painting, he seems to decline in his ability to experiment, in his willingness to take risks, and, consequently, in his spontaneity and his pleasure in using art media.

The child's first representational drawings of flowers, tables, and people lack trueness of size and perspective; when he looks up at objects he sees the undersides, which adults do not see. A child's perspective is different from an adult's. There is a point beyond which height or distance is meaningless to the child. This is the child's means of comparison and must be accepted at this time as his true observations. He sees and thinks in terms of tall or small, tiny or great-big, long or short, not in terms of inches or feet, height or weight, volume or area. Concepts develop slowly, and as they develop he uses them in all forms of communication, including art expression, while constantly refining his ability to express himself.

The teacher should accept the child's trees, houses, and flowers even though they are not in proper relation to each other. She should encourage the child to paint exactly what he feels and sees, for by so doing she helps him to develop his ability independently. As he grows he increases his powers of observation and communication. The ability to reproduce objects exactly as he sees them can be utilized in making new and meaningful arrangements on paper. Children's paintings should be interpretations of their own experiences and interests and not random reproductions of someone else's visual impressions. Art is a unifying activity for children.

According to Lowenfeld and Brittain, this stage is characterized by a removal of geometric lines (schema). The child now shows more independence, an unwillingness to cooperate with adults, and a great awareness of self and of sex differences.[15]

In his human figures, he now gives his attention to clothes (dresses, uniforms) and emphasizes the differences between girls and boys. There is apt to be a stiffness in his figures as a result of his egocentric attitude and the emphasis placed on his own clothes, hair, etc. There is a tendency toward use of realistic lines for the human figure rather than schema.

Space is treated in a new way in his paintings. The base

15. Lowenfeld and Brittain, *op. cit.*

line is not the base of all expression.   There is overlapping—the sky is brought to the base line.   The child discovers the plane; space between the base lines is filled in.   He experiences difficulties in spatial correlations as a result of his egocentric attitude and unwillingness to cooperate.

The objective use of color is replaced by an emotional approach to color.   Color is now used to reflect subjective experience.

The child makes his first conscious approach to design. He becomes acquainted with materials and their functions.

The Pseudo-naturalistic Stage

The pseudo-naturalistic stage begins at about age eleven or twelve when the child, who is becoming increasingly aware of his natural surroundings, begins to worry about such things as proportion and depth in drawings.   This is also referred to as the age of reasoning.

Lowenfeld and Brittain describe this period as follows:

> There is a great deal of self-criticism, and drawings are now hidden in notebooks or are attempts at cartoons.   The drawing of a human figure shows a great deal of detail and, as might be expected, an increase in the awareness of sexual characteristics.   There is also a greater awareness of differences and gradations in color, although some youngsters are not able to develop this visual awareness.   For some, this stage marks the end of their artistic development and we often find that adults, when asked to draw something, will make a drawing that is typical of the twelve-year-old.
>
> At about the age of fourteen or later, youngsters are at the age of development where a real interest in visual art can take place.   They develop a conscious awareness of art and are often eager to develop artistic skills. . . .[16]

They go on to say that although intelligence is developed, unawareness still predominates.   An unconscious naturalistic approach to art is prevalent.   Children during this stage have a tendency toward visual- or nonvisual-mindedness.   They exhibit a great love for dramatization and action.

In drawing the human figure, joints are now used readily. Body actions are well portrayed, indicating visual observation.

16. *Ibid.*, p. 39.

Proportions are included.   The nonvisually-minded place emphasis on expression.

Children at this age seem to have an urge for three-dimensional expression.   Distant objects are portrayed in diminishing sizes.   A horizon line is common among the visually-minded, whereas the nonvisuals use environment in their drawings only when it is significant.

The visually-minded use color changes in nature to denote distance and mood, whereas the nonvisually-minded still show an emotional reaction to color.

The children make their first conscious approach to styling.   They use design especially in depicting the function of different materials with related designs.

At the pseudo-naturalistic stage a child's drawings begin to show a lack of integration.   This may be accounted for by the fact that the child develops an awareness, as he matures, of the attitudes and values of other children, other adults, and eventually of society as a whole, especially in relation to art.   Sometimes this awareness produces conflicts within him which affect his art expression.

All around him he sees and is influenced directly or subtly by these opinions and values.   One idea he is apt to be exposed to is the concept that whereas math and language arts are really basic and fundamental subjects that must be taught each day, art is a frill for which a once-a-week visit from the art teacher is sufficient.   He notes that the regular teacher even leaves the room.

He may discover at this time that society demands conformity and that he had best surrender his own uniqueness and personal expression in art if he wants to retain the approval of his teacher, his art teacher, and his parents.   He may discover that art, as well as the artist, ranks low on the value scale of society.

The type of art he sees at home and on the walls of his school helps establish standards for his own use of art media. Magazines, motion pictures, comic books, and the books and workbooks he uses at school all influence his standards and values at this time.   The emphasis placed on intellectual development and convergent learning may cause him to lose interest in developing his divergent thinking skills and his enjoyment of learning.

Other factors may account for the decline of spontaneity and symbolism in children's art by the time they reach their middle-school years.   One is the overconformity of formal learning, which has been declared a barrier to creative productivity since Lowenfeld's time. Secondly, art is frequently used poorly as a tool for teaching reading, numbers, social studies, and science (see Chapter 7). Through the uncreative use of a creative area, the concept of art in children has become fixed chiefly as that of trueness in drawing. Such use of art has depersonalized the experience and has made drawing skills another way of conforming in order to gain a coveted grade or needed status.

Situations that encourage sensitivity to aesthetic forms and the joy of experimenting and taking risks become fewer and fewer as the child goes through his formalized schooling. Consequently, the experiences of pleasure and success obtained from engaging in activities of this type are so few and far between that the senses become dulled to them and they gradually fade from the child's repertoire.

Lastly, teachers are not trained to develop creative expression. The child's drive to come in close relationship with his world is in conflict with the school's desire to teach him (in unnatural ways) to become acquainted with a particular set of happenings provided by adults which may or may not bear any relationship to his world. Consequently, his ability to express his ideas and feelings through the use of art media diminishes.

Empirical Generalizations concerning Children's Artistic Development

Some research studies regarding the developmental stages indicate that instruction in drawing does not have much influence upon the stages in young children.[17] Applegate found that children who appeared to be in a higher stage of development than their chronological age warranted were higher in mental age also.

In his book *Educating Artistic Vision*, Eisner made the following very worthwhile list of empirical generalizations con-

17. Salome, *op. cit.* Ronald W. Nepreud, "An Experimental Study of Visual Elements, Selected Art Instruction Methods and Drawing Development at the Fifth Grade Level," *Studies in Art Education*, 7, 2 (1966). 3. Betty Lark–Horowitz, Hilda Present Lewis, and Mark Luca, *Understanding Children's Art for Better Teaching* (Columbus, Ohio: Charles E. Merrill Publishing Co., 1967). Meidel Applegate, "Relationships of Characteristics of Children's Drawings to Chronological and Mental Age," Univ. of California at Berkeley, unpublished doctoral dissertation, 1967.

cerning children's artistic development.[18]   These principles, gleaned from research in art education, are of invaluable help to the classroom teacher and the art teacher in planning art experiences for children.

1. The characteristics of a child's art change as he ages chronologically.
2. The level of complexity of a child's art increases as the child matures.
3. The sense of cohesiveness or the Gestalt quality in a child's drawing increases as he matures (the form holds together visually as relationships between forms strengthen).
4. A child tends to exaggerate those aspects of a drawing, painting, or sculpture that are most meaningful to him.
5. During late preschool and early primary years, a child creates works that emphasize pictographic purposes. Later he expands these purposes to include problems of representation.
6. The scribbles that a preschool child makes tend to be motivated by kinesthetic and visual satisfaction emanating from actions.
7. The types of shapes that a child is able to produce are related to his age.
8. The degree of differentiation in a child's drawings is related to his conceptual maturity.
9. Drawing and painting tend to serve different purposes for the young child; the former is used for the expression of feeling.
10. The use of form, color, and composition is related to the child's personality and social development.
11. Children living in different cultures create visual forms with a remarkable degree of similarity, especially at the preschool level.
12. The human figure is the most common subject matter of school-age children's drawings.
13. When drawing, a young child tends to neglect a model or still life even when it is placed before him.
14. Drawing skills tend to be arrested at about the period of adolescence.
15. During the preschool and early elementary grades a child tends to focus exclusively on forms to be drawn, with little regard to the larger context or visual field in which they are to function.
16. No significant sex differences have been found in skill in the productive realm.
17. Children tend to prefer art forms that are visually unambiguous in character and that are related to their level of drawing ability and their age.

18. Adapted with permission of Macmillan Publishing Co., Inc. from *Educating Artistic Vision*, Copyright © 1972, by Elliot Eisner.

THE SPECIAL CHILD: HIS ART

The Gifted Child

Frequently one child in the classroom appears to be able to express his relation to his environment in a very unique way. For one of many reasons, he is identified as being outstanding in art. It may be that this child is considered "outstanding" simply because he fits the teacher's predetermined pattern of proper art behavior. Sometimes it is because he is able to add clever or cute touches to all that is done in the room. Occasionally it is because a child who is unable to read or write well is able to find a means of expressing himself or communicating through art, or a child who speaks little in class finds an outlet for his speech in the use of art media.

Whatever the case, the teacher must be careful about labeling the child's products as good or bad, or about attempting to evaluate them (see Chapter 10). The children described above are probably perfectly normal children. Gifted children, like normal children, may be seriously squelched when their art

FIGURE 3–1. A drawing by an exceptional seven-year-old of Snow White.

products are evaluated negatively.   The teacher should be concerned that the children relate to their environment, but not that they paint according to the teacher's standards and tastes.

Just as highly creative children tend to vary from the norms of development, so do highly intelligent children.   They represent one special group located in one special place on a continuum of intelligence.   The work of Getzels and Jackson has contributed substantially to our understanding of differences between highly intelligent and highly creative children.[19]   Their research helps teachers to realize that the relationship between creativity and intelligence is vague; highly intelligent children are not always creative, although highly creative children are always highly intelligent.

Their work showed that highly creative adolescents, for instance, were significantly superior in writing stimulus-free themes with unexpected endings, humor, incongruities, and playfulness.   They showed a marked tendency toward violence in their stories.   They tended to exhibit a mocking attitude toward conventional success.   High I.Q. children tended to be stimulus-bound, that is, they needed incentives and motivation to get them going.   High creatives tended to be stimulus-free, that is, they were easy to get going and often motivated themselves to a multitude of activities.

High I.Q.'s were unable, or at least unwilling, to risk the possibility of being misunderstood, whereas high creatives did not seem to worry about such risks.

In comparing a highly intelligent group of adolescents with a highly creative group, Getzels and Jackson found that both groups were superior to the general student groups.   Teachers exhibited a clear-cut preference for the highly intelligent group, although the highly creative group was preferred over the general student body.   When asked what qualities they would like to possess, the creative group placed high marks, pep and energy, character, and goal-directedness lower than members of the high I.Q. group and rated a wide range of interests, emotional stability, and a sense of humor higher than members of the high I.Q. group.   This is interesting, because Torrance's studies showed that these particular qualities were characteristic of highly creative children.[20]   All three of these researchers found that the one characteristic that set the creative group well apart from the

19. Jacob W. Getzels and Philip W. Jackson, *Creativity and Intelligence* (New York: John Wiley & Sons, Inc., 1962).
20. E. Paul Torrance, "Explorations in Creative Thinking," *Education*, 81 (December 1960), 216–220.

high I.Q. group was a sense of humor. The high I.Q. group wanted those qualities now that they believed would lead to success in adult life. The creative group was more realistic in selecting qualities more related to present aspirations. The high I.Q. group's personal aspirations were closely related to those that the teacher preferred, whereas the highly creative group showed a slightly negative correlation with those aspirations imposed by the teacher. They aspired more toward the self-ideal. In written responses the creative children showed more imagination and originality than the high I.Q. students.

These studies give us some inkling of the type of behavior teachers can look for in attempting to identify the highly creative child and of the degree to which these characteristics are reflected in the artwork of the highly intelligent child.

The Handicapped Child

Handicapped children have unique problems. Because their relationships with their environments (because of their handicaps) are ordinarily altered, the teacher cannot expect the art products of handicapped children to resemble the art products of other children in the classroom.

The Emotionally Disturbed Child

Often the paintings of the emotionally disturbed child contain in no small measure the problems that are disturbing him, drawn or painted in pictorial or symbolic form. A shy girl in one teacher's class painted an enormous hand through which one eye was peeking. A culturally deprived child known by the authors made endless numbers of beautiful things that she had seen for sale in the store windows. One paints shyness; the other paints longing. Only a very conceited teacher would feel she had the power or ability to grade such feelings. (See p. 344 for further discussion of evaluation.)

Such children are not capable of meeting head on those tasks that are mastered by the average elementary school child. A great deal of readiness is required to help them to begin to learn.

What these children need primarily is sensory experience with materials—a chance to manipulate and explore water, paint, blocks, clay, puzzles, toys, sand, dirt, etc.—and an opportunity to talk with adults and other children. The experiences normally included in the art program are excellent for these children, not solely from the standpoint of teaching them art but from the standpoint of helping them learn.

The Culturally Deprived Child

What is a deprived child? Generally a deprived child is one who has been insulated or isolated from external stimulation. This child has had impoverished experiences in feeling, smelling, tasting, seeing, and hearing. Even when he has experienced thought, sight, or sound, he has not been encouraged to relate it to himself as he functions within his environment. His sensations have been numbed; often his senses are used as a means of protection rather than as a means of providing him with sensations or pleasure.

In studying deprived children Malone found that these children were not alert or responsive to the teacher's spoken directions or to a display of colored paper, scissors, and paste.[21] Malone interpreted their behavior to mean that their vision was used primarily for self-protection and for other reasons different from those that motivate children in a more stable environment.

Most art programs for deprived cultures have been developed on the premise that pupils whose out-of-school experiences differ to a large degree from those of average middle-class children should be provided with in-school experiences that compensate for these differences.

In projects conducted in poverty schools, low scores on all tests with national norms have caused school personnel to examine in some detail those factors that keep children from learning. As might be expected, many of the learning problems are caused by the child's inability to perceive, to analyze, to visualize, to imagine, to compare, to interpret, or to create.

This is the effect on a child of a home where he is addressed in surly and minimal terms, where he uses his vision mainly as a means of protecting himself from fisticuffs, where he has little experience with toys, simple games, songs, and conver-

21. Charles Malone, "Safety First: Comments on the Influence of External Danger in the Lives of Children of Disorganized Families," in Harry L. Miller, ed., *Education for the Disadvantaged* (New York: The Free Press, 1967), pp. 53–64.

sations with parents, and where he lives in an atmosphere that is antisocial and emotionally packed.

In two poor, urban Philadelphia elementary schools, a learning dimensions program has been initiated. In reporting on this program, Margaret Bingham states: "The main purpose of the program is to find ways of helping turn the trend in these two schools away from hopelessness by acknowledging and responding to some of the children's needs."[22]

The program is not an art program in the conventional sense. It is a program that attempts to get to the basic learning patterns of children five to eleven, and in so doing has come to realize that the arts must become a part of the total curriculum because they are related to man's basic learning processes. The emphasis is on *who* is learning and *how* learning takes place rather than *what* is being taught. Bingham goes on to say:

> The important thing that evolved was that "discoveries" of patterns and relationships are as new to the child as they were for the first person who discovered them. The implications for teachers were that they not only had to ask children the kind of open-ended questions that would lead them to discover some patterns but also to structure activities so that each child would be free to explore within a framework that is clear and meaningful to him.

The program is influenced by the theories of Jean Piaget. Piaget deals with how we act on new information in order to learn it—how we organize it by classifying, ordering, matching, and verifying.

Two profound ideas that emerge from Piaget's theory are applied in this project:

1. No two people adapt or learn information at the same rate or in the same way.
2. Thinking skills develop only when we work with and organize concrete objects for ourselves.

The people who developed the project organized it with some new concepts in mind:

22. Margaret Bingham, "Learning Dimensions: A Change Model for the Elementary School," in Al Hurwitz, ed., *Programs of Promise: Art in the Schools* (New York: Harcourt Brace Jovanovich, Inc., 1972), pp. 61–74.

1. Activity is important to learning. The arts must have a crucial role in the total learning process because of the activity involved in learning about them.
2. Thinking rather than reading must be a major priority.

Then

The creative experiences associated with the arts, humanistic interaction associated with exchanging ideas, and comprehension of what one is doing and reading must be the threefold approach to a total educational package from five years on up.[23]

To accomplish their goals, the teachers in the project organized their classrooms around the idea of the open classroom (see p. 157) where art activities are an integral part of the total learning program. In teacher education emphasis was not placed on learning art skills and techniques, but rather on developing skills in classroom organization through activity centers, on knowing how and when to ask questions of children, and on finding ways to evaluate children's work.

The artwork of socially handicapped children reflects their own background of isolation from others and their inability to correlate their experiences with those of others. It is characterized by spatially unrelated items, by inconsistency among the items, and by the fact that most of the figures are drawn in isolation.

Bronfenbrenner found that children raised in an atmosphere of deprivation and sterility fell far behind normal development in their growth.[24]

White reported in his studies that children who were exposed to an enriched visual environment during the first few months of life developed faster than children who did not have anything to focus on.[25]

Eisner conducted a study of the developmental drawing characteristics of culturally advantaged and culturally disadvan-

23. *Ibid.*, p. 64.
24. V. Bronfenbrenner, "Early Development in Mammals and Man" in G. Newton, ed., *Early Experiences and Behavior* (Springfield, Ill.: Charles C Thomas, Publisher, 1968).
25. Burton L. White and Peter W. Castle, "Visual Exploratory Behavior Following Postnatal Handling of Human Infants," *Perceptual and Motor Skills*, 18 (1964), 476. Burton L. White, "Informal Education during the First Months of Life," in R. H. Hess and R. M. Bear, eds., *Early Education* (Chicago: Aldine Publishing Co., 1968), pp. 143–169.

taged children.[26]   He concluded that, on the average, children who came from advantaged communities tended at all grade levels to be more advanced in their ability to create visual depth through the use of overlapping forms than did children from ghetto areas. On the variable measured, namely the treatment of space, children from disadvantaged backgrounds were so far behind their more advantaged counterparts at the first-grade level that it took until fifth grade for their average achievement in drawing to rise to a level achieved in the first grade by the advantaged group.

Eisner also found that the variability at each grade level for each group tended to decrease as the children got older. Children's abilities in drawing at the first-grade level were more heterogeneous than they were at the third-grade level; third graders were more heterogeneous than fifth graders, and fifth graders were more heterogeneous than seventh graders. Eisner stated: "In short, the older children become, the less they differ in ability on the variable measured in this study."

It is interesting to note that the advantaged group reached a plateau around the fifth-grade level and did not advance noticeably until the disadvantaged group almost caught up. Eisner felt this was because drawing was "taught" to the disadvantaged and time was allotted for them to experiment, whereas it was not taught to the advantaged group. He found that drawing skills were developed up to a typical level and then ignored.

Obviously conditions for teaching art in one school vary from those in another, even when similar goals are established.

THE CREATIVE CHILD: HIS CHARACTERISTICS

Although the contributions of the behaviorists have been invaluable in helping teachers recognize and understand natural art processes, more recent research on the personalities of children identified as creative has also made valuable contributions to an understanding of how conditions can be set for all children to better develop their total creativity. These studies indicate that the creative child is not like other children. Because of his high creative drive, he develops certain characteristics that alter his behavior and make him different. Studies of these children show

26. Eisner, *Educating Artistic Vision*, pp. 127–133.

that they are not liked by their teachers and are often treated by the teachers along punitive lines.   They are often discriminated against, and they are not always accepted socially by their peers. To date, no studies have been made to determine whether or not these children deviate from the "normal" stages in art development as defined by Lowenfeld and others in the early part of this chapter.   The chances are that they do, that their own uniqueness exempts them from some of the stages described above.

It must be remembered that the characteristics discussed here are generalizations of studies made of hundreds of children and that no one individual is likely to fit the total pattern.   Children possess varying degrees of creativity, developed or undeveloped, largely because of the environment in which they have grown up.   The characteristics described below are largely descriptive of those children who fall near the "highly creative" end of a continuum.

1. *Creative persons are superior to noncreative persons in their fluency, flexibility, originality, and elaboration.*[27]   The teacher in the regular classroom can readily observe these qualities in her children.

Fluency refers to the ease and ability with which a child expresses himself in a constant stream of communication.   In art products, fluency can be observed in the ease and rapidity with which children adapt to a medium and the frequency with which they use one medium or a variety of media.   In a nursery school situation one child painted ten pictures of the human figure in ten minutes.   Each was snatched off the easel and thrown in the wastebasket as soon as it had been completed.   This child felt no desire or need for a "polished" art product.   He was obviously in the manipulative and exploratory stages of painting.   But his fluency was certainly showing!

In early studies, verbal facility, the ease with which children talk, was a separate category.   It referred to the ability of children to articulate well and to spout their opinions and feelings at the drop of a hat.   Later studies have considered verbal facility to be an aspect of fluency.

Flexibility is defined as the ability to jump readily from one idea to another.   Children who possess verbal flexibility are not deterred when idea-killing statements are used to discourage them.   They generally rally instantly to the situation and propose

27. Original list in J. C. Drevdahl, "Factors of Importance in Creativity," *Journal of Clinical Psychology,* 12 (1956), pp. 21–26.

alternate solutions. In art products, flexibility is indicated by versatility in the tools and media used in creating an art product and by the ease with which the creator goes from one topic to another.

Originality is determined by the degree to which art products (or verbal statements) differ from other products in any given group or from the total population. Originality is the mark of individuality. Sometimes the style of an artist develops from his own unique type of originality.

Elaboration, which was added to the list by Torrance, is defined as the ability to embellish or expand on an idea—the skill of filling it out to realize its greatest potential. In art products it is recognized in the degree to which a child uses detail or, in reverse, expresses a multitude of ideas in one unique way. The sketches in Fig. 3–2 show the differences in the drawings of children who were given an egg shape and told to create something from it.

These four characteristics have been so predominant in the studies of highly creative children that they have been used by E. Paul Torrance as a basis for measuring creativity in the Torrance Tests of Creative Thinking.[28]   (See Chapter 10 for a discussion of evaluation.)

Other studies have identified other general characteristics of creative children.[29]

2. *Creative children tend to be more withdrawn and quiescent than noncreative children.* They tend to be low in sociability and are often estranged from their peers and their teacher. Creative children are accused of having wild and silly ideas. Many times their work is off the beaten track. These children tend to work in isolation.

This cluster of behavior characteristics may make the creative child stand out in the regular classroom. In terms of art behavior, an observant teacher notes that his products rate high on originality. In working on his art products he may often be by himself mentally even though he is physically near other children at the same table. In discussions he is the one who often has his hand raised and when called upon may have unusual or even unreasonable ideas. Teachers who tend to scoff or belittle such

28. E. Paul Torrance, *Torrance Tests of Creative Thinking* (Princeton, N.J.: Personnel Press, Inc., 1966).
29. C. W. Taylor, "Finding the Creative," *Scientific Research,* 27 (December, 1961), 6–11.

FIGURE 3–2.   Egg-shaped creations.

ideas from such a child often build up a similar attitude in his classmates. The creative child is not often chosen to be on teams or to work with other children. Creative children may take active part in discussion and may speak fluently when called upon, but for the most part they work and study by themselves and do not often have a buddy, nor do they mingle with the total class group.

    3. *Creative children are more stable than the average*

child. They are more self-sufficient, more self-accepting, and more independent of judgment. They control their own behavior more, although they are often uncooperative and egocentric.

A creative child tends to go to work more quickly than others. He does not ask for help from his teachers or classmates as often as other children. He has ideas of his own that he intends to carry out regardless of interferences and interruptions. This often leads to selfish acts on his part, such as hoarding certain materials that should be shared with others. He seems to be emotionally mature and able to cope with abuse, ridicule, sarcasm, and antisocial acts inflicted upon him. Often he is forced to make a decision as to whether he will take social status with his peers or sacrifice it to promote the creative (or original) behavior that is bringing about his social estrangement. The "drive of passion" mentioned by Rugg (p. 13) is apparent in these children. They seem to feel compelled to complete a creative job once they have begun. In so doing, they often bulldoze their way toward a finish, pushing out of their thoughts and minds anyone or anything that gets in the way. They seem to possess unlimited amounts of energy and enthusiasm to complete the jobs they begin. Because they become so absorbed in their own particular product, they are often inconsiderate of and uncooperative with others. They are regarded as self-centered and egotistic by their peers.

4. *The creative child is characterized by his excellent sense of humor and his playfulness.* He is adventurous; he is willing to take risks. He does not like to judge, but he is superior at perception. He is more resourceful than the average child.

In all the studies conducted on the characteristics of creative people (children included) there is more agreement on these matters than on any others. The sense of humor of the creative child is obvious in his wisecracks, his witticisms, and his daring remarks. In his work little touches appear that bring a giggle or a smile to the observer's face and such reactions as "cute," "clever," or "charming." In John's painting of the destruction wrought by a bombing raid in Viet Nam the air was full of planes and the bombs were exploding in terrifying colors all over the paper. On the ground buildings were toppling and burning, people were running, and vehicles were lying about blown to pieces. In the center of all this color and confusion sat a crying baby with a sign in her hand which the viewer might tend to pass over quickly. A close examination revealed that it read: "Jesus saves."

Creative children will be more willing to try out new

media or to experiment with paint and clay. They are often the ones who place their papers at a different angle when they work. When tie-dyeing they tie their cloth different ways, dip the cloth in a different manner, or mix the dyes. They seem to be better able to use materials at hand or to invent tools and media if the desired ones are not available.

Deborah, for instance, was intrigued by the silk screen process which she saw demonstrated in a high school class one day. Lacking the standard equipment, she took materials she found in the junk box and invented her own printing process. A set of crochet hoops was her frame. With heavy crayon she drew a design on some scraps of silk and organdy her mother came up with. Then, clamping the organdy between the embroidery hoops, she pulled it as tight as possible. She then used a soft rubber spatula to force fingerpaint through the fabric. The wax crayon resisted the paint, whereas the organdy allowed it to go through onto the paper below, creating the drawn design in silhouette. Later Deborah discovered that melted wax was a better medium than wax crayon and resisted the fingerpaint as effectively. Deborah had used the principle of *adaptation* mentioned in Chapter 1 to invent a new way of printing. Her own flexibility and resourcefulness were apparent in this process.

5. *Creative children are more nonconforming than other children.* They tend to conform less than noncreative people even under group pressure. They are interested in unconventional careers. They are more radical and more complex as persons, and they are less subject to group standards and controls.

Creative children do not generally like to follow models or examples. They sometimes perfect a skill by copying. Buddy learned "trueness" in art by drawing comic strip characters for a period of time. As soon as the copying had served its purpose, however, Buddy was encouraged to create comic characters and cartoons of his own and his work again became individual and nonconforming.

Whereas the average girl tends to identify with film stars, airline stewardesses, nurses, and other glamorous people in the middle-school years, creative girls are more likely to identify with roles such as television producer, airplane mechanic, space explorer, or costume designer. Creative children do not change their opinions and beliefs simply to go along with the crowd; they must be convinced that they have been wrong by new evidence. The art content of their pictures and sculptures may be different from that of the more conventional child. The creative child is neither compulsively conforming or nonconforming. He is either, depending how it affects him or his group.

6. *Creative children are more emotionally sensitive than the average person.* Boys are more feminine in their interests and characteristics, especially in their awareness of one's impulses. They have fuller access to their own life experiences because they do not suppress impulses and imagery as much as conventional children do. Creative children react to experiences more fully in thought and feeling, although some, such as the artist, react more with feeling, whereas others, such as the scientist, react more with thought.

To say that a creative child is more emotionally sensitive to life experiences does not mean that he is more emotional.

One morning in nursery school, Douglas, a brilliant four-year-old, drew a scene he had witnessed the evening before. He and his father had followed the fire engines to a neighboring apartment house that was burning. The sirens screamed, the firemen shouted, people cried out, smoke and flames poured from the building, and all was confusion and noise for a long time. Douglas's picture was drawn with red crayon and he caught all the action. The building was covered with ladders and crawling firemen hacking away with hatchets. The ground was alive with firemen, serpentine hoses, and huge fire and ladder equipment. The smoke and flames poured from the windows, water shot into the roof from hoses held firmly by firemen, and a police car stood by.

When Douglas finished his painting he took a blue crayon and, starting at the top left-hand corner of the drawing, he made a blue swing to the right and then back from the right to the left, making a blue spiral that ended in a point in the middle of the page at the bottom. Looking at the teacher Douglas said, "And that's the noise of the siren!"

Everything was in Douglas's picture except the noise of the siren, one of the most exciting parts of the panorama of the fire. This creative child found a way to express the siren in his picture. Less creative children would not have attempted to do this.

Douglas's ability to draw representationally at his age indicated what in this case was true—that he was a brilliant boy. His ability to symbolize noise by linear movement was a product of his keen thinking abilities. However, this is not necessarily the case, as slower children have also been known to do this.

Creative children often comment in the classroom on things they have seen in a film or a play that other children have

FIGURE 3–3.   Creative children are highly original: Norma's drawing for her story of the Larken family, settlers of the West.

missed.   Often they ask questions about seemingly insignificant parts of an experience.   In attempting to answer these questions, a teacher may find that they are, after all, highly significant.

Because creative boys tend not to limit themselves by strict identification with sex roles, they enjoy exploring female

roles. Many men like to knit, to cook, to practice interior decorating, and to care for children, roles generally assigned to the
female in the American culture. Of late, the sex role lines have
been greatly diminished; this will probably contribute to some
extent to creative development.

Creative children are much freer about transferring life
experiences into symbolic or pictorial representation. At times
this can cause problems in the schoolroom, as when Bobby
painted a scene depicting his trip to the YMCA over the weekend
to swim with his Dad and other friends. It was obvious that one
swam at the "Y" in the nude. But Mr. Cary, Bobby's teacher,
made no special fuss about it. He reassured Bobby that he
should paint what he felt like painting but that some pictures
were for them to share together. Creative children are impulsive,
less inhibited, and more honest in their reactions than other
children.

There is another characteristic or quality of creative
children that the teacher should keep in mind.

7. *A creative person becomes, to a high degree, the indi-*
vidual he is capable of becoming. He is more likely to fulfill his
life potential. Sometimes he is judged to be socially irrespon-
sible, but this may be due to the fact that inner security makes it
unnecessary for him to seek approval from others by following all
the conventions of society. In reality, he may be very responsible; he simply is not a conformist.

SUMMARY

In this chapter the literature on the nature of children and the
normal developmental patterns of their art growth has been
reviewed. It was pointed out that disadvantaged and gifted
children need a special kind of environment in order to develop
in art expression. This may also be true of the creative child,
who exhibits characteristics that differ from those of normal
children.

Smith summarizes the problem of creative children as
follows:

> Often they must choose between social acceptance and their
> own personal intellectual challenge. When they choose in-
> tellectual challenge they may alienate friends, or, driven by

enthusiasm and passion to follow through on an idea, they may appear to be different or not well-rounded.

Creative children like to attempt challenging, diffi-cult, and dangerous tasks; they strive to bring order out of disorder, sense out of chaos; they seek for a purpose. Be-cause of their willingness to cope with the unsolved and the unusual, they may become psychologically estranged from other children. Because the problems they attack differ from purely "intellectual" problems, their behavior is different; they demonstrate characteristics different from accepted norms and their problems of adjustment are more difficult.

Creative children, therefore, may exhibit some types of behavior not readily accepted by the traditional teacher: low sociability; feminine interests, domination and self-assertion; introversion; boldness; silly ideas; playfulness; egocentricity; lack of cooperation; a certain amount of Bohemianism; radical outlooks; lack of interest in small de-tails; nonconformity; lack of courtesy or adherence to conventions; emotionalism; self-satisfaction; excessive ques-tioning; stubbornness; capriciousness; timidity; withdrawal; and resistance to teacher domination.

It is difficult to determine whether the less acceptable personality factors in the creative child *result* from social pressures created by his teachers, parents and peers because they do not understand the social–emotional problems he en-counters in his daily living.[30]

Smith goes on to say: "Creative children do, however, also exhibit behavior that we would like to see more often in all citizens of a free society." He then lists several of these charac-teristics; among them are high motivation, sensitivity, the ability to define problems, the drive to bring order from disorder, the ability to abstract and analyze, the willingness to stick to a goal or belief until disproven, the ability to evaluate and to synthesize, and many more.

Smith points out that we need to take a fresh look at the behavior of children and seek new interpretations of it. He says:

If the less-accepted factors of personality in the creative child result from classroom organization and structure, new patterns of organization may be necessary so that creative children stand a strong chance of developing and are not plowed under—victims of their conforming teacher and their conforming peers—seeking status in the cocoon of so-

30. James A. Smith, *Setting Conditions for Creative Teaching in the Elementary School* (Boston: Allyn and Bacon, Inc., 1966), p. 77.

ciety, rather than developing their own particular contribution to society.

Studies need to be done to show how these characteristics affect the development of art expression in creative children.

ACTIVITIES

1. Look through the samples of children's paintings in this book (other than those in this chapter) and classify them under the following headings: scribbling stage, preschematic stage, schematic stage, stage of dawning realism, and pseudo-naturalistic stage.
2. After reading this chapter, could you agree with the following statements?
   a. "The best teaching at times may be no teaching at all." When would this be true in art? When would it not be true?
   b. From Lowenfeld and Brittain:
      Art education, as an essential part of the educative process, may well mean the difference between a flexible, creative human being and one who will not be able to apply his learning, who will lack inner resources, and who will have difficulty relating to his environment.[31]
   c. From A. G. Sibley:
      As long as a child is in the preschematic stage he cannot learn how to read. Nor is he able to reason in an abstract manner so that he can understand the logical relationship of numbers. A child may learn to recognize words and to count but he does not really understand what he is doing.[32] Does this quote give you some clues as to how children's art may help a teacher determine a child's readiness? Discuss how his artwork shows other things about him.
3. Can you identify the creative children in your classroom? How? Could you devise a checklist of items that would help you, using the material in this chapter as a reference?
4. Make collections of children's paintings that do not have meaning to you but that obviously mean something to the child. Using the interview technique described in Chapter 10, talk with them about their paintings and observe their behavior on succeeding days.

31. Lowenfeld and Brittain, *op. cit.*, p. 6.
32. A. G. Sibley, "Drawings of Kindergarten Children as a Measure of Reading Readiness," Cornell University, unpublished Masters thesis, 1957.

5. Make lists of all the unusual media that you might introduce to children in order to have a basis for studying development at varying age levels.   Think of media not mentioned
in this chapter, such as water, sand for sand painting, colored sawdust, ceramic tile, and colored glass.

6. Check yourself during a day's time and note how many times
you ask your students to follow some pattern—an art pattern,
a pattern of thinking, or a pattern of doing.   Ask yourself
how many times this is necessary and how you might better
allow the children to set their minds to work in their own
manner.   Introduce the children to new ways of thinking and
to helping you in new ways of planning.

7. Can your present art program be improved through a realistic
team-teaching approach?   Make a list of all the ways you
could work more beneficially with your art teacher.

8. Anna Jones was a kindergarten teacher.   One day she stopped
behind Billy Manning's table and held up the crayon drawing
he was working on.   "Boys and girls," she said, "I want you
all to look at Billy's crayon drawing. Isn't it lovely?   See how
nicely he has made his flowers.   Today he has put petals and
leaves on his flowers.   Last week he didn't have them there.
This is so much better, Billy.   You are a good boy!"
     What is wrong with this situation, considering what
you have read in this chapter?

9. Make one creative teaching device to use with your children
each day; it need not be elaborate.   Try it out and examine
your own feelings when you see the children enjoying it.
Think of this statement: "To be creative means to care
about things and places and human beings.   When you care
enough about people to do things for them you release creative powers in yourself."

10. Laura Zirbes, author of *Spurs to Creative Teaching*, has made
some tapes that stimulate classroom discussion.   They may
be available in your audiovisual center.   The following are
suggested for use at this particular time: No. Z-5, *Child Development through Art Education*, 16 min.; and No. Z-6,
Music and the Creative Urge in Child Development (2 parts),
45 min.   You can get them from the Teaching Aids Laboratory, Ohio State University, Columbus, Ohio.

11. Using the same "subject matter" (such as a woman, a child,
a house, or a tree) find all the different ways it can be represented.   Or, better yet, see how many ways you can represent
it.   Sometimes Christmas cards illustrate the concept of adaptation and modification very well.   Collect old Christmas
cards and note, for instance, how many ways artists draw a
Christmas tree, a wreath, and a partridge in a pear tree.

SELECTED BIBLIOGRAPHY

Alschuler, Rose H., and La Berta W. Hattwick. *Painting and Personality: A Study of Young Children.* Chicago: University of Chicago Press, 1969.

Association for Supervision and Curriculum Development. *Perceiving, Behaving, Becoming.* Washington, D.C.: National Education Association, 1962.

Barbe, Walter B., ed. *Psychology and Education of the Gifted.* New York: Appleton-Century-Crofts, 1965.

Barkan, Manuel. *Through Art to Creativity.* Boston: Allyn and Bacon, Inc., 1960.

Bloom, Benjamin, Allison Davis, and Robert Hess. *Compensatory Education for Cultural Deprivation.* New York: Holt, Rinehart and Winston, Inc., 1965.

Brittain, W. Lambert. "Some Exploratory Studies of the Art of Preschool Children," *Studies in Art Education,* 10, 3 (Spring 1969), 14–24.

Bronfenbrenner, V. "Early Development in Mammals and Man." *Early Experiences and Behavior.* G. Newton, ed. Springfield, Ill.: Charles C Thomas, Publisher, 1968.

Brookover, Wilbur B., et al. "Self-Concept of Ability and School Achievement." *Education for the Disadvantaged.* H. L. Miller, ed. New York: The Free Press, 1967.

Cole, Natalie. *The Arts in the Classroom.* New York: John Day Co., Inc., 1940.

———. *Children's Art from Deep Down Inside.* New York: John Day Co., Inc., 1966.

Corcoran, A. L. "Color Usage in Nursery School Painting," *Child Development,* 25, 2 (1954), 107ff.

Dennis, Wayne. *Group Values through Children's Drawings.* New York: John Wiley & Sons, Inc., 1966.

Deutsch, Martin. "The Disadvantaged Child and the Learning Process." *Education in Depressed Areas.* Harry A. Passow, ed. New York: Bureau of Publications, Teachers College, Columbia University, 1963.

Dreyer, Albert S., and Mary Beth Wells. "Parental Values, Parental Control and Creativity in Young Children," *Journal of Marriage and the Family,* 28, L (1966), 83.

Eisner, Elliot. "Children's Creativity in Art: A Study of Types," *American Educational Research Journal,* 2, 3 (May 1965).

———. "Curriculum Making for Wee Folk: Stanford University's Kettering Project," *Studies in Art Education,* 9, 3 (Spring 1968), 45–46.

————, et al. *Teaching Art to the Young: A Curriculum Development Project in Art Education.* Stanford, Calif.: School of Education, Stanford University, November 1969.

Gaitskell, Charles D. *Children and Their Art.* New York: Harcourt Brace Jovanovich, Inc., 1958.

Guilford, J. P. "Creative Abilities in the Arts," *Psychological Review,* 64, 2 (1957), 110–118.

Harris, D. B. *Children's Drawings as Measures of Intellectual Maturity.* New York: Harcourt Brace Jovanovich, Inc., 1963.

Kellogg, Rhoda. *Analyzing Children's Art.* Palo Alto, Calif.: National Press Books, 1969.

————. *The Psychology of Children's Art.* New York: CRM, 1967.

Kozol, Jonathan. *Death at an Early Age.* Boston: Houghton Mifflin Co., 1967.

Lark-Horowitz, Betty, Hilda Present Lewis, and Mark Luca. *Understanding Children's Art for Better Teaching.* Columbus, Ohio: Charles E. Merrill Publishing Co., 1967.

Lowenfeld, Viktor. *Creative and Mental Growth.* New York: Macmillan Publishing Co., Inc., 1947. (Revised fifth edition by Lowenfeld and Brittain, Macmillan, 1970.)

————, and W. Lambert Brittain. "Summary of All Ages." *Concepts in Art and Education.* George Pappas, ed. New York: Macmillan Publishing Co., Inc., 1970, pp. 341–348.

Mead, Margaret. *A Creative Life for Your Children.* Washington, D.C.: U.S. Department of Health, Education, and Welfare, 1962.

Mendelowitz, Daniel M. *Children Are Artists,* 2nd ed. Stanford, Calif.: Stanford University Press, 1963.

Nelson, Thomas M., and Merle E. Flannery. "Instructions in Drawing Techniques as a Means of Utilizing Drawing Potential of Six and Seven Year Olds," *Studies in Art Education,* 8, 2 (1967), 58.

Nepreud, Ronald W. "An Experimental Study of Visual Elements, Selected Art Instruction Methods and Drawing Development at the Fifth Grade Level," *Studies in Art Education,* 7, 2 (1966), 3.

Piaget, Jean, and Barbel Inhelder. *The Psychology of the Child.* New York: Basic Books, Inc., Publishers, 1969.

Reichenberg-Hackett, W. "The Influence of Nursery Group Experience on Children's Drawings," *Psychological Reports,* No. 14 (1964), 433–434.

Russell, Irene, and Blanche Waugaman. "A Study of the Effect of Workbook Copy Experiences on the Creative Concepts of

Children," *Research Bulletin* (The Eastern Arts Association), 3, 1 (1952).

Silverman, Ronald H. "Art Education for Disadvantaged Seventh Graders: An Experimental Approach." *Programs of Promise: Art in the Schools.* Al Hurwitz, ed. New York: Harcourt Brace Jovanovich, Inc., 1972.

Thomas, R. Murray. "Effects of Frustration on Children's Paintings," *Child Development,* 22, 2 (June 1951), 123–132.

Wodtke, Kenneth H., and Norman E. Wallen. "The Effects of Teacher Control in the Classroom on Pupils' Creativity-Test Gains," *American Educational Research Journal,* 2, 2 (March 1965), 75–82.

CHAPTER IV

The Nature of the Art Team

*They are highly skilled in human communications
and understanding as well as in their subject matter.
In addition to this, in much the manner of a child,
they seemed to have kept something of the wonder
and magic of seeing things new and afresh day after
day.*

BETTY TISSINGER[1]

Changes must be made in the organizational structure of most of
our elementary schools if art teaching is ever to become effective
enough to meet the goals of art education. Objectives must be
spelled out much more clearly and specifically than they have
been in the past, and the roles of both the art teacher and the
classroom teacher must be defined. Most important of all, both
the art specialist and the classroom teacher must modify their
current roles to the degree that both can be called art teachers.

Many elements of artistic behavior are also elements of
good classroom behavior: conceiving, structuring, organizing,
presenting, responding, evaluating. Using these common activities as a base, art and classroom teachers must learn to work in
some sort of team arrangement to develop art and creative
expression in children.

In this chapter the authors identify the problems of the
art and elementary school teachers and attempt to help each
formulate his new role.

1. Betty Tissinger describing master teachers in "Search of a Model,"
Art Education, 24 (April 1971), 27.

THE ROLE OF THE SPECIALIST

A glance at the Preface of this volume reveals a startling fact—
the common belief that the public schools of America are well
staffed with art teachers is a myth! The following statement is
from an article by Guy Hubbard and Mary J. Rouse which
appears in a recent book by Hurwitz.

> The statistics speak for themselves. Approximately 90 per-
> cent of elementary art is taught by classroom teachers of
> whom only 15–20 percent receive help from art specialists.
> Of all the 10 percent of children who are lucky enough to
> have art instruction from professional art teachers, most are
> likely to meet their art teacher with a frequency of anywhere
> between twice a week and once a month.[2]

The authors of this article point out the critical state of
art education in the elementary schools of America and offer
some suggestions for remediation.

"Without a doubt," they say, "the best solution is to have
a talented art teacher in every school." They emphasize the
importance of enlarging the possibilities of personal contact with
each child.

This statement is obviously true in itself, but it is not
necessarily the answer to the problem of the teaching of art in the
elementary school today. Having a talented art teacher in every
school will not solve the problem; *it is what that teacher will do
in that school that counts!*

The elementary schools that do have art teachers do not
all have good art programs. The presence of the art teacher does
not always account for a good art program. Just as there are
poor classroom teachers, so are there poor art teachers. The
percentage of poor teachers cuts drastically into the ten percent
of America's schools that do have art teachers.

The authors recently visited a spring arts festival in a
central school. The festival was held outdoors and the entire
community was invited. (See p. 234 for a more detailed account
of this festival.) It was, without a doubt, one of the best experiences in art and human relations they have ever seen.

2. Guy Hubbard and Mary J. Rouse, "Art Meaning, Method and Media:
A Structured Art Program for Elementary Classrooms" in Al Hurwitz,
ed., *Programs of Promise: Art in the Schools* (New York: Harcourt,
Brace Jovanovich, Inc., 1972), p. 15.

FIGURE 4–1.   A festival of the arts: a community project.

The art teacher was a dynamo. Her personality was warm, friendly, bubbly, and happy. The children related to her extremely well. Art was the hub of learning in that school. The art teacher served as a member of the primary teachers' team and met with them during their regular curriculum meetings; she also met with the middle-school teachers at times as a member of their team. The artwork was planned so that both the principles of curriculum development and the principles of art were applied. The classroom teachers taught art as a part of every school day, but they did it under the guidance and direction of the art teacher. The art teacher visited the classrooms frequently and supervised the organization of committees of children to keep the halls and classrooms attractive with displays. An art studio was available to classes and, at prescribed times, to individuals.

In a classroom in another school the authors visited, the door opened at exactly 10:30 and the art teacher entered pushing a cart. She asked some children to help her, and then she proceeded to pass out corrugated cardboard, blunt cutting knives, paper, paints, and brushes. Next she gave a demonstration of how to cut one layer of corrugated cardboard away from the other in order to make a print. It is interesting to note that when the art teacher walked in at 10:30, the classroom teacher walked out. At exactly 11:20, the art teacher announced that the class had ten minutes left to clean up before she would have to leave. Some children eagerly cleaned off their desks and placed their materials on the art cart. Others groaned and complained, knowing that they would not finish their work during that period, if ever. At 11:30, after a mad rush, the art teacher passed the classroom teacher in the doorway as she left the room. The classroom teacher walked to the front of the room and told the children to prepare to take their spelling tests.

Between the two examples mentioned above there is a continuum of types of art teachers and elementary school teachers, each with her own concept of her role.

One of the authors has taught and worked in elementary schools for over thirty-five years. His own history in elementary education parallels the history of art education in this country. As a teacher in a country school, he taught his own art. His only preparation for this was a college course on arts and crafts, which was taught twice a week for one semester by an art educator. To secure a normal school diploma and to be certified to teach in New York State, he then took courses in art appreciation, crafts, and "art in the elementary school." Some of these courses were electives. Because he was extremely interested in art, he took all the electives he could in art.

The first art teacher with whom he worked became available to the two-room rural school where he taught when the school became a part of a central school system. Following is an account of his experiences.

Miss Banning came twice a week for forty-five minutes and during that time she "taught" art. The experience was pleasant. Miss Banning was congenial, she knew her subject, she knew boys and girls, and she knew how to motivate them. The children loved her and they liked art. They looked forward to her visits. During her visits, I sat in the rear of the room or assisted Miss Banning when she taught. Sometimes Miss Banning found time to talk with me and we made plans, trying to integrate or correlate art activities with the children's classroom experiences.

Art was basically a garnish. Occasionally—for example, during a social studies unit conducted by the entire community on religions—art became a potent force in communicating ideas and in promoting visual aesthetics. However, most of the art activities were planned by Miss Banning, and the execution of the art program was her responsibility.

During the remainder of the week, I carried out a rich art program. Miss Banning was always on tap when she was needed—she gave each teacher in the district her schedule, which she arranged so that she could be in her office at specific times to meet our needs. She brought materials, planned with me when she could, and kept the schools under her jurisdiction buzzing with excitement.

But time took its toll. The post-world war baby boom was on and our schools became more and more crowded. At first Miss Banning was forced to cut her visits from forty-five minutes to half an hour. Finally she was coming only three times in two weeks. Obviously, she began to show signs of fatigue. But we still had a good art program! Under her guidance I assumed more of the responsibility for teaching art and things went quite well. I know I learned a lot. Miss Banning was a natural-born teacher!

Then came Miss Banks. With Miss Banks it was another story. She made it known from the very beginning that she was in charge of art—and hands off! Miss Banks asserted in no uncertain terms that she felt *no* elementary school classroom teacher was trained well enough to take charge of any of the art learnings of the children. I was relegated to the rear of the room and was made to feel that I was in the way. Miss Banks did not believe in integrating art into other subjects, so we had little to talk about. She frowned on the teachers' exhibits of crafts and paintings done by the children—art should be taught under her jurisdiction, I was told, and not as a tool, a means of communication, or a visual representation. Art should be taught for art's sake.

A strange silence grew between me and the art teacher. What was worse, a strange silence grew between the children and the art teacher. Art became an isolated "subject." Children were taught facts and techniques, but the relationships among them diminished. Something strange began to happen to their artwork—it did not seem to be a part of them, yet some of it was indeed very beautiful. Miss Banks often taught "appreciation" lessons where the children were asked to repeat the stories she told about the pictures. In all the time she came, however, she never once brought a modern painting or a free-form art object. I "sneaked" these objects into the classroom on the days when the children did not have art.

After a succession of types like Miss Banks, a change in position brought me into contact with another art teacher, Mrs. Kedney. This experience was a joyous one from the beginning. Mrs. Kedney dropped in to meet me during the orientation period when I was working alone in my classroom. She asked when she might have an appointment.

"What about now?" I asked, and she stayed and talked. Soon she had me telling about all the background I had in art and related fields. She took notes while I told her of my training and experience. She asked me about the units I thought I might teach in social studies, science, and language arts. She asked for my views on art and art education and asked how I liked to teach art or see it taught. She asked me how much of the art program I would like to teach with her or carry when she was not there.

I had already learned that the policy of this particular school was to integrate art into the total life experience of the child. I knew that Mrs. Kedney saw her job as that of an expert whose workers carry out her goals throughout the week. Under her guidance art became a real experience in that school.

"You know a great deal about art and art education," she told me at the close of our conference. "It seems to me that you will not need me as much as some other teachers will. May we get together again soon after you have met the children and plan in more detail what we can do for each individual?"

I taught a great deal of art in that school. Mrs. Kedney dropped in almost every day to keep in touch or to offer help. The teachers worked out a system whereby Mrs. Kedney posted schedules for a month ahead outside her office, with each day divided into half hours. When we needed or wanted her, a committee of children was dispatched to her office to sign up for a block of time.

I remember once when my class was planning to make a film for a social studies unit. The children asked if they could make titles for their film and photograph them as is done in a real movie. They wanted some help in lettering, in photographic composition, and in preparing appropriate art objects for each title. Other problems that they confronted included the making of scenery (especially ways of covering large areas of cheap paper with paint), the creation of props (especially fake ones), the printing of programs and advertisements, and the designing and sewing of costumes.

Many of these skills fell outside my talents, so I sent my committee to sign up for a conference with Mrs. Kedney. Seeing my name on her schedule, she dropped in after school to see what the problems were. After she knew what we wanted, she prepared for her visit. For a half hour Mrs. Kedney, my students, and I planned a series of arts and crafts experiences. For the next four weeks she came to our classroom at a scheduled time three times each week, sometimes for an hour, sometimes for a half hour, to help us accomplish the job at hand.

Her teaching was truly related to art. While I shared those objectives that I hoped to accomplish through the teaching of my unit, she suggested where we might logically include those objectives that fulfilled the principles of art expression. Thus we were both able to provide many sensory experiences to sharpen the children's perceptions and to bring them into a closer, more emotional relationship with their environment.   Children were afforded many aesthetic experiences and the opportunity to develop a nomenclature of art.   Our unit brought us into natural contact with many famous artists from all parts of the country, so we studied them and their work.   Mrs. Kedney saw to it that the children learned to use new tools and to develop new skills at the appropriate times.   Our work together on the film was centered around the art activities and art products of the children; it never occurred to us to determine who was teaching what or when. Our work was enhanced when the music teacher, at times, joined our team to enrich our experience and to suggest musical activities that might be included in the production.

Mrs. Kedney did not work with all the teachers as she worked with me.   A few of the teachers in our building felt so insecure about teaching art that Mrs. Kedney blocked out a portion of her program so that she could visit these classes on a regular basis.   Gradually she helped these teachers gain confidence in themselves so they could integrate more and more artwork into their own program.

One other thing she did to help us with the teaching of art was to conduct art classes for the faculty.   We became interested enough to devote one faculty meeting every two weeks to this cause.   I can still remember the fun we had at those meetings, playing around with a variety of art media and viewing children's work while Mrs. Kedney explained it.   We also discussed problems and viewpoints which Mrs. Kedney encouraged us to put frankly on the table.   Under Mrs. Kedney's guidance we all became more learned as art teachers and better as human beings.

Of the line of art teachers with whom I have come in contact, I have briefly described a few.   All of these, plus all of the others, were qualified, certified art teachers.   Like all teachers and like all humans, they were very different.   Their presence in the elementary school did not necessarily make a positive difference in the program.   I would even write Mrs. Banks off as doing more harm than good.   Perhaps it is the word "talented" that makes a difference—"to have a talented art teacher in every school"—although I am not sure about that either.   People with talent do not always make the best teachers nor do they make the most cooperative colleagues.   Talent is not enough.   An art teacher needs special characteristics, qualities, skills, and knowledge in order to function effectively in any school program, just as an elementary teacher needs certain characteristics to function effectively in her classroom.   Her talent, used as Mrs. Banks's was, can be useless to a large portion of the school personnel.

My experience over the years with the special teachers in my school was indicative of the changes in attitude which, for a variety of reasons, affected the growth of art education.   It is interesting to note that, while the times have changed, the problems basically have not.   Teachers and art teachers still recite to me each other's viewpoints and gripes—the same ones teachers encountered years ago.

Because of the authors' interest in the viewpoints of both the art teacher and the elementary school teacher, we have attempted to note their respective problems on the following pages, hoping that art teachers and elementary school teachers will try to resolve their differences and work together for effective change.

We do not attempt to dictate the role of the specialist in the changing school of today.   We feel that the role of the art specialist must grow out of the unique qualities and characteristics of any situation: first of all, the needs of the students and then, as a close second, the needs of the teachers.   We believe that the art program, to be effective, must be related to the setting and environment of the school.   We feel that part of the program must be educating the school patrons in art and aesthetics.   We believe that, whatever the roles of the art and classroom teachers, they must be founded on mutual trust and respect for each other as professionals and human beings.   We feel certain that any program is doomed to bypass its objectives if the teaching of art is not an integral part of the total school program and the day-to-day planning.   We are certain that one of the major roles of the art teacher is that of helping the classroom teacher identify art objectives and strategies for teaching that she can incorporate into her classroom work (see p. 117).

We have attempted to list below the characteristics that make an art teacher effective in today's schools.

1. The art teacher must be flexible.   In the organizational patterns of today's schools the art teacher may find herself playing a diversity of roles.   She may find herself in a traditional role where her program of so many minutes per week to teach art works in isolation from the rest of the school (see p. 108).   Or she may find herself playing a consulting role in an open-education school where she has free reign to teach on an individual basis, she has no set schedule, she is an important part of

a teaching team, her classroom includes several art centers *and* a studio, and art is the universal language (see p. 124). In order to make full use of any situation on a continuum between these two, she must be well versed in the philosophy, purposes, and goals of modern organizational plans.

2. She must be a congenial, friendly person, capable of leadership, guidance, and understanding. She must be able to work with many types of people. (See the quotation by Betty Tissinger at the opening of this chapter.)

3. She should know what children are like and she should possess a healthy fondness and respect for them.

4. She should plan her schedule so that her time is used in the most frugal way. She should not be bound by schedules that allot her a certain amount of time with each teacher, but rather should maintain a flexible time schedule that allows her to spend time where she is most needed to complete her objectives.

5. She should work as part of a team in cooperation with classroom teachers and other special teachers, contributing art objectives to the general and specific classroom planning.

6. She should take the responsibility for helping the classroom teachers to develop knowledge and attitudes, techniques and skills. She should serve as a consultant to faculty or to individuals when needed. She should play an integral role in the faculty meetings and report to the faculty on special projects or problems with children.

7. As an art resource person, she should advise staff on the ordering of the supplies and the introduction of new materials.

8. She should not permit herself to become the victim of predetermined roles. She should evaluate her schedule each term. She must have the power to make changes and adjustments when she sees the need and the privilege to plan with the administrator.

9. She should select the help of her co-workers discreetly and encourage the talents of each teacher working with her in order to put all the art talent in the school to work. She should help plan art experiences with each teacher for the entire time, not just the art periods.

10. She should be in touch with the total program of the school constantly.

11. She should strive to keep art on a personal and individual basis. This is not to say that she should not encourage group art projects, for they have their value; but she should be

careful about using the type of instruction that "teaches" all children the same thing at the same time.

12. She should strive to maintain a studio center for the purpose of working with special problems and unique and unusual cases and situations. Such problems might include providing a place for talented children to work in their spare time or taking a small group of retarded children for a special experience. An unusual case might be a small group of children who need help on a specific project, such as the film production mentioned above, or a small group of students who want to sketch a live baby lamb that was brought to school. Unique situations might include those where an entire class is working on different art projects and the diversity of materials needed necessitates proximity to the source of supply in the studio.

13. She should see as some of her major goals the development of vision, perception, and intuition.

14. She should aim to help all personnel to understand the significant historic role of art, and she should be certain that art fulfills its historic role in the life of the school.

THE ROLE OF THE ELEMENTARY SCHOOL TEACHER

We have said that the elementary school teacher is an art teacher. If our statistics are true, more art is taught by elementary teachers than by art teachers. Yet candidates for elementary school positions are not generally interviewed with the art function in mind. Almost never is the elementary school teacher prepared to teach art, and almost never is her art role spelled out for her. Elementary teachers are often confused about their roles by the inconsistencies that are levelled at them by experts in the art field.

This confusion is compounded by the fact that in the literature on art education, art educators are aligning their defenses against each other and choosing sides in exploiting one theory against another, rather than helping the frustrated, untrained classroom teacher to clarify her goals and strategies in teaching art. Actually, experts have yet to prove which is the best method of teaching art; it is probably a composite of the best aspects of many theories. In this text, we use the principles of creativity to evaluate the usefulness of each theory as it applies to the classroom curriculum.

To complement the work of the art teacher, the elementary classroom teacher should exhibit the following behavior:

1. She should be congenial, friendly, and open to suggestions. She should be able to work with all types of people and ask key questions.

2. She should focus her attention on the individual development of each child. She must know what all children are like and must respect them, but she must also know the individual differences and strengths of the children in her classroom.

3. She should familiarize herself with the art teacher's schedule and class loads, so she will know exactly what the art teacher is capable of giving her in terms of class time and time for individual students.

4. She should plan her art experiences so that they rise out of the life experiences of the children. She should not think of art in terms of a period of time, but in terms of a discipline with its own objectives and its own body of knowledge. She should see art as one means of developing each child's total creativity.

5. She should include the art teacher and other special teachers on her teaching teams and seek the assistance of the art teacher in incorporating art objectives into her work units.

6. She should seek the advice and help of the art teacher in ordering art materials and supplies.

7. She should be flexible in scheduling art experiences. When she needs the help of the art teacher, she should schedule events at a time best suited to all concerned.

8. She should work with the art teacher in helping the children, contributing her own art skills and knowledge to the development of the art program, if possible.

9. She should strive to keep art on a personal and individual basis. This is not to say that she should not introduce group art projects; she should merely allow for individuality within the group.

10. She should try to make allowances for individual differences in art abilities among her students, striving to care for the deprived, the talented, and the handicapped.

Above all else, the art teacher and the classroom teacher must be warm and friendly people. Studies of a thousand junior high school children showed that the amount of work, the quantity of self-initiated work, and the quality of the working student-teacher relationships correlated strongly with the warmth and friendliness of the teachers.[3]

3. Harry Levin, Thomas Hilton, and Gloria Leiderman, "Studies of Teacher Behavior," *Journal of Experimental Education,* 26 (September 1957), 81–91.

COOPERATION IN THE ART TEAM

Evidence seems to support the fact that, in order to survive in the modern elementary school, art education programs must grow out of a cooperative effort between the art teacher and other teachers. The art teacher must be considered an important member of some type of team.

Goodlad feels the answer to the problem of art education is to make certain of the presence of art specialists in the schools.[4] Goodlad considers the problem organizational in character and demands the following organizational solution: One out of every ten teachers is trained as an art specialist. The schools are organized according to a team-teaching plan—every team has an art teacher on it. At certain times the art teacher becomes the head teacher, and the other teachers serve in the capacity of consultants.

The trend toward open education places the art teacher and the elementary teacher in a situation where they must plan and work together. As members of a team, they must come to grips with problems that have gone unvoiced and unsolved over the years.

We attempt to identify below those problems that tend to form a block between school staff members, between art teachers and classroom teachers, and between fine artists and scholastically oriented personnel. We try to discuss each in relation to all aspects of creativity.

Planning Objectives

It is obvious from the cases cited above that an art teacher often comes to a classroom with objectives different from those of the classroom teacher. The classroom teacher may have developed a lesson on some subject and may have included various art activities for the attainment of her objectives. The art teacher, especially if she does not work closely with the classroom teacher, may walk into the classroom and find products that she feels violate the art objectives she has in mind. Before constructive

4. John Goodlad, "Advancing Art in U.S. Public Schools," in George Pappas, ed., *Concepts in Art and Education* (New York: Macmillan Publishing Co., Inc., 1970), pp. 274–279.

criticism can take place, each must know the other's objectives and methods.

Inasmuch as process in art is at least as important as product, it is very important that both understand *how* any particular product was made.   The best way to accomplish this fusion of differences is for the classroom teacher, the art teacher, and any other personnel involved in an experience to plan together at the onset of the experience and to continually evaluate progress together during the process of the unit.

Introducing Art Media

Some art educators suggest that the introduction of art media be slow, that children have the opportunity to exhaust the possibilities of one medium in depth before another medium is presented.   Some even suggest that certain materials not be presented before certain age levels or certain levels of development.   They suggest that the presence of too many media becomes confusing and befuddles a child.

These conclusions, often based on older research findings, are felt by many classroom teachers to be old-fashioned, outdated, and unrealistic for today's child.   Educators tell them that teaching art means helping a child come into close relationship with his environment and providing him with techniques and skills to express that relationship.   By narrowly restricting the use of media, a teacher is negating the very concept of relating to the environment by falsely assuming that the school is the child's environment.   All day long, today's child is exposed to new experiences of sight, taste, smell, feel, and touch, many of which are direct and many of which are vicarious.   His ride to school on a large school bus and his activities in school all day provide the background of experience that makes up his life.   His vicarious experiences at school and home from television, radio, movies, and simply from talking develop his concepts, increase his knowledge, and build his skills.   He is motivated to his life activities by his life experiences almost every step of the way, from withdrawing a book from the school library to sending in a box top for a superduper model jet plane.

The classroom teacher senses a conflict between the one idea that media be presented slowly and at specific times, and the other concept that media be presented whenever they are needed by a child to solve a problem.   In the total educational program of her room she is aware that media presented too fast will confuse and befuddle some children.   In like manner, presenting media too slowly is very likely to bore other children.

Children are exposed to all kinds of materials through films and TV programs.   They see a clay demonstration, tell about it at show and tell, and ask if they may try clay at school. Many children seem excited about the idea.   The classroom teacher considers this one of those "teachable" moments and introduces clay to the children.   It is done in a creative manner at a time when the children most need and want it.

On the other hand, realizing that there is value in developing the use of one medium in depth, the classroom teacher may choose to use techniques that accomplish this objective.

However, the classroom teacher also remembers that creativity means putting past experiences into new relationships. She has learned that the more knowledge a child has, the more skills he knows, the more techniques he has developed, the richer and broader his experiences are, then the more he is able to create.   So, while development of the use of any one medium may be important, knowledge of the existence of many media and of how to use them is also important.   The latter gives a child a greater chance to make choices at the onset of his problem solving.

Another aspect of this problem is that the teacher's interpretation of children's behavior may not always be accurate. Sometimes a child does not choose paints for the reason we suspect.   For instance, Corcoran found that three-year-old children used colors in a sequential order when painting at an easel—the children used the jars of paint one after the other regardless of the colors in the jars.[5]   This study implies that something other than color motivates these children, or that color at this stage is subordinate to movement or order of jars.

The basic problem here will be discussed more fully when we consider individuality (see p. 125).   If art is to develop individuality, it must begin where each child is and move forward from there to where each child is capable of going.   The solution to this problem is not that it be done one way or another.   It is a matter of knowing the child, adjusting the environment, and setting the conditions that best promote his growth.

---

5. A-L Corcoran, "Color Usage in Nursery School Painting," *Child Development,* 25, 2 (1954), 107.

Introducing Skills and Techniques

Another source of misunderstanding among classroom and art teachers lies in deciding when and how various art techniques should be introduced.

Many books on art education feel that, important as skills and techniques may be, they must be the means to an end and never an end in themselves. Yet even today, teachers are confronted with the situation described previously where the classroom teacher leaves the room when the art teacher enters and an isolated lesson transpires. There is little or no integration with any of the experiences the child has had or will have with the classroom teacher.

At the same time, the classroom teacher is often faced with the problem of developing very meaningful art lessons along with her social studies units (such as having children express their feelings in various media of their own choosing), only to be criticized for using art as a tool rather than as art for art's sake. Actually, the experience she provides is a highly integrative one for each child in the class and for the teacher. Some stunning results can be achieved.

Some art educators are dogmatic about the presentation of technique. They advise teachers to encourage the child to manipulate, discover, and explore each technique and thus learn about its disadvantages and its uses. Rarely do books on art education relate the presentation of technique to the total classroom situation, although they continually point out that art expression must show the relationship between the child's work and his life. There are many opportune times for the classroom teacher who is attempting to respect individual differences and interests among the children to present art technique. Some of these situations are listed below.

For Enjoyment. A new tub of clay has come. The children are excited and highly motivated by it. The teacher allows them to play with it, manipulate it, and explore its properties. Some of the children want to know how things are made from clay. The teacher tells about the kiln in the art room. Some children begin to make creations, so the teacher explains how to throw the clay to eliminate air bubbles and introduces the technique of scoring.

Out of Need. The class is studying a unit on pollution. Out of this study grows a play written by a committee of three children. These children tell the class they would like to present the play on Parents Night. Scenes, props, lighting, and staging are studied. The teacher uses this plan to develop lessons in art. One such lesson is in brainstorming—the children brainstorm to determine ways they can paint large areas in a short period of time. Out of this discussion come art lessons built around the exploration of various techniques.

As a Special Creative Lesson. The teacher seizes an opportunity in the classroom experience to develop creativity through art in a special lesson, such as the lesson on prints in the opening of this volume. There the teacher was brainstorming for the purpose of developing techniques for creative thinking.

After a Demonstration. A local potter has been to the school to demonstrate the manner in which pots are made. The children are anxious to try the technique.

A house is being built near the school. Children become interested in plastering and sawing, so the teacher introduces the techniques and materials.

The teacher demonstrates the exciting effects of the way polymer glue penetrates tissue paper, but she does not suggest design or product. She merely suggests they might want to explore this medium and use it in solving some of their problems someday.

To Develop Aesthetics. A new building has opened; the class visits it and discusses architecture.

A visit to the art museum brings out many excellent discussions about children's feelings and the use of technique in the art objects they saw.

The children attend a play in another classroom or in the auditorium and discuss the staging.

See Chapter 6, p. 190 for a more detailed discussion of the meaning of aesthetics.

As a Safety Precaution. The teaching of particular techniques in art may interfere with or check the child's own exploration and experimentation, but in some instances this is justifiable.

The "teaching" of techniques should be done at times as a

safety precaution, as in teaching children how to cut a block print.

Determining a Sequence

A problem that plagues the curriculum planner these days is that of sequence. For over a hundred years the problem of sequence of instruction has been batted around in all fields, art instruction included. We have noted above that some art educators feel a developmental approach to teaching is warranted by the maturation studies,[6] whereas others believe the maturation studies of children (see Chapter 3) simply show natural stages of art development that can be influenced by sensitive teaching.[7]

One of the reasons why sequentially planned programs in art have not been any more successful than nondirected or free programs is that the programs have appeared in a logical sequence from the standpoint of the art teacher, but not from the standpoint of the child. To the student, art classes may appear to be interruptions of more important learnings when he is working on a task for which he is highly motivated.

In one classroom the authors recently observed, the teacher and the children were having a discussion about the recreation activities of the pioneers. One group of children reported to the group that, among other activities, pioneers liked to gather around a fire at night and do dances they had learned to do back home. The teacher of the group arranged with the physical education teacher to teach some of these dances; among them was the Virginia Reel. At 10:30 the children went to the gymnasium and there they spent a delightful half hour learning American pioneer folk dances.

At 11:00 they hurried back to the classroom because the art teacher was due to arrive. Full of excitement, they settled into their seats, the art teacher distributed materials, and they proceeded to have a lesson on plaster casting of junk forms. Now, this was a well-planned lesson and was part of a sequence

6. Viktor Lowenfeld and W. Lambert Brittain, *Creative and Mental Growth,* 5th ed. (New York: Macmillan Publishing Co., Inc., 1970).
7. Elliot Eisner, *Educating Artistic Vision* (New York: Macmillan Publishing Co., Inc., 1972).

of goals and experiences planned by the art teacher. But the activity at this time was inappropriate and out of step. The children had a difficult time settling down. They were highly stimulated and much of the time allotted to the art teacher was wasted while she tried to remotivate the children.

The art teacher complained about the children being over-stimulated and not ready for her. The classroom teacher was apologetic about the high spirits of the children. The gym teacher was sorry they were a little late in getting back to the classroom.

Why were these teachers apologetic and threatened by this situation? Inasmuch as the ultimate goal of the school is to make learning possible, why shouldn't all teachers be happy when children are learning? The setting of rigid schedules and the staking out of small empires and domains has nothing to do with children's learnings: it only has to do with the egos and personalities involved in the teaching act. It has been said that American schools are more concerned with teaching than with learning. The above example illustrates that phrase.

In failing to work out problems of coordination, teachers lose important, teachable moments. Any good teacher knows that almost any motivation or interest can serve to teach many things. *It is not the sequence that matters as much as the degree to which each experience can be integrated into the child's total experience.* Sequence is sometimes necessary for a variety of reasons: building skills in order of difficulty, interpreting in relation to experiences, evaluating in terms of new facts.

Think of the things the art teacher could have taught had she planned with the classroom teacher and the physical education teacher! The body is a marvelously fluid and pliable form. A multitude of lessons could have emerged for which no motivation would have been necessary. Using the motions of the Virginia Reel, the art teacher could have taught a painting lesson on the linear expression of body movements or abstract movement on paper. She could have taught a number of lessons on perception with the children posing for each other. Any number of new media could have been introduced. Three-dimensional materials could have been explored—for example, the children might have caught the pliable motions of the body in clay. Had she taken the time to find out about the children's schedule, she could have taught the plastic casting technique using hands, feet, and junk in order to show each child's perception of the dances abstractly.

Establishing a Pattern of Organization

In the new, dramatic reorganizations of the American classroom, the role of art has not been clearly defined. Consequently, it has often been lost in the shuffle.

New types of classroom organization come about supposedly because new philosophies and new goals evolve in education. In developing the curriculum, planners first state goals in general and specific forms. Then they ask the question: What experiences can be planned to meet these goals? After an exhaustive list of possible experiences has been made, the learnings and behavioral changes expected of the children are stated in terms of outcomes (when possible). Then schoolroom organizations are studied to find the most effective means of carrying out the experiences. After the experiences have been carried out, evaluation is done in terms of the instructional and/or behavioral objectives. Experiences are then planned for the purpose of reteaching those learnings not mastered and planning new learning experiences.

Unless the teachers are included in the total process of planning, they may find themselves harnessed with a schoolroom organizational plan that they do not understand. This is why so many art programs become superfluous to the main learnings of the children. Art teachers are seldom invited to curriculum planning conferences; thus art is added to the curriculum after the basic objectives and learning experiences have been planned.

The most recent of the organizational plans to sweep the country is the open classroom, founded on the open-education plan of the British. This plan is a throwback to John Dewey's philosophy of child-centered learning and the activity school, which was popular in the 1930s and 1940s. The plan includes some innovations, namely the structure of school buildings. Anyone who visits the open primary schools of Britain cannot help being impressed with the happy faces of the children, the eager, enthusiastic manner in which they approach learning, and the obvious values and effective skills being developed. The excellent artwork in these schools is also very exciting.

The role of the art teacher in these schools is quite different from the role commonly played by the art teacher in America. In the open schools, the art teacher is a consultant, not to a teacher or classroom, but to a child or group of children. Because of the open nature of the physical plant, the art teacher can be anywhere and everywhere where help is needed; art instruction almost becomes an individual teaching experience.

In such programs, sequence in planning is carried out, but almost on an individual basis. Integration is a must, because all art experiences rise out of classroom experiences and studies. Art is so heavily integrated into the environmental experiences of these children that there is not a moment of the day when they do not see art being used to solve some life problem or to express a mood or vision. The art teacher is literally on tap, and the classroom teacher is sensitive to the objectives of the art teacher to the degree that she capitalizes on every child's experiences to encourage some form of visual imagination. Anyone visiting these successful schools has the feeling from looking around the classroom that art is the one humanizing, unifying element. It is used as a tool for decorative purposes, as a means of communication, as a means of self-expression, as an experience in itself, as a method for aesthetic improvement of the environment, and as a subject for study.

Other organizational plans, such as the ungraded and nongraded plans, tend to place art education in the back seat. In these plans art is included as a part of the day. Creative approaches to art can be used effectively, but often they are not. Children are allotted only a scheduled period of time each week for art, and the lesson takes place in a room physically and intellectually isolated from everything else in the school.

The name of the plan unfortunately does not give a clue as to what part the art program plays in the overall scheme. It depends on the school; some schools have eliminated art altogether. The place of art teaching in these various plans can be resolved to some degree if the art teacher plays an aggressive role in the formulation of the plans and in the setting of objectives for each age level. The pattern of organization that is determined as the best means of fulfilling these objectives must allow children to receive art instruction and the art teacher to meet her changing role in the modern school.

Incorporating Individuality into Art

In our modern technological society, individuals have lost, to a great extent, their ability to identify with what they do. The lack of ability of the average man to identify with his environment results in a decline in the development of his sensory abilities and his ability to express himself through art media. Man loses

FIGURE 4–2. Motivated by the theme of Halloween and the technique of making papier mâché, each child tries making a mask: individuality shows through even though the theme is the same.

his power to become self-realized.   This phenomenon also accounts for the increase in mental illness in our society; man is preoccupied with adjusting *to* an environment determined by someone else, rather than experiencing *with* an environment he helps to invent for himself.

Unfortunately, the drive to adjust to an environment created by others may well be caused by the child's teachers, who impose art activities on him to the degree that he abandons his own ideas and his own creativeness.   Group stimuli may be presented profitably in a class, but not to the degree that a child's own ideas become secondary.

Unit teaching and the art activities that grow out of it can provide a broadening, enriching experience for children.   On the other hand, a group project, such as painting a mural or presenting a puppet play, may serve no other purpose than to repress the individuality of some children.   Consequently, in the planning of any group project care should be taken to make provision for individual expression and the fulfillment of each individual's ideas.   The emphasis is, of course, on cooperation, but in planning a mural, a play, or a puppet show the teacher can guide

the discussions so creative thinking takes place, justifiable com-
promises are made, and each child contributes his own ideas to
the project.

Miss Barber's class visited a small circus which came to
town immediately after the opening of school.   In discussing the
circus on the following day, the children expressed the desire to
recreate the experiences they had enjoyed most at the circus.

Miss Barber included many worthwhile multisensory experiences in her circus unit.   The children learned circus songs
and animal songs, and they wrote two circus songs of their own,
which they played on a metallophone.   They made cotton candy,
candy apples, and popcorn, and they experienced many situations where they had to deal with numbers.   The children
dramatized the movements of circus animals and created movements to simulate a circus, including a parade.   As one of their
culminating activities they asked to construct a circus in miniature at one end of a dead-end hallway outside their classroom.

Miss Barber saw many opportunities for cooperative experiences in this idea: measuring, scale drawing, adding, sub-
tracting, multiplying, dividing, and using fractional parts.   She
saw the opportunity to develop many social experiences: the
opportunity to make decisions, to pass judgment, to cooperate, to
share, and to think divergently.   She also saw the opportunity to
provide more multisensory experiences in tasting and smelling of
candy apples, popcorn, and cotton candy; in hearing the sounds
of the circus, including music, people, and animals; in seeing the
sights of the circus and various related films and pictures in the
classroom after the trip.   This wealth of sensory and factual
experiences served as a motivation in planning for the miniature
circus.   Miss Barber made sure the children did not limit themselves in their planning to pictorial representation entirely.   In
her discussions with the children she asked thought-provoking
questions which helped them translate their experiences into
other forms of art expression.   One planning period produced
this fragment of conversation:

Miss B: Yesterday we decided that we would make our circus on the floor at the end of the hall outside our doorway.   Today
we are going to plan what we are going to put in our exhibit.   I
would like to talk to all of you together and let each one give his
ideas.   Now, who has some ideas about what we should put in our
circus?

Freddie: We should have a big tent with a ringmaster and
clowns and people.

Joanne: We want to have trapeze people ready to fly through the air.

Artie: We want the sideshows too.

Bill: I want to make a popcorn man, an ice cream cone man, and a frozen custard wagon.

Helen: I think we've got to have elephants.

Jane: I want zebras.

Mike: And horses and cowboys.

Jill: Bareback riders.

Eddie: A carnival with a merry-go-round and a ferris wheel.

Joanne: We ought to have midgets in their funny cars.

Miss B: I have been listing all these ideas as you said them. They are good ideas, but one thing bothers me. How can we show all these things in the little space we have? Do you have any ideas on that?

Bill: Well, we could paint some things flat against the wall and not really make them all.

Miss B: Like what, for instance?

Eddie: Like the carnival—that could be in the background against the wall.

Miss B: Good idea.

Carrie: We don't have to make everything in the tent either. Can't we paint the people's faces on the inside of the tent so that it looks like hundreds of people watching the circus?

Miss B: Hey, that's a good idea! While we're talking about what we can paint, I'd like to ask a few questions that Carrie has brought to mind. With all the fun we have had with the circus I think that we might show the circus in ways other than a "picture" of what we saw. We had many tastes from the study of the circus. We also had many feelings; remember the list we made in language arts that described how the circus made us feel—excited, happy, joyous, gay, friendly, warm, full of awe, fearful, frightened, and all those other things? How can we make the other boys and girls feel this excitement, this fear, and this happiness? Can anyone think of a way?

Mike: We could use a lot of bright colors to make the circus gay.

Miss B: Good idea. Anyone else?

Jimmy: I think we should have a special day for other classes in the school to come and visit, and we can show them all our things and make candy apples for them.

Miss B: I like that idea. What else could we do?

John: We could sing our songs and do our circus parade.

Jane: We could have an exhibit of all our circus pictures and charts.

Artie: We could make a tape recording of circus noises to play with the exhibit.

Miss B: These are all good ideas and I have written them down. Let's get back to the actual way we'll show our miniature circus. We'll use color and sound to help the other boys and girls feel the way we felt about it. Now how will we actually show it?

At this point there was a great deal of discussion until Linda finally summed up the problem.

Linda: It is going to be too much work to show everything in the circus. Can't we just show the things we liked most?

Miss B: Good idea. This would be a good opportunity for me to hear from each one of you. Let's go around the group and see what we've got. Maybe then we will have some ideas as to how we can put it together. Let's begin with Mike. Mike, what would you like most to put in our circus, and how would you like to show it?

Mike: I want to show trapeze artists flying through the air.

Miss B: Have you thought of how you could best do it?

Mike: Yes! I'd like to make pipe cleaner sculptures and and wire them in a box in flying positions.

Miss B: That sounds good. Yes, Joanne?

Joanne: I'd like to make trapeze artists too, but I want to paint mine.

Miss B: Sounds good. Carrie, you're next.

Carrie: I'd like to make a color painting showing words like excitement and happy.

Miss B: Good idea. Bob?

Bob: I'd like to make some performing elephants out of clay.

Jimmy: I'd like to make some clown masks out of the paper pie plates in the junk box.

Miss B: I like all these ideas. I like the fact that you each have a different idea.

Freddie: I want to make a circus collage.

Bill: Miss Barber, can't I make a real little cart with a little man selling candy apples and cotton candy?

Miss B: Of course.   Maybe someone else would like to work with you and make a popcorn man with his cart.

John: I would.

Alvin: I'd like to make a clown puppet.

Bea: And I'd like to draw lots of clown pictures.   I love clowns!

And so the discussion went.   Miss Barber limited the children to a fifteen-minute planning period and then allowed them an incubation period.   Later in the day when she returned to the planning many children had firmed up their ideas, many had changed their original ideas, and almost all had come up with new ideas.

The end product was far better than the idea that had originally been proposed for the miniature circus.   Instead of a reproduction of the circus grounds per se, a large tent graced the end of the hall.   It was cut away in the front so viewers could see inside, where people of all sorts were painted on the walls as though they were viewing the circus.   Some of the boys had reconstructed the three rings in great detail with a handsome ringmaster doll (made by one of the girls) in the center ring.

Charlie's clay bareback rider was performing in one ring. Bob's performing elephants graced another ring.   Overhead Mike's trapeze artists (constructed from pipe cleaners and papier mâché) appeared to be tumbling and falling all over the tent. Mike and his pal Joey had worked long and hard to suspend these action-packed figures in mid-air on nylon thread.

Almost all the children at one time or another had made clown figures out of a variety of materials; these figures were placed everywhere around the tent.

Outside the ticket office stood a booth in which there was a pretty lady selling tickets.   Nearby was Bill's cart with a man selling snowcones and frozen custard.

The walls at the end of the corridor were covered with mural paper and here the children had combined realism with fantasy in trying to paint their feelings about the circus and the sounds of the circus.   Directly behind and to the left of the large tent was painted Eddie's carnival and to the right were the side-shows.   These tents and signs were painted in hues of the same color which suggested the physical presence of the tents, the ferris wheel, etc.   Streaming out from these more somber paintings and filling the sky in bold, fresh, bright colors were the feelings and sounds (as the children saw them) of the circus.   Colors were made to look like explosions to show the racket made by the

FIGURE 4–3.   One child's clay figure of a clown.

motorcycles. Orange and red concentric circles raced out from the ferris wheel to fill a portion of the sky. Actual words appeared here and there as part of the design—"Buy here," "Only seventy-five cents," "Pow," "Bam." Bright lines jerking up and down showed one child's feeling about the sound of the calliope. Wild streaks of color represented whip rides; lightening-like strokes communicated the feeling of the ride on the tumble bug; lone black dots painted within large yellow spots in close succession suggested the "empty stomach" feeling that accompanied the sky ride. A huge sweep of color that twisted back and forth until it ended in a dot was one child's interpretation of the sound of the siren.

In order to capitalize on the children's individual interests, the thrust of the miniature circus concept had been completely changed as the project progressed. The children had not developed all the details that had been mentioned in the first planning session; another plan had evolved. Above and in front of the big tent and mural a frame had been constructed with shelves. On these shelves were the individual creations of the children—their own expressions of the sights, smells, feelings, sounds, and images of the circus. Many beautiful animals had been cast in clay or molded in papier mâché. Among them was an enormous black free form. A winding, twisted trunk emerged from it and circled around it to make a massive, heavy

131

design.   No doubt about it; it was *Elephant*.   Some children had tried soap and plaster of Paris sculpting, and some striking figures graced the exhibit.   Jimmy's clown faces were fastened there.   In fact, the children enjoyed the many clown faces Jimmy made so much they asked him to make a series of clown faces and hands to hold the sign that told the theme for the exhibit, "The Greatest Show on Earth."

So enthusiastic and productive was the group that Miss Barber was forced to solicit the cooperation of the other teachers in her wing of the building in order to find enough space for all the murals, individual tempera paintings, collages, masks, pastel paintings, drawings, and other forms of art expression.   The entire corridor of that wing became the circus wing.   The children presented their program to other classes as they had originally planned.

The circus unit in Miss Barber's classroom is an example of a unit project where the teacher is able to guide the children into developing their own individual ideas creatively.   In some units, however, such as the one described below, children may need to surrender their own creativity to some degree for the successful completion of the total project.   In any case, it is important to make certain that each individual child has ample opportunity to develop his own means of expression.   If properly conducted, group activities can provide an experience of great value to children and can broaden their opportunities to practice many skills, to adventure with new media, and to express themselves in divergent ways.

Mr. Barth's middle-school group became involved rather deeply in a unit on the history of the local community.   The unit began with a study of local industries.   Trips were made to each of the local industries to gather information and to see products being made.   Among the industries studied were a chocolate products factory, a china factory, and a paper-manufacturing plant.

Mr. Barth planned art activities that would result logically from these experiences.   He used scrap materials from the china and paper plants to place his students in situations where they would employ creative thinking.   Discarded china plates were brought back to the school so that the children could explore circular designs and ways to fill a circular space.   China paints and glazing processes were introduced and the children went to the art room to fire their work.

The paper scraps brought back to school from the paper factory provided a motivation for all sorts of experiences; strange and wonderful things made from paper appeared around the room. The children were encouraged to find out all the things they could do with paper—folding it, crumpling it, cutting it, tearing it, rolling it, wadding it, twisting it, etc. Brainstorming sessions produced many new uses. The principle of forced relationships was applied here to develop creative thinking.

The children used the recipe from the chocolate factory to make candy; then they experimented with recipes of their own. One highly exciting day they divided into five groups and each group developed, cooked, and tested a recipe. Many excellent language and mathematics experiences resulted from this experience.

The class then decided that they would try to communicate the history of the industries of Mudville by making a huge mural along one bare wall in a hall. It was to depict the story of each industry in the material manufactured by that industry. For example, the story of paper was a composite of designs about papermaking constructed completely from paper. The china story was told completely with china; much of it was broken pieces arranged in a mosaic pattern. The chocolate story was told completely in chocolate candy and pastry.

Subcommittees were chosen to work on the different aspects of the mural, and then each group brainstormed ideas. Sketches were drawn, decisions made, judgments passed, and finally agreements were reached that constituted a composite of everyone's ideas.

In a project such as this, the individuality of each group member becomes so absorbed in the emerging product that much of it is lost, much as the creativity of individuals is lost when they work together to produce a play. The pooling of the ideas of many individuals results in a level of creative thinking and a creative product that is different and often superior to the thinking and creating that an individual does alone. It also provides excellent practice in organization, a necessary quality in all art expression.

Dealing with Stereotypes

Stereotypes in paintings and in other classroom situations often become a matter of concern to people who work with youth.

Stereotypes are a natural part of the child's art development (see Chapter 3), especially during the schematic stage. Although the teachers of children can accept these stereotypes as normal parts of children's growth, they must attempt to help the children grow to more creative modes of expression. On p. 164 are some suggestions of ways teachers can help children to move on from the stage of stereotypes.

Among the many problems confronting the teacher when a child becomes hung-up on the use of stereotypes is that of the child's addiction to model construction and to the use of kits. Kits for making art products show someone else's relation to his environment and not the child's. They result in hours of busy-work which produce little growth, if any, in art expression. The teacher may well ask why these kits appeal so strongly to adults and children.

First, they satisfy to a degree that drive to create which lies in all humans. Those who have not learned to produce products that they can accept receive the satisfaction of seeing products evolve under their own hands if they follow the careful directions of other people—people who are perhaps more creative than they are—who have laid out the process.

Secondly, these kits remove the psychological barriers of creativity: the fear of taking risks, the uncertainty of acceptable results, the fear of failure. But, in removing psychological qualifications, the kits also remove those experiences that build creativity.

Art education texts often scold the teacher for promoting the use of kits, models, and other forms of art-experience substitutes, but the experienced teacher knows that hardly a week passes without some child, highly motivated by seeing such a kit advertised on television or in a local toy shop, coming to school displaying one he has assembled or asking if he might not make a boat or a plane. A good teacher feels that this is a teachable moment and that the introduction of wood, plastics, yarn, and other materials at this point helps the child use his intense motivation artistically and creatively and *steers him away* from the commercial kits and models which lure him to a false sense of "product-creativeness." The timely introduction of the principles of macrame to a highly motivated fifth-grade girl may result in some very beautiful and creative knot-tying rather than the purchase of a do-it-by-numbers kit. Art books not withstanding, the authors found that the introduction of acrylics to a very intelligent and gifted sixth-grade boy at a time when he was excited about discovering form, shape, texture, and design in flowers led him into experimentation that produced some beautiful paintings and provided him with great aesthetic enjoyment.

Once more, the basic solution to developing each child's growth is to know and plan for individual differences. Texts are making a mistake when they suggest a dogmatic solution to complex problems.

If there is any good that comes from the use of kits it may be that some children learn techniques from them that can later be used in more creative ways. John was given a clay molding kit which he played with for several days until he had perfected the technique of preparing and pouring slip. Then he asked his art teacher how molds could be made and whether or not you could make big pots in the same manner as he had prepared slip for the small molds in his kit. John soon launched into a project that held his interest and stimulated his imagination for months.

Motivating the Students

In the beginning of this chapter the importance of motivating children for their art experiences was stressed. As in other areas of planning, the types of motivation often cause disagreement.

Art teachers are often concerned with motivating the child to produce art products. Therefore, they strive to motivate the child with basic art principles, such as developing his perceptions, his imagination, his sense of color, and his reaction to texture, color, and space. The classroom teacher, on the other hand, may see the art product as one step in the child's development toward self-realization; it is a pinpoint on the path of time. She may feel that other objectives are important, such as the communication of an idea or the mastery of a skill.

Art books often suggest motivation techniques geared to developing the art principles mentioned above. These strategies are usually carried out through the use of questions or media that build in the child a keener sense of observation and imagery and that spark ideas for his art expression.

"Why did you go on the space ship? What did it look like? How did you fit into it? In what position did you sit? Show me. Why did you sit like that? How did you eat and what did you eat? How did your legs feel after you sat in that position a long time? your arms? When did you sleep? How did you feel floating around in space? Were you afraid? lonesome? happy? sad? What smells did you experience? How did your food taste? How did your skin feel?" etc.

Such questions appeal to the child's senses and help him

to perceive, imagine, and interpret experience, real or imagined, in a variety of ways.

The classroom teacher, however, tends to feel that children grow weary of this unchallenging mode of questioning, especially when it is used too often. They may feel that more children are highly motivated at one time and to a higher degree when they engage in regular or contrived classroom experiences that result in some form of art expression.

The light show described on p. 14, the puppet show described on p. 10, and the circus unit described on p. 127 are all examples of the type of motivation that grows out of classroom activities and that arouses children so much that they seek some form of art medium as a natural way to express tastes, smells, feelings, sights, emotions, or sounds.

Any motivation ceases to be effective when it is used to excess. Sometimes a motivation strategy loses its effectiveness after being used once. A realistic solution to the problem lies in the discreet and balanced use of experience or action motivation and verbal motivation.

Basically, motivations fall into three general categories:

1. Offering a contrived experience (such as the puppet show) to a child.
2. Helping a child to recall an experience he has already had directly or vicariously and massaging his sensitivities to squeeze deeper mileage from his interpretation of it.
3. Providing the child with a "normal" life experience, an experience that has become a part of the child's particular environment for that particular time through some natural circumstances. Such "natural" experiences, such as a visit to a museum or a beautiful park, the viewing of an art film, or the study of a tree or a landscape, sharpen his interest and enthusiasm.

One problem faced by both the classroom teacher and the art teacher is a common one in today's world. In light of the fact that parents are bombarded at home with advertising for all kinds of kits and art materials and that the general public has been conditioned to accept the benefits of these materials, children often come to school already familiar with many materials and media. They are not motivated by a presentation of the same material in school.

Not only do the things people buy influence their children before they come to school, but the things people do influence

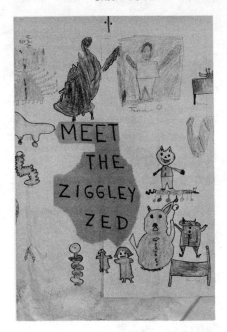

FIGURE 4–4. In Miss Smith's second grade each child created a story about a Ziggley-Zed: art is a tool in illustrating these stories.

them as well.   Weisberg and Springer found that the home influence is a significant factor in the encouragement of creative thinking.[8]

This home influence can, of course, be an excellent aid to the teacher.   The job of the school is to try to find out what experiences children have had at home and capitalize on them. This may mean remotivating the children to new uses of the media or adapting one skill to another one.   In the creative lesson on prints described at the beginning of this book, the teacher called on Beth to demonstrate the making of a block print.   Beth's father had taught her this technique at home.   This is one way children can be motivated—by sharing their skills with others.

8. Paul S. Weisberg and Kayla Springer, "Environmental Factors in Creative Function" in Ross Mooney and Taher Razik, eds., *Explorations in Creativity* (New York: Harper & Row, Publishers, 1967), pp. 120– 134.

FIGURE 4–5. Branches collected from the school yard after a storm are modified by papier mâché build-ins: art and life.

Assessing the Role of Art

One conflict that often confuses teachers is the objection on the part of the art teachers to the use of art in relation to other subjects. Some art teachers tend to adopt a sentimental and mystical outlook, enshrining art in a "holy" atmosphere and regarding it as something hallowed. On the other hand, classroom teachers find that art relates best to children when it is used to help solve their everyday problems, artistic and otherwise.

Art is a means of self-expression, a way of communicating life experiences. Art educators believe that the best way to learn art is to practice it. Art, then, is more than self-expression; it is experience itself. As an experience in itself it becomes a method, a means to an end, and an end in itself. In the classroom it may be justifiably used in all three roles. Unless it is related to other areas of the curriculum, it is never going to be an experience with which children can identify and in which they see a reflection of their own relationships to life. The use of art in the subjects is discussed in Chapter 7.

Gifts, Favors, and Busywork. Pretty little products such as baskets made of decorated milk cartons, crushed egg shells pasted on paper, and macaroni-covered, gold-sprayed pencil holders are like the dittoed sheets that overwhelm our children in some schools—they serve little or no purpose in developing a close relationship with the child and his life experiences. Too often in primary school hours are spent keeping a child busy, rather than furthering his artistic development. Rather than having art merit, the products of such experiences often make the child more dependent, more insecure, and less able to develop his art expression normally.

Obviously some children enjoy these products. Often, however, these are the children who already experience great indecision in self-expression. Activities that make them more reliant simply push the crutch, however gently, into the child's waiting hand.

Lowenfeld and Brittain state:

> There is no place in the art program for those activities that have no meaning for the scribbling child. Occasionally a nursery school or kindergarten teacher may plan certain art activities such as pasting, tracing, folding, or cutting: these are designed for a particular end product, such as a May basket, Pilgrim silhouettes, cute snowmen, or products for Halloween, Christmas or Mother's Day. Such activities are worthless and should never be included in a program planned for scribbling children, because they only point out the inability of the child to perform on a level to his understanding and ability. Sometimes teachers have an interest in discovering new and novel activities for children. Any new material should be looked upon with a great deal of care to make sure that it can further the natural development of children. It must not obstruct the opportunity for the child to gain control over his material, rather, it should promote his own creative expression.[9]

What these authors say about the scribbling child applies equally to children of all ages.

What, then, is the answer to the problem of providing meaningful art experiences for young children? Should such efforts be abandoned? The teacher who does not understand the place of art in the life of a child and who does not understand how children develop may have a difficult time in keeping children gainfully occupied with worthwhile art experiences day after day. Most teachers say that there is value to these "busy-work" experiences. This may be true, but when one principle of education is violated or when one aspect of the child's growth is

9. Reprinted with permission of Macmillan, Inc. from Viktor Lowenfeld and W. Lambert Brittain, *Creative and Mental Growth,* Copyright © 1970, by the Macmillan Co.

denied in order to accomplish another, the results are highly questionable.

What are the values of such activities?

First, when introduced at the proper time they provide children the opportunity to learn cutting, pasting, folding, and painting skills. They allow the children to work with a variety of shapes and forms of different dimensions. They afford children an excellent opportunity to manipulate and explore new media and new forms in a *somewhat* controlled environment. If not too tightly controlled, these activities may contribute to the child's divergent thinking and consequently to his creativity.

For instance, a teacher was asked by her second grader what they were going to make for Dad for Christmas. She took advantage of the interest of the children (which proved to be rather general) and had the children brainstorm for ideas. In evaluating the list, the children became aware of the fact that they were limited by their supplies. They finally settled on an idea offered by one of the boys—that they collect small tin cans like the few in the junk box and decorate them as pencil holders.

The cans were collected. Each child painted his can a color of his own choice. So far, conformity had had little value, inasmuch as all the children had had the experience of painting tin before.

Miss Farnsworth, the teacher, wanted to make this a personal experience for each child, so she asked the children if they would brainstorm all the ideas they could muster about materials to use to decorate the cans so each would be different, reminding each child at once of his father. The following list resulted:

felt	raffia
macaroni	silver and gold paper
seashells	glitter
stones or pebbles	spray paint
cloth	papier mâché
paper	leather
polymer and tissue	plastic
paint	rope
yarn	sand
string	sticks

Miss Farnsworth collected the necessary materials and each child was encouraged to work out his own design and decorate his gift in his own way. Miss Farnsworth was able to fulfill many objectives of creative development in this experience, chief among them being the development of open-ended, divergent thinking. The children were able to find many uses for new materials and many adaptations and modifications of the same basic shape. They got some experience in organization, and each one produced something different. The experience contributed to creative development and was meaningful to each child. Consequently, it must be evaluated fairly as a technique for developing creative thinking.

Secondly, experiences such as the one described at the beginning of this chapter can be of value in developing human relationships. A teacher must remember the cherished experiences of his own childhood when he thinks of making gifts in school for others. One of the authors of this book was born and brought up in a small rural town. He remembers to this day one school experience he had:

I remember so well the excitement that electrified the air one particular morning as I jumped the bobsled of old Mr. Striker, the milkman, on my way to school. Today was the day! We were going to start making Christmas gifts for mother—next week we would make father's. What would it be? We had already decided the previous day that we were going to make mother a decorative sprinkling bottle to use while she worked at the ironing board. I already had my ketchup bottle hidden safely and carefully in my old mackinaw. I remember how I jumped on and off the bobsled with the utmost care so I would not fall and break the bottle on the ice.

To this day tears sting my eyes when I see mother working at the ironing board, just as they stung my eyes then. I still don't know why this simple scene wrings such emotion from me—probably because it symbolizes all that mother stood for. She was always working, always tackling one job as soon as she finished another. Her work was never done. And while she was at the ironing board it was as though I had caught her unaware and she revealed to me in one simple scene all that mothers do: they sacrifice for their daughters and sons, they wear their fingers to the bone for them, they love them, they stand by them, and they are patient with them. "Oh, mother, mother," my heart cried out silently, "Let me show you how much I love you! Someday I will be rich and I will buy you warm blankets and wonderful furs. Someday I shall pay someone to do ironing for you. Someday I shall show you how much I love you!"

But she did not know, and pregnant moments passed as I studied her while she swept her hand from the old kitchen stove to my fresh clean shirt stretched over the aging ironing board and ironed the starch into it under enormous heat and amazing weight.   She deftly manipulated the heavy, old, heated flatiron (which really was a chunk of flat iron); the room was filled with her incessant chatter and laughter and the hot smell of cloth near scorching.   Two baskets were heaped high with the mountain of unironed clothes she would press flat before sundown under that huge hunk of hot iron she glided smoothly over the wrinkles.   I saw the flipping of the clothes onto the big ironing board piece by piece and smelled the fragrance of their cleanliness as they spread their outdoor smell all through the small kitchen.   I saw the graceful dip of her cupped hand into the small mixing bowl of water on the side of the ironing board as she sprinkled the fresh, starched articles with droplets.   I saw it all; I had seen it all for ten years of my young life.

And today, today I was going to be able to help my mother!   I was going to make her a sprinkling bottle so she could shake the droplets evenly on the clothes to iron them!   Today I was going to make her job a little easier, a little more bearable.   She had never owned a sprinkler.   And it would be all mine—I would make it!   Miss Kelsey on that very day was going to show us how to marbleize a ketchup bottle.   We had each given her three cents to buy a sprinkler top and after the bottle was painted we would put the top on, make some pretty wrapping paper, and have it all ready for mother under the Christmas tree.   Truly this was the greatest day of my life!

I have never forgotten this intense moment of living and many others like them.   Something beautiful and wonderful happens to children when they are able to create and give to others; it happens to adults too.   All my boyhood was lived in an environment where we "made and gave" and we were the better for it.

As an elementary school teacher first starting my career I remember how I, like many teachers, searched for things that my students could do to share in this most joyous of all human relationships, giving of yourselves to others.   I know I violated all the art principles in the book at one time or another.   I can't say that my children were hurt; they just weren't helped much— artistically, that is.   In terms of their social relationships and their concepts I saw things happen to them that did not come about in any other way.

So, such activities are not all bad, nor are they all good. Children need to take things home, to give extensions of themselves freely to others, to share, and to love themselves and each other.

Nothing is solved by the critic who enters a classroom, sees the teacher involved with her students in such activities, and condemns her. A more positive approach is to examine the teacher's objectives and to try to plan alternative ways of meeting them so that the social needs are met without violating the principles of art processes and creativity development.

Miss Kelsey's objectives, I suppose, were simply to allow us to make gifts for our parents within the limited means of the school. She knew we were all too poor to afford them. She might have had other objectives, such as providing us with the experience of marbleizing, providing for free expression in designing wrapping paper, and encouraging us to manipulate three-dimensional shapes. At any rate, this was an experience with which I related with high emotional impact. It definitely had carryover; my buddies and I gathered up all the old, partially emptied paint cans from our fathers' barns and garage workshops, thinned the contents with turpentine, dropped and spread the paint on water, and marbleized everything in sight. It was truly a sensory and emotional experience, a positive relationship with the environment.

Miss Kelsey probably did the best she could in trying to develop artistic expression, but she needed help. This is where an art teacher can bring her skills to bear and help the children encounter experiences loaded with the rich emotional impact of this one, but also full of opportunities for meaningful art expression. Some of these types of activities are listed in Chapter 7. They may be helpful to the elementary school teacher in persuading her that experiences in art can result in products that are worthy of being called gifts and worthy of the child's time inasmuch as they contribute to his development.

An easy but highly unsatisfactory way to dismiss this problem is to say that children should give to parents only art products that are good art in themselves. As such they may be appreciated and enjoyed. This idea is excellent except that a child can only paint just so many pictures or work just so many clay objects before he rebels and/or loses his motivational drives. Like all humans, he needs change, new experiences, and new materials with which to work. Elementary teachers who must be sure thirty students are motivated to engage in art processes all day and every day are well aware that their resources often become overtaxed.

In a brainstorming session held after a group of fifth graders asked if they could make Christmas gifts for their parents, Mr. Dennis guided the children into a situation where they had many options and many opportunities to make highly individual and personal gifts.

Candlemaking was the activity selected in connection with a social studies unit for which the children had read about how to dip candles. First Mr. Dennis discussed all safety precautions that would have to be taken to make the project plausible. The children then studied the properties of wax and observed that it could be melted at a certain temperature, it could be cooled and molded at a certain stage of plasticity, and it could be poured into shapes. New processes were explored; tin and aluminum foil were crumpled into bowls and containers with unusual shapes to serve as forms for the candles, and sand candles were poured, dipped, and molded.

One boy asked if it was possible to paint on candles. "I don't know," said Mr. Dennis, "but we can try to find out."

Old colored crayon stubs were melted (according to colors) in cupcake tins. Bob tried painting with warm colored wax on the surface of the candle. It worked! So free-hand paintings blossomed on many of the candles.

The classroom resembled a factory for the next few days, but the products did not; each was different and highly individualized. New processes were explored and discovered; old ones were tried simply so the children would know how each one was done.

One of the values of activities of this nature is that they give children an understanding of the industrial arts of the country. Candlemaking is a large industry in this country today. When candles are mass-produced, production is cheaper and quicker, but the candles are all the same. Individualizing the process so that the candles are unique and different makes them personal, yet it takes more time, and makes them more expensive.

In the work periods that followed, Mr. Dennis talked with the children about reclaiming wax and ways wax is used, such as in paper-resistant products and in batik. He encouraged children to create their own shapes, forms, and designs. The entire candlemaking experience turned out to be a very creative one. It also helped to some degree to develop the art skills in the children. Few of the copying, patterning, and nonemotional types of experiences were apparent.

Parties. Closely allied to the problem of gift-giving is that of decorating for a party. The problems tend to be similar: How can the experience contribute to the art expression of the children?

Certainly a child is never in closer relationship with his environment than when he is having a party. He always wants to paint or use some other art medium to express himself about it. Aside from these activities, can other experiences be contrived to spur his artistic development? Can the art teacher and elementary teacher work together to plan for the children experiences that are new and challenging and yet present the children with experiences in art expression?

Children are born with a natural sense of design, balance, rhythm, harmony, contrast, line, texture, and form. All of these senses come into play when a child is using paints or compositions unless, of course, he has been subject to experiences that destroyed his native equipment. Now is the time for a teacher to broaden the children's concepts of design by encouraging them to work in bigger areas. This is always on the intuitive level, and not a conscious act of the teacher to teach them design. Any plan that serves to weaken the design sense of the child or to impose fixed plans or a preconceived design sense on him is of little value.

A child's sense of design is evident in his reactions to houses, rooms, buildings, bridges, and trucks. "I like your house," a child says, or "I don't like it." If you ask him what he means, he says, "It is nice here; the colors are pretty," or "I like the fireplace." What he is trying to say is that you have created an environment that is warm, friendly, and pleasant. His eye, sweeping around the room, causes his aesthetic senses to react— he knows somehow intuitively that this room or this house suits the occupants "to a T"; he feels comfortable about it.

It is the development of this intuitive sense that we are aiming for when we encourage the child to create for himself (or for himself and his friends) an environment that is physically happy and comfortable and in which an emotionally happy event can occur: a birthday party. To be emotionally happy the environment must be in accord with the children; it must be gay, harmonious, and comfortable. It must be balanced, interesting, and exciting.

Consequently, rather than having the children express reactions in paints or collage on paper, have them explore other media and other forms of expression. The situation is not a child working before an easel, but a child working with his friends before a room.   Many opportunities for new experiences and for creative adventure can be provided in examining the qualities of crepe and tissue paper, in working with paper plates and cups, and in manipulating, preparing, and decorating food such as gingerbread men, homemade ice cream, and popcorn balls.

For example, one group of boys in Mrs. Mayo's room became intrigued with papier mâché techniques which Mrs. Mayo had shown them when they were building a huge clown head for a play.   These boys asked to be on the table decoration committee for the Easter party.   For the centerpiece they made an enormous hollow egg out of wadded paper which they decorated beautifully with handsome designs.   Then they asked each child to make a smaller egg from a balloon and to paint it like an Easter egg for the table.   These boys had a large-scale idea in mind that called for a total design; each child made an item to complete the total picture of the set table.

Very childlike, yet very beautifully executed, their table was covered with a large green construction-paper tablecloth. Sitting in a shredded crepe paper nest in the middle of the large table was the beautiful, big, papier-mâché Easter egg.   Ribbons of crepe paper running out from it to each placesetting ended under the small Easter eggs made and decorated by each child. Each of the smaller, balloon-sized eggs had been split open, a "lip" of cardboard had been glued around the inside, and then it had been put back together.   Each was filled with colored popcorn made by the food committee.

After the refreshments had been consumed, the boys lifted the top off their big egg, and it was full of prizes that another committee had collected or made as rewards for winning the games that were to follow.

The remainder of the table contained some creative as well as some noncreative things.   Homemade cakes decorated by some of the children were very unusual and unique.   Each child had made his own placemat and colored his own napkin and cup. The entire room was decorated with crepe paper, cut and twisted in unusual ways as a result of the experimentation done by the children.   The walls were decorated with huge pictures painted voluntarily by some children who wanted to paint their impressions of an Easter party.

When the room was ready, Mrs. Mayo took time on the day of the party to have the children stand around the walls and react to the effect of the room on them.   Some children put some items away (Scott put a garbage pail behind the door) because these items were unharmonious with the rest of the contrived environment.

After the children had reacted to the environment they had created, Mrs. Mayo pushed their perceptions farther with questions such as: What does this room make you think of when you see it like this? How did you feel when you first stood back and looked at it? Why does it feel so good to you? What do you think is going to happen here? Is it a sad place or a happy place? You have used your minds well to create this place; how will you use your bodies in it? How do you think you will feel when you have to pull down your decorations? How do the cakes make you feel? I see eyes widening—what is happening in your mouth? Does something seem to hold the room together? How many feelings have you had in the room since we made it look like this? and on and on. Awareness of an environment, especially one you have created, can result in art expression for days to follow.

Teachers need to be concerned about children who copy or produce things alike only if those specific children are insecure or overly dependent on adults. Children often copy simply to practice a technique or skill (see p. 172).

In a classroom where the art and the classroom teachers work together to help children relate well to their environment and to express that relationship in art forms, children are too busily engaged in their own work to copy the work of others.

An occasional venture in creating a totally harmonious or special environment on a larger scale for a specific purpose such as a party, a show, or a circus justifies some degree of mass production of items or articles when these finished products are a necessary part of a larger creative process.

SUMMARY

The most likely solution to the problem of staffing the art department in the elementary school in the next decade is to join the art teacher and the elementary classroom teachers in some type of team arrangement where they share objectives and they plan procedures and evaluations of art experiences together. In a team relationship, certain characteristics and behavior are essential on the part of all teachers in order that the team may work together for the good of the children. This calls for sacrifices on the part of all involved; chief among these sacrifices is the need for teachers to surrender the prestige of *teaching* for the development of *learning*.

Such an arrangement demands that all art problems—including all uses of media—be resolved through dialogue. The final decisions must respect the background, experience, and knowledge of each member of the team. Problems must be solved, not ignored.

ACTIVITIES

1. This chapter has dealt with only a few of the problems that often go unresolved in the average classroom. List others and engage in dialogue about them. Seek out opinions different from your own. Try to resolve the problems to the satisfaction of all. Here are a few to get you started:
   a. Art periods are more profitable when held the first period in the morning.
   b. Every art program should provide for a time to learn about the great paintings of the world.
   c. Every classroom should have an art center.

2. Statements for discussion:
   a. If classroom teachers are to assume the role of art teachers, teacher training institutions must offer more preparation in art for the classroom teacher.
   b. Conversely, if the art teacher is to serve as a member of the classroom team, her teacher-education experience should offer her more background in curriculum development.
   c. Professional education tends to neglect the human element that might help create a more human education process.
   d. A curriculum in art needs continuity to develop, refine, and internalize skills.

3. Try to locate an art teacher who is serving as a member of a teaching team and invite her to talk to you about her job. Find out what adjustments she has had to make in her new role and what problems she faces.

4. Try to invite a visiting teacher from England or a person at a nearby college who has visited the British infant school to explain to you the part that art plays in the daily program of the school. Consider the role of the art teacher in this plan.

5. Read the nature of art teaching and the role of elementary classroom teachers on p. 34 and p. 115. Could you fulfill

both of these roles? Did you ever know a classroom teacher who seemed to be a "natural" at teaching art, although she was very inadequately trained to do so? How do you explain this?

6. Examine your own feelings about working with art media. Most adults do not respond positively to situations where they are asked to create with art materials. Why do you think this is so?

7. What feelings do you associate with your elementary school art and music periods? Try to analyze them. Take a consensus of these feelings among your colleagues. Who taught the creative arts in your school? What kind of person was she? Did she follow the basic principles of this chapter? Do you think she helped you develop your creativity? How?

8. Make a list of all the techniques you have seen art or classroom teachers use in the teaching of art that really discouraged creativity.

9. Following is a list of quotations overheard by the author in recent classroom observations he made. Decide which ones encourage creative development and which ones discourage it.
   a. "I told you to cut the leaf to the edge of the paper. Now it will be too small and won't look like the others on the bulletin board."
   b. "That doesn't look like a log to me. Where are the lines that show the bark?"
   c. "I told you to be careful not to cut outside the lines!"
   d. "Listen to Molly's tune—she has an idea that is different from all the others."
   e. "Bill, I never saw a lumberman chop like that!"
   f. "Helen, I think you're not acting like a doormouse should act."
   g. "Children, look at what Bill is doing. Does that help to give the idea that he is a doormouse?"

10. A college student has been unjustly accused of cheating on an exam and has been called to the professor's office. To free himself of suspicion would mean placing the blame on a fraternity brother. With a group, role-play the scene in the instructor's office. After five minutes have the players reverse roles and replay the same scene. Note what happens. What clues does this experience provide for developing perception in children?

11. If you are currently working with children, focus on a unit you are teaching and list all the possible art experiences that could be taught in conjunction with this unit. Examine the objectives of teaching the unit, add art objectives, and

note how you would evaluate them.   If you are an art teacher, do this with a classroom teacher.   Plot ways new media, skills, and techniques could be introduced in an artistic manner.

12. Think of all the ways you have used art as a tool this past week.   Then think of the times you have engaged in art activities simply for the joy of creating.   When you compare your lists, what can you conclude?

13. Make a list of all the "real" art experiences that could be incorporated into the celebration of Halloween in a middle-school classroom.

14. Try this exercise in forced relationships: Put a black light and fluorescent invisible paint or chalk before you on a table. On the chalkboard list the words *literature, social studies,* and *math.*   Now ask yourself how you can use the black light and chalk or paint to teach a lesson in each of these areas creatively.   Force yourself to come up with solutions. Was your creative-thinking ability challenged?

SELECTED BIBLIOGRAPHY

Anderson, Warren H. *Art Learning Situations for Elementary Education.* Belmont: Wadsworth Publishing Co., Inc., 1966.

Burgess, Lowry. "The Hidden Landscapes: Art for the Open School." *Programs of Promise: Art in the Schools.* Al Hurwitz, ed. New York: Harcourt Brace Jovanovich, Inc., 1972.

Davis, Hazel. *Music and Art in the Public School.* Washington, D.C.: National Education Association, 1963.

Goldstein, Harriet, and Vetta Goldstein. *Art in Everyday Life.* New York: Macmillan Publishing Co., Inc., 1954.

Goodlad, John. "Advancing Art in U.S. Public Schools." *Concepts in Art and Education.* George Pappas, ed. New York: Macmillan Publishing Co., Inc., 1970.

Hausman, Jerome J. "Teacher as Artist and Artist as Teacher." *Concepts in Art and Education.* George Pappas, ed. New York: Macmillan Publishing Co., Inc., 1970.

Herberholz, Donald, and Barbara Herberholz. *A Child's Pursuit of Art.* Dubuque, Iowa: William C. Brown Co., Publishers, 1967.

Hubbard, Guy, and Mary J. Rouse. "Art Meaning, Method and Media: A Structured Art Program for Elementary Classrooms." *Programs of Promise: Art in the Schools.* Al Hurwitz, ed. New York: Harcourt Brace Jovanovich, Inc., 1972.

Jefferson, Blanche. *Teaching Art to Children.* Boston: Allyn and Bacon, Inc., 1969.

Keiler, Manfred L. *The Art in Teaching Art.* Lincoln, Nebr.: University of Nebraska Press, 1961.

Lansing, Kenneth M. *Art, Artists, and Art Education.* New York: McGraw-Hill Book Co., 1969.

Pappas, George, ed. *Concepts in Art and Education.* New York: Macmillan Publishing Co., Inc., 1970.

Wampler, James. "The Warehouse Cooperative School." *Programs of Promise: Art in the Schools.* Al Hurwitz, ed. New York: Harcourt Brace Jovanovich, Inc., 1972.

PART 2

The Nurture and Use of Art in the Elementary School

CHAPTER V

Setting Conditions for Teaching Art in the Elementary School

Art is the surest and safest civilizer. . . . Open your galleries of art to the people, and you confer on them a greater benefit than mere book education: you give them a refinement to which they would otherwise be strangers.

CHARLES FAIRBANKS[1]

In Part 1 of this volume, many illustrations were presented to demonstrate the principles of creative teaching, the nature of art teaching, the art growth of children, and the nature of art teachers in action. Consequently, we have already ventured deeply into specific ways to nurture art in the elementary school. Other aspects of the development of art expression need to be explored: the conditions necessary to carry out an exciting, fruitful art program, the nurturing of art for art's sake, the further development of art through the school curriculum, art media and how they may be used creatively, the resources available to teachers of art, and the manner in which teachers evaluate art.

All art education is, to a great extent, dependent on the environmental conditions set for its operation. We will deal with that topic in this chapter.

Art educators have observed that a particular kind of environment can be constructed to offset some of the conditions

1. Charles Fairbanks, *My Unknown Chum* (Paris), p. 139.

under which children have been denied normal expression through art media. From the discussion in previous chapters an obvious fact emerges: a particular environment created to develop a sound art program will not be the same in all schools for all children. The child in a culturally deprived school, for instance, needs different materials, motivations, and processes from a child in a wealthy suburban school.

However, there are certain general principles that every classroom teacher and art teacher should consider in creating a teaching environment. Favorable conditions are brought about through manipulation of the environment, motivation of the children, and introduction of materials. It is hoped that under good conditions children will continue to grow or at least show less decline in their ability to express ideas and feelings uniquely with aesthetic form.

When the authors use the term *environment* in this book, they are using it in the context of Ridlon's definition:

> When one refers to environment he is referring to the sum total of influences that constantly surround us and affect our many senses. Environment also refers to intangibles that affect attitudes, transactions, and dreams. It is environmental awareness that activates our senses which in turn activate the process of perception. Therefore, man's perception of his environment forms the base for which he exists, responds, communicates and creates.[2]

The conditions discussed below have been grouped into physical conditions, intellectual conditions, social–emotional conditions, and psychological conditions. They are clusters of principles basic to a worthy art environment, so there is a great deal of dependency and overlap among them.

PHYSICAL CONDITIONS

First, the teacher must recognize that *the ability to express oneself* through art *is developmental,* as we discussed in Chapter 3. In his first encounter with new materials, the child experiments and explores. Later, as he reaches the schematic stage,

2. James A. Ridlon, "The Dialectics of Synaesthetic Education," in M. Andrews, ed., *Synaesthetic Education* (Syracuse, N.Y.: Syracuse University School of Art and the Division of Summer Sessions, 1971), p. 43.

some of the things the child paints become recognizable. Still later, the child paints for the joy of painting; we call this the aesthetic stage.

Stages of growth in art expression must be considered as part of a developmental process and therefore temporary. Too much stress should not be placed on the permanency of children's paintings, for they often paint by the hour, discarding painting after painting. The standards the child has set for himself may be lowered when a teacher insists on putting one of his paintings on the bulletin board. To the child this may not have been a finished product, and for the teacher to praise it as such discourages the child from going further in his experimentation.

In order to set conditions for art experiences in the classroom, *materials must be easily accessible.* If children are to develop new uses of art media, they must be given unlimited opportunity to experiment and explore. Locked cupboards do not provide incentive for frequent use of art materials. Art centers in classrooms should be equipped with easels, large tables for working, and open shelves containing paints, crayons, various kinds of paper, paste, scissors, and interesting scrap materials. Clay and Plasticene, dyes, block prints, fingerpaint, and other artistic media add richness to the child's art experiences. Frequent opportunities should be planned for the children to use these materials and to apply them to bulletin-board, flower, and room arrangements.

The concept of "centers" now popular in the open classroom plan is one of the most encouraging movements in education, for it places materials in the classroom so they can be used and enjoyed by the children. The "center" concept is one that can be successful in all types of schools.

Most art activities can be best accomplished when the student is standing up. Sitting, especially if the chair height is not exactly right, inhibits free movement of the muscles of the arm. Painting is really an activity that involves the whole body; complete freedom to move is almost essential. It is also necessary that the painter be able to move from one area to another; the painter needs access to the water and to the supplies. A good art center has these traffic patterns arranged to reduce the possibility of confusion in the area.

Tools such as brushes need to be in a place where they are readily available, rather than stored in drawers. An easy way to keep brushes washed and stored is to punch some good-sized holes in the bottoms of two suitably sized cans. If the brushes are placed bristles down in the first one, they can then be placed under the faucet and a little dunking up and down will remove the paint without soiling the hands.   It is easier to have one student wash all the brushes in this way than to have a sinkful of paint-covered helpers.   Once the paint has been removed, the brushes can be stored right side up in the other can.

It is a good idea to avoid glass containers in the art center; they are washed often, and the sink is a bad place to spot broken glass.   Plastic paint containers can be cut down to make ideal water pots.   Large bleach bottles make ideal bowls for mixing such things as paste for papier mâché, and they are surprisingly easy to clean.   Scissors are best kept in a rack.   If you do not have a commercial one, a suitable cardboard box with holes punched in the top to hold the scissors is a good substitute.

Any work area that is to be used by a large number of people needs a definite organization that all will agree to maintain; otherwise a great deal of time is wasted looking for misplaced supplies.   If possible, there should be a central supply point, the golden rule being to return everything to this point the minute the user is finished with it.   A tea trolley or a cart works well for supplies for special projects and makes for easy storage.   Scrap boxes are indispensable.   If there is enough space, it is a good idea to have more than one and to sort the materials.   Experience will determine the most valuable things to collect.   Some suggestions are left-over sewing materials, buttons, ribbons, fabric, plastic meat containers (ideal for making prints), egg cartons, plastic bottles, styrofoam packaging, aluminum foil and plates, broken plastic toys, corrugated cardboard, and construction-paper scraps.   These boxes should represent materials that can be recycled.   If you can provide a few simple tools, a box of wood scraps is useful.

A box of newspapers is a must.   If the tables are covered with newspapers before work commences, clean-up consists simply of throwing them away.

If space permits, a table with a sloping top makes the ideal working surface.   The slope should be nearly at a right angle to the child's line of sight.   It is not generally realized that from his lower viewpoint, the top of the paper actually appears foreshortened.   Ideally sloping benches are built against the wall with slight ledges to prevent things from sliding off.   If this is not possible, a sheet of plywood with some blocks behind it can be set on a table.   If this type of working surface is provided, provision must be made for setting paints and water pots down on a level surface.

A very real problem in a small work center is what to do with wet, finished paintings and other work. Hanging them up is a good solution. A line of clips can be made by threading spring-type clothes pins onto a line. The line can be threaded through the center of the spring. Bulky things, such as papier-mâché objects that can take several days to dry, can be stood on the cafeteria trays that have been used as paint palettes. They can often be stored in another part of the building until they are needed again. It is a good idea to label each item. It is amazing how often children are unable to identify their own unfinished work.

Clay is a highly desirable material, but it presents many problems and almost requires a separate area. Traces of clay are very persistent, so clean-up has to be meticulous if traces of clay are not to be found on other work for days afterwards. It is a pity that these difficulties deter teachers from using clay. If there is a kiln available, the best clay to buy is terra cotta. It fires to a beautiful dark red, works easily, and, best of all, it does not crack easily during working or firing. If space does not permit the use of clay indoors, it can provide the ideal outdoor activity. Terra cotta can be fired in a bonfire if no kiln is available.

The final form that the work center takes is an outgrowth of the way in which the class operates. There is no one form. Very often the careful arrangements planned by architects are far from workable. It is better to find out exactly what your requirements are and leave enough flexibility in planning and construction so that changes can be made without too much difficulty.

If the school is fortunate enough to have an art room, every classroom can benefit from a work center in which the child can work at odd times of day. The rigid scheduling that is necessary to permit time for students to use an art room is often an inhibiting factor in creative production. If art is to be an integral part of the learning situation, then provision should be made for it within the learning environment.

Materials selected for art instruction (and for children's play) *should provide stimulating sensory experiences.* They should be chosen because of color, texture, shape, or moving parts so that the experience of using them is, in itself, pleasurable.

Materials placed in the child's environment *should stimulate experimentation and inventiveness.* They should tease the child's own ideas and evoke feelings so that the child easily discovers something he wants to express and unique ways of expressing it.

New media should be introduced to children *with no set of preconceived adult standards.*

Some classroom teachers and art teachers have made statements to the authors like "I don't believe in allowing children to use enamel paint. It is too difficult to handle." "I feel carpentry materials are too dangerous for young children to use." "Clay is too messy."

In these cases the problem is the teacher's; she is restricting the child's environment to her own tastes and prejudices. If John constructs a toy car that he wants to leave outdoors in the play box, he needs to know about enamel paint in order to protect it from the elements. By confining him to her tastes and prejudices, she is limiting his art expression just as dogmatically as if she were limiting his art expression by confining him to her ideas.

The answer to the problem is to introduce John to the proper medium to help him solve his problem, but also to instruct him in the clean and proper use of it. He should simply be told that he must wear a protective covering, that he must cover his work areas with papers, that he must work carefully, that he must clean up accidents with turpentine or other appropriate solubles, and that he must allow his product to dry for a longer period of time than usual. Depriving children of experiences with media or techniques thwarts their creative expression.

Materials should be adaptable to varying abilities and ideas, varying degrees of muscular control, varying attention spans, and varying interests so each child can set his own goals and have a reasonable amount of success.

When materials are selected to make up the environment for the classroom and/or the art room, *the teacher should* certainly *be aware that* all *materials* she sets out for children's use *influence,* and even determine, their *learning experiences.* One of the greatest misconceptions about the open classroom is that children choose the materials they want to work with and do what they want with them. Actually, each open-classroom center is carefully stocked by the teacher with materials and equipment that guide the children's learning along necessary lines. Every change in this equipment is made with a definite purpose in mind.

Just as the materials themselves set limits and suggest avenues of learning for a child, so does the manner in which they are set out greatly influence or control the child's learning. This is especially true of art materials.

It has long been the custom for teachers to set out the primary colors in paint pots along the bottom of the easel, each with a paint brush in it. This is done mainly to encourage children to go to work at once. Teachers often feel that children who must prepare their own paints grow so tired of the task that they abandon painting.

Although this reasoning applies to some children, other perils are equally as important to consider. Setting out brushes and primary colors mixed to a certain consistency deprives a child of the sensory experiences of manipulation and exploration that he needs not only to learn about art, but also to learn about paint! (See p. 203.)

Somewhere along the line children have got to learn that water added to pigment thins it and weakens the color. Somewhere along the line children, to be literate in art, must learn (hopefully by experimentation) that red mixed with blue becomes purple, that the mixing of paints with other paints produces various hues, shades, and tints. Sometime a child must learn that if he uses dry paint, the paint on the paper will be thick and chunky; if he uses wet paint, it will be pale and smooth and allow the paper to show through. Sometime along the way a child must learn the differences in brush strokes and the multitude of effects he can obtain from painting with wide brushes, narrow brushes, dry brushes, wet brushes, flat brushes, and pointed brushes and from rolling, dripping, blowing, pushing, and running paint on paper. It is better that he learn all of these facts through experience and discovery.

When teachers set out materials for children to use they should consider carefully how they are to be set out. They might consider setting many jars of different colors and many different-sized brushes and other applicators on a table. As the children come in they are instructed in how to thin the paint and how to clean the applicators. The teacher then shifts roles at once by stepping back and allowing nature to take its course. (See p. 15 for further discussion of this point.)

INTELLECTUAL CONDITIONS

To be creative, experiences in art must be open-ended. The teacher should place the child in situations where he is confronted with a problem that he can solve by using various art media. The providing of motivation and the teaching of necessary convergent-thinking skills are in the realm of the teacher, but the child provides the solution to the problem—the art product.

The teacher should strive for individuality and uniqueness; each art product should differ from all others.

The teacher should try to understand what art is and the processes involved in creating, and not expect realism in the products.

The teacher must understand that when children reach the schematic stage in art where they desire to reproduce objects and people in their paintings as they see them, they do so in various ways according to their development. A child cannot see the world through his teacher's eyes. In the process of growing up, he receives impressions of the world around him. For instance, after a trip to the zoo, a five-year-old made bold, black stripes across a sheet of paper and brought it to her nursery school teacher. "Tell me about your painting," said the teacher.

"Why, it's a tiger at the zoo," said the five-year-old in a tone that implied that the teacher should have recognized it at once. The child was impressed by the bold color of the tiger's coat. She did not see the head, feet, tail, and body in detail. Obviously she knew they were there, but this was not a new discovery for her. She painted what impressed her most.

Although the product is an important gauge of the child's growth, emphasis should be placed more on the importance of the process as a means of receiving pleasure and growing in art appreciation. A teacher needs to remember that the stages of growth mentioned in Chapter 3 are not common to all children at the same age levels.

A teacher's role must vary with the maturation of the child. For young children she provides an environment rich in materials and ideas and a permissive atmosphere so the child is free to explore, manipulate, and discover. For the early intermediate grades, the teacher provides more guidance, helps the child discover new techniques, and motivates him with a rich environment full of many ideas and suggestions. When children begin to evaluate their own work, much of the vocabulary of art technique can be mastered. The teacher can encourage and promote art for art's sake, she can provide children with many techniques and an opportunity to try them out, and she can develop art principles and art standards through experience and discussion.

Many teachers feel children's techniques and paintings are influenced and restricted when other paintings are set before them. The desire to copy tends to reduce the child's own attempt to think and paint creatively. Carried to excess, this can be true. But children who have frequently experienced the joy of creating in many ways are interested in observing how others create. They paint when they have something to say and are not eager to copy other people's work. They may, however, borrow ideas and accumulate techniques for building standards of original expression and skilled workmanship.

Art objects and fine paintings should be used in the classroom. The teacher should choose the subjects according to the age level and the interests of the children. She should draw attention to the pictures, discuss them with the children, and acquaint the children with the artist.

A fourth grade was discussing a beautiful winter scene that the teacher had borrowed from a nearby college picture library for a week. Paul said, "You know, Miss Perkins, the artist really painted the snow green but it looks white." Some of the children doubted the snow was green, so Paul cut a hole in a piece of paper and placed it over the rest of the painting so that only an area of the snow showed through. It was green! An excellent discussion followed on ways to get effect through use of color. Many children, looking out the window, pointed out the fact that the snow outside really was quite blue and that the shadows cast by the tiny hills were almost purple. This class had made an exciting discovery and a whole period of investigating and exploring with their own paints resulted. This teacher was using a good painting wisely.

Children also enjoy knowing the stories of paintings. They thrill to Raphael's *Madonna of the Chair* and the story of its creation. Stories about pictures are best told after the children have had an opportunity to enjoy the aesthetic qualities of the picture, so their pleasure comes from the painting as well as the association connected with it. Greater appreciation of pictures often comes when children know something about the artist.

A continual flow of stimuli must be present to encourage mental images that challenge the child to express himself through the media at hand. The subject matter at hand should vary for different age levels, for what a child paints is determined by his own development, his particular needs and interests, or his own particular feelings (see Chapter 7). However, some subjects (holidays, for example) are common to all children and can be utilized for planned art lessons. Much of good art teaching must be done on an individual basis, even when the interest is common. The following plan worked out by an art teacher illustrates the type of lesson that utilizes a common interest, Lincoln's Birthday, to foster true creative effort on the part of each child.

A fifth-grade class had asked to paint some pictures for Lincoln's Birthday. The results were a stereotyped silhouette pasted on the conventional white background. Realizing that a carryover from former sterile art experiences had caused this, the art teacher set as her objective the development of a creative experience from this very uncreative one.

The art teacher opened her lesson by stimulating the children's interest in painting about Lincoln.

She said, "You know, when I think of Abraham Lincoln a whole flood of pictures come to my mind. One of them I like very much. I see a tall, lanky, muscular young man in the middle of a clearing. He is stripped to the waist and he swings a gleaming axe in the sunlight as he splits rails for a fence. His legs are spread firmly apart and the sunlight makes ripples across his tanned body as the muscles flex with the movement of the gleaming axe. Behind him in the distance is a cabin with a thick spiral of smoke rising into the air. Behind that is the dark green forest. Above is the clear, blue sky, and in all that loneliness the sound of the axe is the only sound, the rippling of the man's body the only movement. What do you see when you think of Lincoln?"

One child raised his hand. "I see a long train draped with mourning and I see a band playing a funeral dirge. The train winds slowly in and out among the hills and stops at the towns where people dressed in black stand along the way sobbing. And the only colors I see are on the flags flapping at half-mast along the way."

Other children were catching the spirit. "I see a beautiful parade marching down Pennsylvania Avenue," said one boy. "There are bands playing and flags waving and thousands of people line the way and cheer. Lincoln is riding to the capitol. It is his inauguration day."

"I see a box in Ford's Theater—a torn flag hangs from the front of the box. A weary man clutches his side and falls forward over the torn flag. Mary Todd Lincoln stands gasping and the crowd below stares in terror at the sight of the man falling."

Each child who so desired told what he saw, and the panorama of the life of Lincoln unfolded. It was painted verbally around the walls of the room in a riot of color, movement, and form. Then it was but a step to transfer the verbal paintings into pictorial ones. The color, imagination, and action that this simple discussion released was a far cry from the row of black silhouettes along the front of the room.

There was one picture done in shocking blacks and purples, full of sadness and despair, of the funeral train winding through the hills. A brightly painted flag and a few bits of colored bunting formed dramatic and startling contrasts. There was an action-filled picture of the muscular Mr. Lincoln in the sunlit field splitting rails. There was an unbelievably sensitive picture of Lincoln at the grave of Ann Rutledge. Some pictures were designs of exciting colors that children labeled *Death, Fear,* and *Sadness.*

The discussion of the paintings was another creative experience; it was an experience in thought-provoking communication. There was some dependence on the art teacher, but she was fulfilling her role well in taking the children from where they were and unfolding new possibilities by initiating freedom to work independently.

Continuous effort should be made by the teacher to help each child develop his creative ability, though the abilities of individual children may vary widely. On occasion, disturbed children or children who appear to have lost their individuality need special help in rediscovering their own abilities. In such instances it is necessary for the teacher to focus careful attention on those conditions that will free this child from his inhibitions. Setting up these conditions may necessitate the use of unusual methods to gain creative art expression.

Oddly enough, the very measures that have dimmed the creative power of the child can be utilized to recapture those powers. Copying or tracing patterns in art experiences, for example, may have restricted the child's powers of interpretation and observation. In order to lead a child away from the concept that his art product is a good one if it closely resembles a pattern or is a replica of someone else's work, the teacher can first encourage the child to make his traced Christmas tree or his turkey different from those of the other children. Soon his individuality begins to assert itself in many small ways. If encouraged, it will perhaps grow. This is not often a quick change, for the child has to unlearn; the teacher must reteach, which is much more difficult than teaching.

If the child has had the greatest of all his abilities killed—his creative ability—almost any step the teacher takes to reawaken that ability is legitimate if it results in a richer life for the child. When he is deprived of his creative powers, a child loses one of his finest means of communication.   Such a child is not equipped for a full, satisfactory life.   He has no way of deriving pleasure from what he has and from what nature has provided him; he seeks pleasure and satisfaction outside himself, never realizing that the greatest satisfactions and pleasures he can find lie within himself and his own inherent ability to create his own happiness.   Our world is filled with people of this sort and the schools of our culture cannot afford to turn out more like them.

Emphasis should be placed on developing perception. Inasmuch as the power of perception is basic to all art expression and to the total development of creativity, lessons must be planned in the art program or the school program for its development.

One such lesson described on p. 215 demonstrates how one teacher handled an individual child's problem by trying to make her more perceptive.   Perception does not always mean helping children to see more clearly or to represent objects more truly.   It may mean developing in children a reaction to life so that the feelings, smells, tastes, sensations, and sounds are

FIGURE 5–1.   A lesson in perception: how does the other half of the face look?

absorbed and classified and normal relationships are used to evoke new patterns in forced relationships.

Our perceptions come from our experiences, not from abstract knowledge. Much of what children paint comes from what they know (knowledge) rather than what they see (experiences); the teacher must help the children to *see* better.

"What color is the sky today?" asks Mr. Thompson. The child has learned that skies are blue and almost without looking he is about to answer, "Blue." But he does look—and it is not blue; it is gray. A discussion of the color of skies brings out the fact that a sky can be black, blue, gray, green, off-white, red, or multicolored, as in a sunset.

In the flashlight lesson on p. 14, Miss Hill was deliberately trying to refine the children's concept of color and rhythm through vision.

When a teacher is setting conditions for art development in elementary school classes, she must include planned lessons in the development of perception with the understanding that although all children may look at the same thing, they will not see the same thing. (For a full discussion of perception, see Chapter 6, p. 207.)

FIGURE 5–2. Sensitivity training: two boys shift roles to develop empathy in an argument.

Emphasis should be placed on developing sensitivity. Sensitivity training has become almost a fad among adults attempting to rehumanize the world. Great efforts are being made to develop the ability to empathize and to "feel" for the other fellow. Courses are being taught everywhere to help people to discover themselves and yet to get outside themselves to become sensitive to the feelings of others.

Children too can benefit from sensitivity training. Some of the techniques being used by the adults can be applied in the classroom. Just as a teacher should make a conscientious attempt to develop perceptual abilities in children, so should she help them to be more sensitive to the needs of others and more sensitive to objects and phenomena in their environment. Perceptual training and sensitivity training in many respects fall into the same category.

Many teachers today are already using strategies to develop sensitivity to the environment. Role-playing and role-reversal are two such techniques (see Fig. 5–2). Others include taste and touch experiences which help the child develop an imagery to improve his creative writing.

"Look what I brought to school today," said Mrs. Balmer. Exclamations of "Oh" and "Ah" and squeals of delight filled the art room as the children gathered around a baby lamb which she was leading from a sheltered corner.

The lamb was for feeling. "Oh, he is so soft. Isn't he sweet?"

The lamb was for smelling. "Phew, Mrs. Balmer, he stinks!"

The lamb was for hearing. "But he doesn't really say 'Baa,' does he?"

The lamb was for seeing. "Can you see any way he might protect himself if he thought you were going to hurt him? How does he hear you? Does he have eyelashes? Is his wool curly or straight?" asked Mrs. Balmer.

All the children experienced the lamb. They talked about his life on the farm—where, when, and how he was born— and they learned what to feed him, how to keep him comfortable, and how to clean up after him. Although it was the same lamb and they all agreed to name him Posie, each experience was somewhat different. And the art expressions of their impressions were all different too.

Shelly made an almost exact replica of Posie in clay. She even put curly marks representing his wool into the wet surface before it was baked. Charlie painted a large, soft eye in a gray, fluffy blob of paint. Frank made a montage from old carpeting he salvaged from the junk box. Jimmy painted a ridiculously funny picture of Posie's rear end. Marcia made a soft, delicate pencil sketch of Posie and her mother in a field of flowers.

"How did you feel when your dog was hurt? How does it feel to be a piece of milkweed down? What color is happiness? What media would you use to show laughter? How did you feel when you hit your best friend that time you were angry?"

Sensitivity training can become a legitimate part of the classroom program.

Empathy cannot be taught. It can be experienced and encouraged but, like creativity itself, it appears when conditions in the environment intuitively demand it.

The capacity to become responsive and sensitive to the dimensions of one's nature, to express oneself as a free entity opposed to the universal forces, to see truth, and the resultant sense of satisfaction, security, and well-being in the doing may be referred to as the essence of creative living (humanism).[3]

If art is an expression of man's relation to his total environment, it is logical to assume that helping children relate to the environment with all their senses will enhance their ability to express themselves through creative art.

Intuitive thinking should be encouraged. In setting the conditions for art expression, the teacher also needs to plan experiences that promote the child's ability to think intuitively. But what is intuitive thinking?

Mr. Lander's children had been experimenting with fingerpaint prints. After the children had selected and mounted their favorites, each child put one on a bulletin board in the front of the room and the children shared them.

"Let's begin with Jamie's," said Mr. Lander. "Do you see anything in it? Does it make you think of anything?"

"Looks like a big dragon sleeping," said Gwen.

"Show us," said Mr. Lander.

Gwen traced her finger along the pattern. "Oh, I see," said Bunky. "But it looks to me more like a bowl of fruit—here, let me show you!"

Mrs. Lane's children went outside to study the exquisite

3. Michael Andrews, unpublished paper.

cloud formations on a certain spring day.   "What do you see in the clouds?" asked Mrs. Lane.

"Lambs," said Jamie.

"A dog's head," said Andy.

"An Indian," said Gailen.

Intuitive thinking is exactly that: letting something inside of you take over and see things that are not really there but could be.   Intuitive thinking is that part of the human system that causes a man to wrinkle his nose, pull off his tie, say "Ugh," and select one that goes more appropriately with his jacket.   It is that set of impulses and senses that causes a woman to feel, "That's exactly the hat I need to go with my new coat."   Intuition is described by Webster as "the direct or immediate perception of truths, facts, etc. without reasoning."

Intuitive thinking is what tells you your dishes match, your clothes look good, the garden has just enough decoration, you are wearing enough jewelry, etc.   It is an inborn trait in humans which, like their creativity, is often disrupted in its development or killed off by the socialization processes of modern times.   It is a blend of knowledge, instinct, emotion, morality, and value judgment.   It is another basic element of art.

The powers of analogy should be developed.

The ability to deal with analogy is the ability to see common relationships between dissimilar things and situations. "In what way are a record player, a tape recorder, and a baby alike?" is a question that sets the mind galloping for analogies." The type of thinking that is necessary to make analogies is in young children and can be developed in the elementary school classroom.

"The moon is a flashlight in the sky," says an eight-year-old cub scout looking for the latrine in the woods at night.   He is using analogy to show his perception of the moon.

An intellectual condition necessary for the development of art ability is the opportunity for children to form analogies in the classroom.   The ability to form analogies is discussed in the next chapter (see p. 213).

The teacher should help the child to build a sense of design.   Just as a teacher needs to develop perceptual abilities, the ability to empathize, sensitivity, and intuitive thinking, she should also strive to build a good sense of design.   This can be done in a multitude of ways.   Materials can be arranged so that they are functionally located, easy to obtain, and yet pleasing to the eye.   The room itself, although it contains many materials and tools, should be attractive.   If it is a functional room, a good

FIGURE 5–3. Developing aesthetic sense with clay.

design is likely to result. However, the concepts of harmony, balance, color, shade, texture, contrast, and line can be so subtly made a continual part of a child's environment that so-called formal teaching of these concepts is not necessary.

The teacher should develop a sensitivity to beauty, an aesthetic sense.

Lowenfeld and Brittain define aesthetics as:

> a means of organizing thinking, feeling and perceiving into an expression that communicates these thoughts and feelings to someone else. The organization of words we call prose or poetry, the organization of tones we call music, the organization of body movements is usually referred to as dance, and the organization of lines, shapes, color and form makes up art. There are no set standards or rules that are applicable to aesthetics; rather the aesthetic criteria are based on the individual, the particular work of art, the culture in which it is made, and the intent or purpose behind the art form. There is a tremendous variety of organization in art. We find that an aesthetic form is not created by the imposition of any external rule but rather that a creative work grows by its own principles.[4]

They go on to say that aesthetic growth in children is shown by development of the sensitive ability to integrate experi-

4. Reprinted with permission of Macmillan, Inc. from Viktor Lowenfeld and W. Lambert Brittain, *Creative and Mental Growth,* 5th ed. (New York: Macmillan Publishing Co., Inc., 1970), p. 31. Copyright © 1970, by the Macmillan Co.

ences into a cohesive whole: the harmonious organization and expression of thoughts and feelings through the use of lines, textures, and colors. Young children organize intuitively. Aesthetics is intimately tied up with personality. (For further discussion of this topic see p. 190.)

Aesthetic growth is an important part of each person's development; it should not be neglected in the classroom. The classroom itself should be not only a workshop but also a place where objects of beauty made by the children can be displayed and appreciated.

The truly lovely paintings of the past and the creations of the present are all part of a child's rightful heritage; they should be introduced in the classroom so the child can evaluate, interpret, and learn from them. The more contact he has with paintings of all kinds, the more adept he becomes at building his own standards and enjoying his own culture.

There is no limit to the resources for finding beauty. In a school in the slums where there was not a great deal of beauty in the environment, one teacher used the following items as her resources for developing art concepts:

color: in the children's clothes
textures: in collections of old wood, broken cement, fruit displays.
line: in maps of the city streets—fences, buildings, sidewalks, blocks.
design: in buildings, windows, oil on water in the streets, automobiles, books, etc.
balance: in the structure of bridges, machines, buildings and in street signs, playground equipment, peddler carts.
harmony: in packages in the supermarket, in the sidewalk sections, in the stone and brick facades, in window dressings.

Situations should be arranged or contrived to permit the application (and practice) *of acquired skills.* The concepts discovered or learned by children and the techniques and skills they acquire need to be practiced to become internalized. This has been discussed previously.

To see a child copying occasionally is not a matter over which a teacher should become alarmed. Children often teach themselves a new technique or perfect an old one by copying someone else's craftsmanship for a while. It is only when this work replaces a child's own expression that a teacher needs to feel concern.

Opportunities must be provided for children to learn to

think. Individuals learn to think when they are given the power to *decide* (to judge, to make choices) and the power to *imagine* (to relate one thing to another to form something new, to integrate two or more isolated facts into a unified whole, to foresee what might happen, to create). Basic to all thinking processes is the ability to question. Children ask questions normally if they are not discouraged. Questions become the basis of a problem statement. Consequently, these skills should become a regular part of the intellectual environment for creative development: opportunities to ask questions, to formulate problems, to make guesses, to imagine, and to make decisions. The problems caused by questions create tensions in the child; the tensions are often released in an art product.

Most important of all, *the teacher must accept and reward creative behavior.*

PSYCHOLOGICAL CONDITIONS

The teacher must provide a permissive atmosphere and a "level of expectancy" in the classroom that will keep the children experimenting, producing, and discovering. She should use as many of the natural experiences of the children as possible to promote art expression, but she should also set up situations that provoke their imaginations to go beyond the realm of the ordinary. In this way she will develop the creative thinking that results in creative expression.

The teacher must realize that, at certain times, the best teaching may be no teaching at all. She must develop a sensitivity to that psychological moment when she should withdraw from the situation and leave the child to summon his resources and fulfill the creative act on his own.

Teachers often express doubts about their ability to teach art because they cannot draw well themselves, but often teachers who cannot draw well do a better job of teaching young children than those who can. Their standards for completed art products are not as high, and they are likely to leave the children to their own devices. The child is free to explore, manipulate, and experience to his heart's content. This is perhaps the most important technique in teaching—allowing the child to have materials to work with and a chance to try them out. The teacher at this point should recognize the child's purpose in painting and not demand sophisticated products of him. She should show interest in the child's painting by asking that he tell about it—not by asking what it is supposed to be.

Children have a natural sense of color, harmony, and balance. The teacher needs to encourage the growth of the child's ability to relate objects and to use good art principles in his pictures. She does not have to stop to teach a formal lesson on perspective or balance, but she should help the child to sharpen his sense of observation and discover these things for himself.

A child who is attempting to say things with his paintbrush may become irritated when the brush fails to say what he wants it to say. When he paints his chimney jutting from the roof at a ninety-degree angle he senses it is incorrect, but by himself he cannot discover the technique for painting it correctly. He does not really see why it is incorrect. A series of such experiences may cause him to surrender the art experience for a more successful one. Repeated failures may result in a disinterested attitude toward art expression. The teacher can play an important part in resolving this failure experience and thus guide the child to a successful experience and on to another step. Noting his problem, she can step to the window and point out that the line of the side of the house across the street goes the same way as the line of the chimney. The child can try again with his new knowledge and sharpened powers of observation to communicate the true picture which has suddenly become so important to him.

Similar techniques are used in good teaching of other subjects. In reading, for instance, the teacher can show the child a technique for tackling the pronunciation of a new word, or she can tell him the word at once. The danger in art teaching lies not in showing, telling, or providing techniques, but in showing the child what to make and thus submerging the child's own ideas. Techniques are necessary for the final attainment of his own creative idea. They should be acquired quickly so they do not hinder him in his accomplishment. The ones he does not learn through self-discovery, manipulation, or explanation the teacher should help him to learn.

The classroom environment should be set up so children encounter daily a reasonable amount of success in their art experiences. (See our earlier discussion of physical conditions.)

When freedom and success are experienced in the classroom, they come to pervade the total personality of the child and they help to build self-confidence and a stronger self-concept. Children appear to become more flexible, more imaginative, freer in taking risks, more adventurous, and better able to relate to people and objects in their environment. All of this is necessary to creative development.

Proper psychological *conditions* in a classroom *should offer* children a rare opportunity to find *positive outlets for their emotions* and for ideas that are not socially acceptable or that cannot be discussed.

"I can't draw a straight line" is a cliché heard time and again. What the child (or adult) is really saying is "I have a problem; I have lost my self-reliance," "I am afraid of failure," or "I am insecure."

In the first place, no one can draw a straight line without a tool, so our friends are not as badly off as they think they are. Nonetheless, to be realistic, this problem confronts teachers at all ages and in all situations.

In setting conditions for art expression in the classroom it is essential that children be considered individually and that *plans* be made to *provide a certain amount of psychological security* and support for each child in his own way. It must be remembered that that which makes one child secure will have little or no effect on another.

Children abandon expression through art for several reasons: pressure from parents not to get dirty, negative evaluation of art products, sarcasm directed at their attempts to be creative, fear of failure in general, lack of familiarity with new media, physical illness, lack of sensory stimulation in the home or school environment, social stigmas they have heard, such as "Painting is sissy," lack of self-confidence, and lack of previous creative development.

Often a child's deprecation of his ability is an attempt to avoid the art experience. It needs to be regarded as a symptom of some deeper cause. The teacher has to find out the cause before the problem can be attacked. Talking to the child or allowing him to do something else at which he is more comfortable until she can probe deeper into the problem is more beneficial than forcing him to perform as the other children are, perhaps at the risk of turning him away from art expression and self-realization forever.

SOCIAL–EMOTIONAL CONDITIONS

Emphasis should be placed on the values of individual differences or uniqueness rather than on conformity. (See the discussion of intellectual conditions above.)

A spirit of exploration and experimentation should be encouraged. Cooperation must be stressed rather than competition. Risk-taking and a spirit of adventure should be developed.

The teacher should try to develop a congenial and accepting atmosphere in the classroom.

Children should be helped to make their own decisions and to use their own ideas (see p. 126).

A conscientious effort should be made to inform and instruct parents in understanding children's art and their growth in art so that the conditions set at school can be extended to the home. This principle is often very difficult to apply in some types of schools; it can be fulfilled only to a minor degree in certain situations. It is included, however, because it is so important.

Art offers a natural, normal outlet for emotions. Often children use art media as a means of giving vent to strong emotion in a constructive way. Almost all art reflects the emotions of its creator. The emotional state of a child can, at times, be identified by his art products.

Because of the relationship between art expression and the inner self, the paintings of emotionally disturbed children are often quite different from those of other children. These paintings, when studied by trained psychiatrists, can give insight into the problems with which these children are unable to cope.

In like manner, the teacher of normal children will find that the feelings of children in her classroom show in their paintings with such frequency that she needs no psychologist to help her understand if a child is sending signals for help. High emotional involvement in painting is generally discerned when a child, his feelings, or something personal about him appears in the painting. Stereotyped repetitions in paintings generally indicate low emotional involvement. Copying from others may also indicate low self-involvement, although this need not always be the case.

Normal encounters with art expression can be tactfully handled, or they can be so poorly handled that the child becomes more and more emotionally upset. He may even abandon one of the tension valves he has for releasing his emotional pressure—his art expression.

The problems of emotionally disturbed children are far more numerous than those discussed above. The average classroom teacher or art teacher may need help from the school psychologist in dealing with the emotionally disturbed child. It must be remembered that art expression contributes heavily to the rehabilitation of emotionally disturbed children. Often these children continue to communicate through their paintings when they can no longer communicate verbally. Fingerpaint was first invented to provide a medium for disturbed children so that they might express themselves without the use of tools such as brushes. Beautiful paintings have been done by people with various types of emotional disturbances.

Educating the emotions does not mean suppressing them; it means helping people find constructive ways of releasing them. Art expression is one way.

SUMMARY

The success of any art program relies to a great extent on the conditions set for its operation. Adjustments can be made in environmental settings to offset the abnormal conditions under which some children grow. However, common principles serve as a guide in all settings. Obviously, certain *physical* conditions must be recognized. The child himself is an animal subject to changes in his own physical growth and therefore his art is developmental. Materials should be easily accessible; they should provide stimulating sensory experiences; they should encourage experimentation and inventiveness; they should be introduced with no set of preconceived adult standards; they should be adaptable to varying abilities and ideas; and they should be placed in the environment for a purpose.

There are *intellectual* conditions that should be considered in setting up the art environment. Experiences should be open-ended in order to foster creative thinking. The teacher should strive for individuality and uniqueness. She should understand what art is and should not set standards of realism in representation as a goal. The teacher's role should vary with the growth of the child. A continual flow of stimuli should be presented. Each child should receive attention and help in a program that includes lessons in developing perception, analogy, empathy, sensitivity, intuitive thinking, and sense of design. Creative behavior should be accepted and rewarded.

Under *psychological* conditions, the teacher should set the following: a permissive atmosphere, success experiences, positive outlets for the child's emotions, and psychological security.

Social–emotional conditions also need to be considered.

The child should be a contributing member of a congenial group, individual differences should be valued, and a spirit of exploration and experimentation should be encouraged. Children should be helped to make their own decisions. The program is enhanced if parents are informed of the program so that they understand what is going on.

A child's art expression reflects a strong encounter with his environment. That environment must contain the essential tools and conditions to allow art expression to take place.

ACTIVITIES

1. One way to get to know art is to practice it. Take analogy, for instance. Try out some of the following activities designed to develop your ability to use analogy.
   a. On the basis of your strongest personal interest, make an analogy for a goldfish pond, geese flying south, a crane swinging a wrecking ball, and a garden.
   b. Write a short letter substituting symbols and numerals for words.
   c. Ascribe human characteristics to inanimate objects such as a jug, an old newspaper, and a half-empty cup.
   d. Make a series of sketches using shape and color to describe feelings.
   e. Invent humorous country-style metaphors for human situations such as "He's as rootless as a mess of beet greens."
   f. Take a photograph or drawing and give it a caption that converts it into a cartoon or joke.
   g. Using paper, invent a substitute for a spoon and a cup.
   h. Using direct analogy, discover how many ways a strip of cardboard can be made to stand on edge.
   i. Consider the ways an artist has available to represent the wind.
2. Janie Edwards is in the third grade. Every art period Janie sits beside Suzie Kelly and waits to see what Suzie does. Then Janie proceeds to copy it. What is Janie's problem and how would you help her?
3. Statements for discussion:
   a. Multisensory perception is implicit in every learning situation.
   b. It takes more imagination than experience to paint.
   c. Education needs to recognize more fully the objectives of humanistic and aesthetic education.

4. Look at the environment in which you work daily. What have you done to make it attractive and functional? Do you think environment plays any part in the way people are able to work? Do you think you might be more creative in your working environment if conditions were set up to make you want to create?

5. If each person were really an individual, it would be reflected in his dress, his speech, his acts. Look at the people around you. Decide which ones are really individuals and which ones conform to almost everything, such as current hair styles, current clothes styles, accepted behavior in class, and current slang and speech expressions. The latter are often status-seekers and name-droppers. What other factors besides the lack of creative development make people, especially young adults, become such conformists?

6. What are your reactions to the following situations?
   a. Seeing an exhibit of children's paintings defaced by the scribblings of a college student.
   b. Finding tawdry posters nailed to trees all over the college campus.
   c. Seeing a man wearing tan slacks, a brown coat, and a dark blue tie.
   d. Seeing someone put a pocketbook down in front of a lovely flower arrangement.
   e. Seeing circus posters pasted over the glass of a beautiful building.
   f. Looking at the window of the average five-and-ten-cent store.
   g. Seeing a heavy girl in tight slacks.
   Discuss these feelings. Do you think the answers to these questions might help you analyze your own aesthetic sensitivities?

7. Are you familiar with the Rashoman technique? It is an excellent way to demonstrate how people's perceptions differ. It comes from a Japanese movie made several years ago in which three different witnesses to one murder see it in three different ways. Plot a scene for your class or group meeting using this technique and discuss the perceptual differences among the witnesses.

8. See how creative you can be. Plan a lesson in social studies that has as one of its objectives the development of perception. Plot a lesson in language arts that has as one of its objectives the development of analogy. Plan a lesson in physical education whose main objective is to build a sense of design.

9. Have the students bring something into class that they think is beautiful. (Better make it an inanimate object. When

your author gave this assignment, one fellow brought in his wife!) Place the objects where everyone can see them and have everyone rate them in order of appeal. The lists will never be the same. Why is it that what is beauty to one is not to another? Is it true that "beauty is in the eye of the beholder"? After you have compared choices, have people tell why they chose that particular item as the most beautiful. What are some of the different elements that constitute beauty? Are there any common elements among your group's choices?

10. Often we encourage children to mix two primary colors in order to obtain a secondary color. For instance, yellow is mixed with blue to get green. Instead of using this approach, ask some of your children, "How many greens can you mix?" In fact, try it yourself—can you fill a whole sheet of poster board with tiny samples of the color green? What did you (and the children) learn and discover with the second procedure that you did not or could not learn with the first?

SELECTED BIBLIOGRAPHY

Andrews, Gladys. *Creative Rhythmic Movement for Children.* New York: Prentice-Hall, Inc., 1959.

Aronoff, F. W. *Music and Young Children.* New York: Holt, Rinehart and Winston, Inc., 1969.

Barkan, Manuel. *Through Art to Creativity.* Boston: Allyn and Bacon, Inc., 1960.

Boorman, Joyce. *Creative Dance in the First Three Grades.* New York: David McKay Co., Inc., 1969.

Bornstein, Elid, ed. *Art and Music.* Wittenborn, 1964.

Burskoff, Gerald, and Lawrence Wheeler. *Making Music in the Elementary School.* New York: Hargail Music Press, 1973.

Chester, Mark, and Robert Fox. *Role-Playing Methods in the Classroom.* Palo Alto, Calif.: Science Research Associates, Inc., 1971.

Cole, Natalie. *The Arts in the Classroom.* New York: John Day Co., Inc., 1940.

———. *Children's Art from Deep Down Inside.* New York: John Day Co., Inc., 1966.

Davis, Elwood C., and Earl L. Wallis. *Toward Better Teaching in Physical Education.* Englewood Cliffs, N.J.: Prentice-Hall, Inc., 1961.

Garretson, R. L. *Music for Elementary Teachers.* New York: Appleton-Century-Crofts, 1966.

Gillespie, Margaret C., and A. Gray Thompson. *Social Studies for Living in a Multi-Ethnic Society: A Unit Approach.* Columbus, Ohio: Charles E. Merrill Publishing Co., 1972.

Hartley, Ruth, Lawrence Frank, and Robert Goldenson. *Understanding Children's Play.* New York: Columbia University Press, 1964.

Hickock, Dorothy, and James A. Smith. *Creative Teaching of Music in the Elementary School.* Boston: Allyn and Bacon, Inc., 1974.

Kirchner, Glenn, Jean Cunningham, and Eileen Warrell. *Introduction to Movement Education.* Dubuque, Iowa: William C. Brown Co., Publishers, 1970.

Kozal, Jonathan. "Death at an Early Age." *Concepts in Art and Education.* George Pappas, ed. New York: Macmillan Publishing Co., Inc., 1970.

La Mancusa, Katherine. *Source Book for Art Teachers.* Scranton, Pa.: Intext Educational Publishers, 1965.

Lanier, Vincent. "The Teaching of Art as Social Revolution," *Phi Delta Kappa,* February 1969, 314.

McCaslin, Nellie. *Creative Dramatics in the Classroom.* New York: David McKay Co., Inc., 1968.

Michaelis, John. *Teaching Strategies for Elementary School Social Studies.* Itasca, Ill.: F. E. Peacock Publishers, Inc., 1972.

National Education Association. *Planning Facilities for Art Instruction.* Washington, D.C.: NEA, 1961.

Peck, Ruth L., and Helen E. Peck. *Art and Language Lessons for the Elementary Classroom.* Englewood Cliffs, N.J.: Prentice-Hall, Inc., 1969.

Piltz, Albert, and Robert Sund. *Creative Teaching of Science in the Elementary School,* 2nd ed. Boston: Allyn and Bacon, Inc., 1974.

Rubin, L. J. "Creativity and the Curriculum," *Phi Delta Kappa,* 44 (1963), 438–440.

Smith, James A. *Adventures in Communication: Language Arts Methods.* Boston: Allyn and Bacon, Inc., 1972.

———. *Setting Conditions for Creative Teaching in the Elementary School.* Boston: Allyn and Bacon, Inc., 1966.

Woods, Margaret. *Creative Dramatics.* Washington, D.C.: American Association of Elementary-Kindergarten-Nursery Education, 1967.

CHAPTER VI

Teaching Art for Art's Sake

"Before I know where I'm going, I must first get there."

CHARLIE CHAPLIN

In Chapter 2 the authors took a stand about art teaching. They believe art expression comes from the child's intensive involvement with his environment. They believe that since most of the child's waking hours are spent in a classroom, the experiences the children have in that classroom have a greater effect on the child's art growth than any other factor. It is hoped that these experiences will be so appealing to the child and will involve such strong sensory reactions that he will develop a love of art and will want to engage in art activities simply because of the inward joys and satisfactions he receives. This desire is a better justification of the art program than any other. In this chapter we talk about teaching art for art's sake, where children put to use in divergent ways all the convergent learnings they have accumulated in art.

THE JOY OF ART

Much of what we call fine art when it is performed by adults, we call play when it is done by children. The child balancing building blocks on the kindergarten table is playing. The artist assembling pieces of sheet metal in sculptural form is engaged in producing fine art.

Play takes place quite naturally in healthy children and animals. We see that play allows animals to learn the means by which they survive. Play takes in more and more of their environment, as they venture further and further afield until they are completely at home on their range. At any one stage of their development it is very doubtful that they know where they are going. The same holds true for children's play; they do not plan it sequentially with an end in view. They are like the wise traveller who enjoys the journey as much as the arrival at a destination.

Play is a highly successful learning process for people of all ages. Consider how much the child learns during the period of most intense play, his first five years. It is doubtful that we ever lose our need to play. It is a pity that the adult tends to confuse play with competition.

We know that all children play; we also know that entwined with their play is the development of a graphic language that they use before they acquire verbal skills. Children's art is a way of playing with ideas and concepts, a way of feeling out a place in the environment. Comparisons of artwork done by children of diverse cultures and backgrounds reveal that it is a language common to all children. It is as if they were telling of the brotherhood of all men. There is also a remarkable similarity in the ways that they all play.

There is a joyousness about both their art and play that suggests that these activities are not being undertaken for the express purpose of training for the rigors of adult life, but for the joy of doing them for their own sakes. Art is not only a tool for learning; it is an intensely pleasurable occupation. Often there is no possible way of knowing where the endeavor will lead when the creator embarks on it.

The degree to which the child can enjoy his art is dependent upon how well it develops. There is limited fun in playing with a punctured ball or a swing without a rope. Full enjoyment is dependent upon fully functioning abilities. We know that during the child's first five years his art is going to go through some predictable, healthy stages if these have not been interfered with by well-meaning adults. These stages were discussed in Chapter 3. We also know only too well how often children are inhibited by their environment and are not able to express themselves freely and adequately. If they are to enjoy art for art's sake, we need to help them to develop their artistic abilities as fully as possible.

TEACHING THE JOY OF ART

Art does not develop in a vacuum. As a means of expression, it requires a supply of internalized experiences to deal with. We all have experiences; the variant is in the degree to which different individuals are able to understand them or to profit by them. We know that people learn best when they are able to make things concrete. One of the ways in which the child is able to do this is through his art. He is performing two activities at the same time: he is bringing together the total input from the reactions of all his senses to experience, and he is involving himself in an extremely pleasurable activity. The one cannot operate without the other. One cannot teach art that people can enjoy for itself alone without also helping them to become fully functioning individuals. This can best be seen by looking at the ways in which two teachers approach the problem.

Mrs. Duffy had not had any art training and she had not studied problems related to art education. She had, however, a great liking for art, and she provided time for the children to enjoy it. Productivity was high in her class and the annual exhibition of students' work that she held each May made her a highly respected teacher.

Mrs. Duffy closed up her books early in the afternoon and said to the class, "We have worked so hard all day that I think it is time we did something different. I am sure you will all enjoy doing some artwork." It was October and the leaves were exciting in their riot of colors. "Now that the leaves are turning, let's make some pictures that we can take home. Let me show you a really fun way to paint leaves."

The children gathered around Mrs. Duffy in her well-organized art center, eager to learn a new technique.

"See, if you put some paint on these trays and pick up just the right amount of paint with a sponge without pressing too hard on the paper, it will leave a mark just like the leaves on the tree." Mrs. Duffy, who really enjoyed these lessons, continued with the demonstration until she had a tree full of colors that the children accepted delightedly. The class spent a happy afternoon sponge painting and went home content when Mrs. Duffy said that she thought they were all better than hers.

On the face of it, Mrs. Duffy was hard to fault: the children were happy in her class, they obviously enjoyed their art, and their parents were glad to see that they were learning so much about trees.

Mrs. Burnham had many of the same intentions as Mrs. Duffy. However, some graduate courses that she had taken had made her question Mrs. Duffy's methods. She wanted the children to enjoy the possibilities of dealing with the fall colors by means of sponge painting, but she wanted to make sure that the activity was enjoyed for more profound reasons.

"Children, before we do any artwork this afternoon, why don't we think of all the ways in which we can put paint on paper? We always seem to choose a brush, but there must be many exciting ways if we can think of them."

Jimmy, whose parents had just done some redecorating, suggested a roller. "Do you think this would do?" Mrs. Burnham produced the brayer that they used for printing. Jimmy was a man of experience and agreed that it would.

"Any other ideas?" Sue suggested putting it on with a stick. "Would you dab it on or spread it with the side of the stick?" Sue considered, and opted for dabbing. Once the concept of dabbing was understood, all manner of things from potatoes to hands were suggested, and finally, because Mrs. Burnham had placed a pile of small sponges on her desk, sponges.

Mrs. Burnham was anxious to have the children enjoy the autumn colors that she knew could so easily be reproduced with a sponge, but she also knew that there was a process that had to intervene.

"Let's try all the ways that we have thought of and see what happens." The afternoon was spent searching for new things to add to the already formidable array of painting tools. At the end of the afternoon, when Mrs. Duffy's children were proudly taking home bright pictures of trees, Mrs. Burnham's class had nothing to show but a wall covered with strange textures, scribblings, dabbings, and shapes.

The next afternoon Mrs. Burnham stood with her class looking at their experiments. "It seems to me that some ways of putting on paint are better for saying some things than others," she said. Up to this point the class had not considered this possibility. A painting was usually begun and ended with the same brush. Nearly everyone had an idea to contribute. James, who had established himself as the expert with the roller, said that he thought it a great way of putting in sky. Mike, who had tried cardboard, said that his dabs looked like a spider's web, and someone else said they looked like twigs.

Mrs. Burnham was surprised to find that the immediate response to the sponge painting was not trees or leaves, but gravel and earth. She suddenly realized that the missing recognition factor was color; the sponge had been used with gray paint. Not wanting to be put in the position of suggesting leaves, she said, "What would you say if we had used green with the sponge?"

This time the response was immediate. "Hey, yes, trees. That's good."

Mrs. Burnham still perceived insights that would make the children's art experience even richer. She put a rhythmic piece of music on the record player and, standing by the window, she said quite simply, "Watch. The leaves are dancing." She began to trace the movements of the leaves with her hands. The background music helped the children, who quickly joined in the activity to find a pattern in the movements of the leaves rather than a blowing mass.

"They are not only beautiful colors; they move beautifully, don't they? Look at the way they dance around, come together, and then dance off on their own again."

James became intrigued with the way some kinds of leaves came down with a zig-zag movement. There was a concerted shout when the leaves were caught up in a miniature whirlwind.

At this point Mrs. Burnham knew that her job was done. When the children started their artwork they were not only ready with new technical abilities that they had discovered for themselves, but they were fascinated by new concepts that as yet they only half understood. These were the beginnings of new aesthetic perceptions that were already starting to widen their horizons.

Mrs. Burnham was the kind of teacher who enjoyed whatever you showed her. Very often what she said made what you were trying to do so much clearer that you could not wait for the next art period to see if you could make it work. Mrs. Burnham, for her part, hoped that she could develop the child's pure and innocent joy in his new perceptions.

In Mrs. Burnham's lesson, art for art's sake was not only a product, but a process. It was not only a given technique, but a deeper understanding of the means available in the visual arts for expressing oneself. Through their art the children were helped to look beyond the obvious for a deeper understanding of their subject. A leaf was no longer only a leaf, but a part of the rhythm of nature and of life. Mrs. Burnham was well aware that her children were unlikely to be able to verbalize such concepts, but she had the feeling that some of the artwork reflected them.

The art lesson was presented for no other reason than to enjoy art for art's sake. It was not concerned with learning in any other curriculum area; technique and skills came from a process of self-discovery, and the resulting benefits were those that only art could provide.

ART APPRECIATION

As with many other things, it is easier to see what art appreciation is not than what it is. It is not art history, which has to do with who did what and when. It has to do with reacting to the painting and to an understanding of the character of the artist, his aims and ambitions, and the means that he employed to bring everything together as a piece of visual art.

Art appreciation, actually, is more than reaction; it is in-depth study. A person looking at a painting may have an immediate reaction to it. This is one type of appreciation. It may motivate the viewer to want to know more about the artist, about the conditions under which he worked, and about his other works. So he seeks out other paintings, reads books, and views films until he feels he knows the man through his work. This is appreciation through identification—"in-depth" appreciation.

It would be difficult to appreciate to the fullest the works of Van Gogh without understanding the man. It is not enough to · enjoy the swirling forms of clouds and trees unless one knows or reads in the paintings his feeling about the oneness of things. This concept—rhythmic vitality—is part of the ancient canons of Chinese painting. Through its use the artist tries to express the creative essence and not the outward form.

Visual arts are never created in a vacuum. There is never a truly original work in the sense that, to a great extent, all art is influenced by what has gone before. The progress of art is not like that of the sciences. One has only to view the cave paintings at Lascaux in southwestern France or those of Altamira in Spain to realize that man was expressing himself 20,000 years ago with basically the same skills, perceptions, and understanding that we have today. In some respects his understanding of the way in which animals move was not matched until the camera was able to freeze the image for us.

There is a timelessness about art. Art, perhaps more

than any other single thing, permits a man in one generation to live with a man in a previous time. When one looks at the encaustic portraits of ancient Egyptians one knows exactly what kind of people they were; they were not unlike one's neighbors.

Art appreciation, then, can serve a twofold purpose: it can help the student to see how others have achieved their objectives and to enjoy their insights, and it can expand his horizons and his sense of the human content of history. It also provides him with answers to his own problems both in the area of skills and perceptions.

TEACHING ART APPRECIATION

In the literal sense of the term, it is doubtful if appreciation can be "taught" as men have attempted to do in the past. We can set the conditions under which appreciation can develop in healthy ways. The right conditions have as profound an effect on art appreciation as they do on creativity.

These conditions have as much to do with human attitudes as they do with the physical. There is evidence to suggest that the artwork we grow up with sets our standards for later life. The environment acts as a conditioning agent. Much depends upon the attitude of the family and the school, though it is entirely possible that the child will reject art forms much in the way that preachers' sons have a habit of rejecting the ministry. The love of good things must be arrived at through freedom of will.

Lessons in aesthetic perception should be part of the entire day, rather than a period set aside for the appreciation of art. The lesson might, for example, be about transportation. Airplanes and airports are now familiar to all children, and they accept the wonder of flight without even considering how it is possible. In talking about flight one can talk about birds, and in talking about birds one can talk about the beauty that others have perceived in this one small part of the child's world. To do this successfully the teacher must have an adequate library right in her room. This might take the form of large, mounted prints or large-sized, well-illustrated art books in color. The teacher might show pages from John Audubon's *Birds of America* or examples of early Chinese brush drawings in which the birds were drawn with a minimum of beautifully controlled strokes. There are the prints of the magnificent carvings of falcons that appear so often in ancient Egyptian art, and there are paintings such as *The Singing Birds in a Tree,* a tomb painting from the twelfth dynasty that is very close to the perceptions of children. Art appreciation used in this fashion is not an added nicety, but an integral part of the learning process. It has as much to do with what the child becomes as with what he learns. In order to help the children appreciate the subtle skills of perception and control that are an intrinsic part of the Chinese print, the teacher herself must be able to appreciate them to the fullest. The process of imparting this appreciation to the student is best done by asking the right kind of questions.

A Chinese print might be used to develop perceptual skills in the following manner: "What kind of brush did the Chinese use and how did they hold it? We have all kinds of art materials; what kind of art materials did the Chinese use? Does their art look like that because of their materials, or did they choose their materials to match the way they saw things? How can we choose materials for special purposes?"

The teacher might tie all the works together with further questions. "In all the examples shown, the artists were interested in birds for very different reasons; can you see what the interest of each one was? When you draw a bird, what is it that interests you?"

The questions are all aimed at making the child relate the artwork to himself. This may be in the way that he sees things or feels about things, or it may have to do with the problems that he has faced in trying to deal with the same subject or area of experience.

The classroom is obviously going to have a tangible effect upon the aesthetic growth of the child. There is a sterility about many classrooms that is echoed in the sterility of our urban culture. The beauty of things is not one of our prime concerns. We are much more concerned with utility and cost. We have come to equate anything that is beautiful with expense. The serene beauty of Shaker products and architecture proves this is not necessary. Here is a careful blend of the utilitarian and the beautiful. There may be little that the teacher can do to alter the physical structure of the room, but there are many things that she can do to stimulate aesthetic growth.

Miss King, who taught fourth grade in a rural school, became concerned when she discovered that very few of her students had visited an art gallery or a museum. Their experiences were limited to an area within a few miles of their homes. There was no money available to bring in exhibits from outside sources.   Miss King discussed the matter with the local librarian, who was also the town historian.   This lady was able to list a number of people who had interesting collections ranging from Indian artifacts to quilted bedspreads.   Miss King realized that, with all her other responsibilities, it would be impossible for her to take on the added burden of arranging exhibits of these materials.   She took her problem to a committee of parents. There was concern for the safety of the exhibits, so it was decided to confine the display to Miss King's room, which could be locked and supervised.   To begin with, the parents gathered handmade antique articles that they had in their own homes, and, together with Miss King, they made one side of the room into a bright display area.   The results were more than successful; the exhibit was visited by every grade in the school, and Miss King's students, placed in the position of hosts, became very knowledgeable.   Things were pointed out not only for what they were, but for special qualities that they possessed.   There was absolutely no damage to any of the pieces, which made it even easier to induce others to loan materials.   One of the teachers who was taking graduate work at a nearby college talked the art faculty into putting together a small exhibit of paintings.   In every room things were displayed for the children's enrichment: flowers and prints of paintings of flowers; found objects and examples of abstract art; a ball of clay, some photographs of a potter at work, and a few ceramic pieces.   These exhibits were even more valuable when they were planned and put together by the students themselves.

AESTHETICS

The important role of aesthetic development in the art program is often mentioned in this book.   This term must be clarified.   The reader may interpret aesthetic development as meaning art appreciation and, in a sense, it does.   But to today's art educators, it has come to mean more, as we shall see.

Aesthetic, according to Webster, is "having to do with the beautiful as distinguished from the useful, scientific, etc. . . . showing good taste, artistic, pleasing."

Aesthetics means "the study of beauty in art and nature; the philosophy of beauty or taste; the theory of the fine arts."

It is impossible to develop the creative powers of individuals without also developing their aesthetic powers.

The need to develop an appreciation of the beautiful is great in our land today. The beautiful and artistic is all too often swept aside or destroyed in the frenzy to construct large, vulgar, and ugly shopping centers or new city centers. The fact that some of these new developments are carefully planned, attractive to look at, and pleasant to shop in attests to the fact that the construction of anything does not need to be a case of "either/or," but can be an aesthetic experience.

Broudy describes aesthetics as follows:

> By the aesthetic dimension of life I mean that part of experience concerned with colors, sounds, textures, shapes, and images, i.e., with the way things look, sound, and feel to our perception and to our imagination. In aesthetic experience, attention is drawn to the appearance of things in nature or created by art, and this appearance is interesting on its own account—not because it leads to something else or because it comes from something else.[1]

He goes on to say:

> Another characteristic of aesthetic experience is that whatever meaning or quality we experience is seen or heard or felt as being in the object, not in ourselves. . . . The aesthetic experience or the aesthetic object in whatever form or medium is never strictly true literally. We say that there is a figurative or imaginative or metaphorical element in it.

Current authorities in art education have concluded that refined aesthetic sensitivity and "taste" (a cultural preference) can be a product of instruction. As a consumer of art, a child must develop his ability to weigh one piece of art against another, and this aesthetic sensitivity is based on personal taste.

A standard of taste often relies on limited art experiences. One way to develop taste, then, is to expose the child to a wide variety of experiences with many kinds of art. Wide experience means that the child encounters art in his life as often as each day. The teacher's job lies in providing many art experiences and in clarifying relationships between the familiar and the unfamiliar.

1. Harry S. Broudy, "Quality Education and Aesthetic Education," in George Pappas, ed., *Concepts in Art and Education* (New York: Macmillan Publishing Co., Inc., 1970), pp. 282–288.

Viewing any art form or participating in any art experience requires reactions from the viewer or the participator. The activity itself calls for development of the critical aspects of art. We are developing the child as an art critic, so he will have values on which to judge one work against another and on which to judge his own work.

Eisner suggests that there are various frames of reference from which one views art.[2] One is *the experimental dimension* wherein the child reports on how the work makes him feel. Another is *the formal dimension* of the work wherein the viewer notes the relationships existing among the particular forms that constitute the work (such as how one area of color affects another, how shapes are repeated, the general form of the work, how the work is put together). A third frame of reference is *the symbolic dimension* wherein the viewer looks for familiar symbols in the work and attempts to decode them. Closely related to this is *the thematic dimension,* which is concerned with an appreciation of the underlying general meaning of the work. Another aspect of the work is *the material dimension,* the artist's use of materials to enhance the visual meaning of his work. Eisner also stresses the importance of drawing attention from the work being viewed to other works of art. He states: "In the contextual dimension a work is seen as a part of the flow and tradition of the art that preceded it."

Broudy says that quality in anything can be developed:

> The problem of quality both in life and education, therefore, comes down to the possibility of systematic instruction and expert judgment in the realm of feeling. Today the masses are direct consumers of art, and paying the piper entitles them to call the tune.[3]

In order for schools to become aesthetically literate, Broudy suggests that they systematically develop:

1. Sensitivity to sensory differences in the work of art.
2. Sensitivity to formal properties in the work of art.
3. Sensitivity to technical features in the work of art.
4. Sensitivity to expressiveness in the work of art.

2. Adapted with permission of Macmillan Publishing Co., Inc. from *Educating Artistic Vision* by Elliot W. Eisner. Copyright © 1972, by Elliot W. Eisner.
3. Broudy, *op. cit.,* p. 286.

He divides criticism into the following ingredients: classification of an art object by style, period, and the like; formal analysis of the aesthetic features in the work of art; application of some sort of standard to arrive at some reasoned evaluation of each dimension of the work; and evaluation of the total effect of all the dimensions.[4]

In Chapter 10 the authors deal with the evaluation of children's art and in that chapter they indicate that evaluation of art is a two-pronged affair. One prong deals with evaluating children's art itself. The other prong deals with the assessment of the children's progress in developing aesthetic tastes and visual sensibilities. The goal is for children to be able to see aesthetic and expressive qualities and their relationships. Part of the task is helping the children describe or express the qualities that make up visual form in spoken words or in writing. Developing the critical realm of art education also means developing effective descriptive modes of communication in children. Following is a narration of an experience in the development of taste, aesthetic sensitivity, and critical appraisal which took place in one schoolroom your authors visited.

TEACHING AESTHETICS

Miss Fox, a middle-school teacher, learned soon after school started that she had a mother artist in her classroom. This mother was persuaded to hang some of her paintings in the foyer one week. Classes went in groups to view the paintings and to talk with the mother. Miss Fox's children seemed to like one bright-colored abstract painting very much, so it was brought into the classroom where the children sat around and talked about it. The following conversation was edited from a tape recording of this discussion. Notice how the open-ended questions are asked in such a manner that no personal values are imposed on the children, yet the teacher is developing creative-thinking skills— the ability to observe a painting and its qualities.

Miss Fox: I am wondering why so many of you liked this painting so much. Would anyone care to tell us?

4. *Ibid.,* p. 288.

Debbie: I love the colors in it; they are so bright and happy.

Bill: Me too, and I like the way Mrs. Mier put them on the canvas.

Harry: I like the way she made some colors close to you and others seem to be far off.

Sue: I like the contrasts in the brights and dulls.

Miss Fox: Would any of you like to give some words that tell me how this painting made you feel?

John: Happy.

Mary: Gay.

Bill: Aggressive.

Allyson: It makes me feel bubbly, but peaceful.

Ellen: It is busy, I think.

Marcia: Sort of excited.

Betsy: Proud.

Miss Fox: Anyone else?

Hank: Heavy.

June: Pleasant.

Miss Fox: Mrs. Mier has been able to make us have many feelings with her painting. I wonder how she was able to do this. Can anyone think why he felt as he did?

June: Well, I felt pleasant because the painting is bright, but the colors are put on the canvas so that they are, you know, evenly spread around.

Miss Fox: Could we say they are harmonious?

June: Yes.

Miss Fox: Why do they make you feel happy?

John: Well, there are no drab colors when you first look at it—they are quiet. I didn't even notice them at first.

Bill: I said the picture made me feel aggressive because the colors are so bold. So are the brush strokes. She painted big and fat.

Allyson: The few round strokes that are fat and bright made me think of bubbles and that's why I said it was bubbly.

Ellen: I said busy because there are so many colors going many ways. There are almost no lines going the same way as the paper.

Fred: It looks busy to me, too. Some of the little rectangles are repeated, but they are not placed the same way.

Miss Fox: Let's see if we can find other shapes that are repeated. (They did.)

Mary: All the bright colors put together that way make me think of a flag flying and that's gay.

Peter: I think it's fences.

Marcia: I think it's a design.

Debbie: To me it's just excitement and happiness.

Miss Fox: You are trying to imagine what Mrs. Mier was trying to say in the painting.

Bill: I think she just liked the colors and wanted to put them together.

John: I don't know why, but when I look at it I think of farms.

Allyson: I don't. I think of city streets on a Sunday morning.

Bruce: Looks to me like colored chimneys.

Bonnie: I was going to say factories.

Ellen: I think of a race track and the colors are the explosions of the car motors.

Jimmy: It looks like cloth to me.

Miss Fox: Mrs. Mier was very clever to create all these impressions. She made the painting in such a way that it means something different to each of us. How did she do it?

Peter: Well, she put the paint on thick. You can not only see the color, but you can see the thick paint.

Miss Fox: Do you mean we can see the texture?

Peter: Yes. That's it.

Miss Fox: What else?

Allyson: She used shapes so you could see many things in them.

Bruce: Yes. I see many things now, but when I first looked at the picture I thought of chimneys.

Mary: I think she made it balance so you could feel it was peaceful even though all the colors are loud.

Miss Fox: Good point.

Jimmy: She uses a lot of contrast in the colors.

Miss Fox: You have described the painting with many words and phrases. I have written them down on this little chart. Let's take a look at what we have and see if we can add to our list.

Her chart looked like this:

bright	heavy
happy	pleasant
gay	balanced
aggressive	harmonious
bubbly	bold
peaceful	big, fat strokes
busy	round strokes
exciting	colorful
proud	

We thought of:

flags flying	happiness
fences	colored chimneys
designs	cloth
excitement	race-track noises
city streets	factories
on Sunday morning	farms

After the children had added to the chart, Miss Fox encouraged them to write descriptive phrases about the painting. She encouraged the children to write a poem, story, critique, or discussion about the painting later in the day. A few excerpts of their work follow:

Great blocks of color
Tumbling before the wind.

DEBBIE

A Poem

Colors move in pretty shapes
Some are round but most are not
Bright and dull and small and big
Some are cool and some are hot
Kaleidoscope!

MARCIA

The painting is an explosion of noises.

ELLEN

A Present

A lady painted a picture and brought it to
school. What she really brought was a
box of funny shaped colors.

CHARLIE

Colors tumbling everywhere
Helter-skelter
Chunks and pieces
Bits and parts
A broken stained-glass window.

ANDY

THE ELEMENTS OF ART

Art, in spite of its apparent complexity, is put together from some very simple elements. The complexity arises from the use to which we put the simple tools. Skills in art consist of being able to handle these elements well enough so that they allow free rein for creative expression.

The basic elements of art are line, texture, color, form, shape, and tone. It is interesting to consider the fact that art deals mainly with three subjects: people, things that people make, and nature. There are, of course, works that do not have a subject but consist of the manipulation of the basic elements. It is the connections between these nonobjective forms and our past experiences that give these works much of their interest. The child at various stages of his development becomes aware of and uses all the basic elements without ever feeling the necessity to name or list them. However, in planning a comprehensive art program, the teacher needs to be very much aware of them. One does not plan a diet without understanding the nutritional elements.

TEACHING THE ELEMENTS OF ART

Line

Line is the first element to engage the child's attention, and it often remains the most important tool for him. It is the element most commonly found in primitive art. Line is an artificial convention that is universally accepted; it does not exist in nature. Trees and animals do not have lines around them. One thing is separated from another visually by changes of color and tone.

Nature abhors anything that is straight. This fact is overlooked by the people who say, "Not me. I can't draw a straight line." Their case should be considered helpless only if they cannot draw a curved one. One of the reasons for discouraging children from drawing with rulers is the fact that it contradicts the nature of things and robs them of their self-confidence and expressive ability.

Line holds infinite possibilities. It can be traced with a stick in the mud, or with a stick and mud on a rock. Any sort of point can scratch or draw a line. Each instrument will impart to the line its own individual quality. Lines can be drawn in any direction. They can be fine, thick, long, short, smooth, or jagged (Fig. 6–1). Lines can be combined to produce other elements, such as texture or tone (Fig. 6–2). Lines are combined to form the basic elements of written communication (Fig. 6–3). Lines as a completely abstract entity are capable of conveying ideas and concepts. They become symbols for our generalized experiences. Test your reaction to the lines in Fig. 6–4.

We tend to associate the vertical lines in Fig. 6–4 with the tall strength of trees or buildings. They have the same strong, static quality that we think of when we look at bridge abutments. If we wish our drawing or painting to emphasize these qualities, then we must find every possible excuse to include as many of these lines as possible. We like to think of our children as being strong and are always admonishing them to stand up straight. The horizontal lines in Fig. 6–4 we associate with quiet landscapes or a body at rest. Any painting in which these lines predominate will give a sense of tranquility and stillness. The diagonal lines in Fig. 6–4 remind us of the human body broken into the angular movements of running or jumping, trees falling, or explosions. The diagonal line is the line of movement.

Two identical images can be given entirely different meanings by simply changing the directions of the major lines.

FIGURE. 6–1   Lines.

FIGURE 6–2. Combination of lines.

The political meeting in Fig. 6–5 may be quiet and orderly, or violent; the only things that change are the major lines of the painting. The still seascape in Fig. 6–6 becomes a stormy scene when diagonals are introduced.

With all this in mind it is possible to plan art programs that capitalize on the child's natural use and acceptance of line. He needs the opportunity to experiment with all the ways in which a line can be produced. The edge of a piece of cardboard dipped in paint will print a straight line; bend the cardboard for a curved one. String and paint produce lines with an entirely different character. Scratchboard allows children to investigate negative lines: white on black. Given the opportunity, the child may well develop a distinctive character to his lines that is entirely personal. It is a pity that writing is practiced with such

FIGURE 6–3.   Communication through lines.

conformity.   A personal handwriting should be regarded as part of the uniqueness of the individual.

Texture

In early childhood, children are little concerned with texture.   An examination of the output of a class will reveal almost a total absence of this element.   In his early years, the child is much more interested in a broad patterning.   We think of texture as the roughness or smoothness of the surface of an object.   Our tactile sense is able to determine if it is wet or dry, hot or cold. The artist's problem is to find a way to express these characteristics with his materials.   Sculpture requires a different technique, but the problem is no less real.   In a child's early paintings, sky, land, and water are all painted with the same texture.   Color is used to define the limits of each.

It does little good to talk about texture to a child.   What is even worse is to show him how to portray it.   The best approach is to create a set of tactile experiences and a set of projects that have as their main emphasis experimentation with texture.   It must be remembered, however, that the child may not be ready to

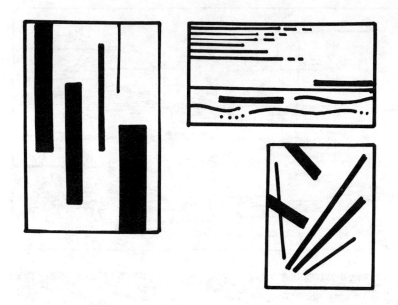

FIGURE 6–4.   Abstract lines.

FIGURE 6–5.   A political meeting: changing the lines.

FIGURE 6–6.   A seacape: changing the lines.

accept the additional element.   His symbols may be sufficient for
his needs.   Texture may fit into a later stage in his development
when he is searching for greater visual realism.

A game involving texture that children enjoy involves
dividing them into pairs.   One, the blind man, is blindfolded; the
other acts as guide and safety man.   The object is for the blind

man to determine where he is through the sense of touch. Another game is to distribute paper sacks containing such things as pieces of fur, stone, and sandpaper. A good trick is to include some different things that have the same texture, such as plastic, glass, and metal. The fact that they are all the same is a way of emphasizing other visual clues to the nature of an object.

Color

In his early years, the child uses color without any concern for visual reality. A horse may be blue and the sky green. Usually at this stage the child is still drawing lines with his brush. As he begins to use his brush to lay in large areas of colors, he becomes more selective in his use of color. It is unfortunate that in so many schools there is such concern with not getting things dirty. If the paints are presented in jars with a brush stuck in them, the child has no opportunity to select color or to experiment with mixing his own (see p. 161). When we admire the color that the child used in his painting we overlook the fact that sometimes the choice was made by the teacher.

To develop a good color sense the child needs the freedom to manipulate colors. Children who are suddenly presented with the freedom to do this for the first time will spend so much time mixing and messing that they have no time to paint a picture, which is fine if you can see the process as being at least as important as the product.

The type of paintbox that grandparents love to give their grandchildren is not always the best selection of material for the child. It usually has forty "different" colors that defy all efforts to make them soft enough to apply to paper. There are only three basic colors: red, yellow, and blue. Every other color that you can think of is mixed from these three primary colors. The child can quickly learn the secondary colors that result from mixing any two: green, orange, and violet. Later on he will have a real sense of accomplishment when he wins his independence from the pot of brown paint by discovering that he can mix any brown he likes from blue, red, and yellow. Some children are much happier when they are allowed to master a few colors at a time.

There are workable theories on the subject of color schemes. What goes with what is not a mysterious insight; the answer can be based on a set of definite rules. This is way beyond the child's interest. There are, however, some broad divisions of color that children take a great deal of pleasure in discovering. Have the class think of all the colors that they associate with fire, ice and snow, a cold rainy winter day, and a warm spring day. List them; the colors have been sorted into warm and cold color schemes. For the child beginning to investigate realism, it is exciting to find that he can use colors in special ways. A subject takes on a new dimension when he can control the mood in which it appears.

For the child who is still drawing symbolic forms, color is merely another opportunity to extend the meanings of his symbols. If he has reason to associate a color with an unpleasant circumstance, then he may use this color in his painting to denote something that he thinks of as unpleasant without any concern for visual reality. Children are prone to seize on color symbolism at an early age. It then becomes important to provide the means by which they can reexamine their symbolism. Water is always blue and grass is always green. Provide small pieces of colored acetate through which the children can view familiar surroundings, or shine a colored spotlight on the class. The children delight in seeing themselves as green or red people. Trees take on a new significance when they are seen in an unusual color. Painting in these unfamiliar colors forces an evaluation of the subject, since the old symbolism—color—is no longer available.

Painting with light, which is described fully in Chapter 8, is an ideal medium for the child to use to experiment with color. It has the advantage of allowing almost instantaneous color changes. The same subject can be seen in many different colors without repainting the picture each time. The child is free to devote most of his interest to the problem of color.

Color has almost universal emotional appeal. It is associated with clear-cut emotional responses. Red is associated with blood and is used as a means of expressing anger, violence, and great activity: red rag to a bull, red racing cars, the fires of hell, sinful women in red dresses. Blue, on the other hand, is strongly associated with sadness. In "singing the blues" there is a feeling of quiet and peace. This feeling probably arises from the blues that overtake the landscape at the close of day.

The association of yellow with the sun is too strong to miss. There is some evidence to suggest that this color is the choice of very young children; it has the suggestion of youth and new growth. White is so strongly associated with purity that most brides still choose it. The example of fresh snow, so easily dirtied, is an obvious connection.

Black is a very dominant part of an image. Traditionally it has been associated with evil, the power of darkness. It is a color readily chosen by children because of its dominance and not because of its associations. Black has the ability to suggest other colors. Black and white films are often viewed and thought of in terms of color.

Green is obviously pastoral; it is a ready-made symbol for all things—other than people and animals—in nature. It is also one of the most difficult colors to see in all its complexity.

Form

Children need opportunities to explore form at the same time that they are offered two-dimensional materials. One of the easiest ways that the child can deal with the problem of three-dimensional design is through the old-fashioned building block. He learns to handle the problems of symmetrical and asymmetrical balance, mass, and volume. Blocks provide an ideal way to create a volume-occupying space or forms that imply the occupation of space. Both concepts become important later on if the student is to form any worthwhile appreciation of three-dimensional design. Architecture, sculpture, and industrial design are all aspects of this kind of design. Ultimately the kind of environment that we create for ourselves depends upon how well we are able to order our forms. A child can make a clear three-dimensional statement with clay long before he is interested in mastering the techniques of perspective that are necessary to imply form in his drawings or paintings.

There are very few children who include lighting or shadows in their paintings much before the fourth-grade level. It is the passage of light over an object that allows us to perceive form.

Producing the illusion of form—of three dimensions on a flat surface—is an extremely abstract concept. The ability to create the illusion comes quite late in the history of Western art. Other cultures accept an entirely different convention for showing that objects are near or far. To show a child how to make things recede into the distance or how to make his pond lie flat may leave him with a pattern, but little understanding.

Form can be demonstrated by presenting children with the opportunity to cast a spotlight on themselves and other objects in a darkened room. The intense light clearly shows how forms turned away from the light appear to be darker. Discussions that help the child to see that things always have a distinct relationship to other things are very valuable. We seldom see anything in its entirety. One form overlaps another; the chair is partly hidden by the table. This clue is usually enough to start the child exploring the possibilities of perspective and form.

Shape

Shape is the term usually reserved for two-dimensional objects. The terms shape and form are often confused. This may derive from the use of shape to describe some aspects of form. The artist, in talking about a landscape painting, might say, "I was attracted by the shape made by those trees." He uses shape here because initially he was not attracted by the form of the trees, but by the edge of the masses as he visualized them forming a shape on his canvas.

Children need ample opportunity to play with shapes; there is a tremendous amount of learning inherent in this activity.

Tone

Tone is another basic element that is usually missing from the work of young children. When they wish to separate an object from its setting, they usually do so by drawing a line around it. Unless they are helped to explore other possibilities and solutions to the problem, they may continue to employ the same means as adults. This is not to say that there is anything wrong with outline drawing. There are many ways to separate images, and the more ways that are explored, the richer the visual experience becomes.

To the young child there is often just green or blue paint. He may not have considered the possibility of light blue or light green. When color is being used symbolically, this is of no importance. Young children painting a snow scene on white paper will ask for white paint to add to the snow even though the white paint does not show. Some primitive people are unable to recognize a tonal drawing of themselves. Their eyes are accustomed to tracing the outline of the form.

In our culture we make extensive use of tone. We use it to produce photographs in books and newspapers, black and white films, and television shows. All of these depend upon the ability of tone to depict our environment with great accuracy.

PERCEPTION

Throughout this volume emphasis has been placed on the term perception. This term has a unique meaning to the art educator, and this meaning is not always clear to the elementary school teacher.

Perception has come to mean seeing and looking. In actual fact, it is the way in which we gather knowledge through the refined use of all our sensory abilities. We discover a flower with our sight, our touch, our smell, our emotions, our intellect, and our intuition. It is impossible to consider the senses without including the guiding intellect.

During childhood we are able to explore things with our total being, for we have not at that stage developed all kinds of preconceived ideas that cut us off from an expansion of our

FIGURE 6–7. Four different children's perceptions of a terrible monster.

understanding. Young children gather in all the information available without making judgments about its usefulness or relevance.

The three-year-old rummaging in his mother's kitchen discovers a saucepan. He investigates it first with his sense of touch: he explores the shape and the weight, the relationship of the parts, the feel of the surface, and the bumps made by the rivets that attach the handle. He brings it to his face and recognizes the smell of food. He makes the comfortable associations with kitchen and mother. He applies it to his mouth, seeking the taste of food, but he is also feeling with his mouth. He drops the saucepan and is intrigued by the sound, so he drops it again, and finally he bangs it against the floor. He takes out a smaller pan and discovers that it fits inside the original larger pan. Putting the two together makes a different sound, so he bangs the two together. He traps his fingers between the two and discovers the pans as a source of pain. He puts them on his head and discovers that they blot out his visual world. Taking them off again, he discovers that the pan has a bright color outside and a dull one inside. He finds the hole in the handle and tries to insert his finger. He recalls his mother using the pot and makes intuitive connections between filling the pot with food and filling it with other things, so everything that will fit is put into the pan.

The child has no other objective but to explore, to learn, and to perceive.

We all undergo experiences, but only the perceptive individual is able to fully understand them and store the vital information for future use. Art springs from the desire to express past and present experiences. The creative nature of the process and product depends upon the degree to which the individual has made the experience his own.

Perception is inevitably modified by the individual's uniqueness and individuality. There is a story about some vacationers staying at a small guest house by a picturesque waterfall. The honeymooners went away talking about the romantic sound of falling water and the dampness of the grass. The engineer was intrigued by the possibilities of hydroelectrical generation. The golfer felt his time had been wasted; the local golf course lacked any challenge. The artist went away with images of refracted light, the intricacies of the pattern of falling water, the subtle change in night smells as one approached the moister air around the falls, and the feel of the moisture on his face. He had climbed to all sorts of viewpoints seeking new visual compositions.

Perception, it seems, is very much a part of experience. If we want our children to develop fully, then we have to help them find both worthwhile experiences and the means to perceive their meanings. Experience can be as significant for the child in the wheelchair as for the healthy, active child. It is not so much the magnitude of the experience as the quality that is important.

There are many theories about the nature of creativity. Most have one thing in common: a vast amount of unrelated information is received by the brain and lies dormant until it is brought together in new patterns and associations. Preceding any creative activity there must be a period of information gathering. The quality of this information and its completeness determine, to a great extent, the quality of the creative act. Gathering is followed by gestation, by insight into the solution of a problem, by creation, and then by evaluation. For these reasons it is vital that children be helped to capitalize to the fullest on their perceptual abilities.

Becoming Aware

Human survival depends to a large degree upon automatic responses to the things our senses perceive. We jump at and shy away from a loud noise. We become wary at the smell of smoke. We recoil from things that feel hot. These responses are necessary, but they can become so stereotyped that there is little awareness of the sensations. Awareness, when it is linked to experience, is more easily recalled. Bang—a gun, the start of fright, the emotion produced by the sight of a bloodied rabbit, the internalizing of the emotion, the sympathy with the rabbit.

Awareness of this situation is easily recalled. It can also become stereotyped so that situations involving "bang" are never again fully explored. No two situations, however similar, are ever the same. The next bang may be from an old car backfiring; the initial reaction may be the same but the creative individual will rapidly perceive new areas of awareness within the experience. The bang may be associated with pleasure, such as fireworks on the Fourth of July. The trick is to maintain a continuous stream of awareness.

Awareness can be extended into areas of extrasensory perception. Primitive people are perfectly capable of knowing of the presence of an unseen lion or the unheard person in the next room.

Repressing Awareness

The more we perceive, the more we open ourselves up to the world and the more easily we can be hurt. Hence the expression "What he doesn't know can't hurt him." We can protect ourselves from failure by refusing to perceive the problem, by protecting the status quo and the imagined rightness of our ways of doing things.

To be fully aware means constant challenge, change, flexibility, and fluency. All this demands the output of physical, emotional, and intellectual energy. It is easier not to be aware.

Awareness can also be the source of sorrow and depression, unless it is matched with the ability to act. To be totally aware of the environment is to sorrow for man's lack of aesthetic and spiritual understanding.

Nurturing Awareness

First there has to be the desire to perceive. There has to be the stability and self-confidence to deal with what one becomes aware of. The total sensory information needs to be accepted without judgment; no element should be ignored because of apparent similarities to other experiences. It is necessary to approach each experience with the innocence of the three-year-old with the saucepan.

The ability to regress is vital to the creative act. There was always a time when we were able to perceive things without the preconceived ideas and associations of adulthood. The child's perception of a box might go as follows: hard, angular, empty, full, color material, rough, smooth, open, closed, lid, size, smell, get in, look out of, stand on, put one inside another, put one on top of another, heavy, light. All this and much more he accepts.

The noncreative adult has long since ceased to be really aware of the box. His awareness now takes the form of judgments: useful or junk, for beer or clothes, etc.

The creative individual is able to add the qualities of flexibility and fluency and to make unusual associations, intuitions, and analogies. For him, perceptions of a box may lead to experiments in prefabricated architecture, rigid cellular structures, musical composition, painting, furniture, or engineering. He cannot afford to prejudge what part of perception he will accept, because he can never know what information he will need.

Perception is often heightened by shock. Our awareness of the automobile undergoes extreme changes after an accident. Gone is the feeling of shining strength and worth. The vulnerability of thin steel is revealed. The same changes in perception can be brought about by providing mildly shocking experiences. Look up at things that you normally look down on, and vice versa. Look at things while standing on your head or lying on your side. Enforce selection by viewing things through a hole punched in a card or through the viewfinder of a camera. Look at things through a magnifying glass or the wrong end of a telescope. Look at things through pieces of colored acetate. Look at the parts separately from the whole.

Record the sounds of things and play them without visual context; play them louder than normal. Locate things solely by the sense of smell. Color meat green with food coloring and discover how one area of perception fools another—in this case, taste. Play the game of filling paper sacks with objects that simulate the feel of other things: wet grapes—eyeballs; a water-filled plastic bag—liver, etc. These activities help to make the point that true understanding and awareness come from an integration of all the senses.

TEACHING PERCEPTION

Through Linear Movement

Linear movement (the development of the path of a line) is basic to all drawing and to an understanding of all painting. Control of the line by the painter indicates a sophisticated form of art and indicates a maturity above and beyond the natural scribbling stages of the young child.

Children have learned to control line in many ways even before they come to school. Playing their out-of-school games at school can become a starting place for developing a sense of linear movement.

• Children push trucks and trains through the sand, leaving an uneven line.
• Children play circle games and games like mulberry bush,

where they join their own bodies with those of others to make
linear patterns.

• Children playing cowboys use a rope as a lasso.   Often the
  rope is dropped on the floor in a variety of linear patterns.
• Children make linear movements in their fingerpaint.
• Children observe animals, and some, like snakes, provide
  specific examples of moving lines.

The teacher can develop an awareness of the variety in
linear movement and can emphasize the child's ability to control
line by using the child's natural experiences, such as:

• exploring linear movement in games like parchesi or checkers
• exploring on a local map the movement made by all members
  of the class on their trip to the zoo, or exploring on a large
  road map the linear movement of the individual class members
  during their summer vacation
• using maps and graphs to show how linear movement, when
  controlled, can communicate specific facts
• demonstrating linear tension through the use of a thick rubber
  band
• exploring string painting
• demonstrating how linear movement makes possible the use of
  line to symbolize something else, such as a number, a letter, a
  group of numbers, or a word
• studying drafts and architectural drawings to show how controlled linear movement can become specific communication
  (rather than the general communication of open-ended linear
  movement in a painting)
• studying science drawings to show how linear movement can
  be used as a means of recording ideas or as representation
• making time exposure photographs that, when developed, show
  (in color perhaps) the linear movement of automobiles and
  other vehicles on the photographic plate
• observing a snail crawl across a surface and studying the type
  of line he leaves
• tracing the linear direction of a group of lines such as telegraph
  wires, noting how the groups develop branches or split as they
  pass each house or follow a new street
• exploring the line of a flashlight spot moved to music behind
  a sheet hung in the classroom
• drawing the invisible linear route of a person dancing
• drawing the invisible linear route of a child playing hopscotch
• noting the linear route of string or ribbon tied around a package
  for mailing
• observing the linear route of a jet plane or a skywriter

Through Analogy

From *Pirate Story*

Three of us afloat in the meadow by the swing,
Three of us aboard in the basket on the lea,
Winds are in the air, they are blowing in the spring,
And waves are on the meadow like the waves there
    are at sea.

ROBERT LOUIS STEVENSON[5]

The ability to deal with analogy is the ability to perceive common relationships between dissimilar things and situations. Without knowing it, the three children of Stevenson's poem were involved in an intense play-learning situation in which they internalized the experience of being at sea in a pirate ship by using the analogy of a basket and a waving sea of grass.

Direct analogy is a method by which significant discoveries are made. It is said that Alexander Graham Bell invented the telephone by making a direct analogy between his work on a hearing aid and the human ear.

Analogy is one of the basic differences between prose and poetry.

From "The Road Not Taken"

I shall be telling this with a sigh
Somewhere ages and ages hence:
Two roads diverged in a wood, and I—
I took the one less traveled by,
And that has made all the difference.

ROBERT FROST[6]

This poem sums up in a few words all the complications of a man seeking creative individuality. The beauty of poetry is in the invitation that it offers the reader to make his own connection with the analogy. The reader becomes an active participant in the poetry.

5. *Story Telling and Other Poems,* Childcraft Vol. 2 (Chicago, Ill.: Field Enterprises Educational Corp., 1954), p. 109.
6. From "The Road Not Taken" from *The Poetry of Robert Frost* edited by Edward Connery Lathem. Copyright 1916, © 1969 by Holt, Rinehart and Winston, Inc. Copyright 1944 by Robert Frost. Reprinted by permission of Holt, Rinehart and Winston, Inc. and Jonathan Cape Ltd.

The same can be true of painting and other forms of art. The artist is often trying to use his visual symbols to express other ideas. At times he can best achieve his ends with non-representational forms. Constantin Brancusi's *Bird in Space,* a tapering and swelling bronze shaft fifty-four inches high, is a visual analogy.[7] One is permitted to connect all of one's associations with birds to this visual symbol without being dictated to by representational detail.

The young child is perfectly capable of developing his ability to use analogy in creative ways. He has already demonstrated that in his play. As his artwork proceeds to more and more realistic forms, he needs opportunities to regress to earlier periods; we all do. He should be encouraged to paint emotions and feelings without considerable knowledge of the world of reality.

No matter how well trained the artist, he can only represent the things about which he has considerable general knowledge. Using nothing but color and shape, the child should be able to express feelings of rage, sorrow, quiet, and love. In order to do this successfully, he must be perceptive and able to establish relationships between things. He needs to be able to do this on many levels and in many ways.

Miss Barclay planned a series of activities that she hoped would develop the ability to make analogies.

"I am going to show you a collection of photographs that I have cut out of magazines. See if you can find things in them that will make them match a second picture."

The first efforts resulted in people being matched with people.

"Very good. Now let us see how many other things you can find that match the pictures."

Jim chose an elephant and a fireman with a hose.

"Jim, that's clever. Why don't you take a magazine and see what you can find."

Analogy can be developed on a more concrete level using art media. Provide paint and paper, but no brushes. The child is forced to look at other materials that have characteristics similar to brushes, things that will hold the paint long enough to allow it to be applied to the paper. Some of the possibilities are pieces of cardboard, sponges, tissues, popsicle sticks, and cotton swabs. Once this has been understood, substitutions can be made for both paper and paint. Paintings can be made without

7. Now in the Museum of Modern Art in New York.

any commercial materials.   Children can be encouraged to discover the possibilities of coffee, tea, ketchup, mustard, and food coloring.   These can be applied to such things as paper towels, paper sacks, cloth, wood, stones, and the sidewalk.   The important thing is the discovery of common relationships.

The ability to deal freely in analogies frees us from having to resolve every problem as a thing separate from all others.   Analogy is a means of speeding the learning process.

As we have indicated, this type of learning takes place naturally at an early age during play.   It is reasonable to suggest that if children lose the ability to deal with analogy freely it is because learning has become divorced from play.   Consider some of the following characteristics required for play and how necessary they are to learning and making analogies.

enthusiasm	curiosity
the ability to use discoveries	the ability to analyze
self-motivation	discriminatory powers
patience	the power to exploit
perceptual skills	imagination
improvisational skills	the ability to fantasize
the ability to abstract	flexibility

The ability to deal with analogy can only be developed if these other qualities are being satisfactorily developed at the same time.   The child's artwork is in many ways a symptom of his emotional, intellectual, and psychological health.

Time after time Sue's paintings included a house, a tree, and a swing set between a ribbon of blue sky and another of green grass.   This repetition of stereotypes was not so much an art problem as a symptom of something else.   Miss Jackson perceived the problem and structured some art experiences to excite Sue's interest and make it difficult for her to rely on the old stereotypes.

"Look what funny shapes these scraps of construction paper make; these two together look like a huge head with a wide-open mouth."

Sue could not see the connection until the jaw was made to move.   "What kind of head is it?" she asked.

"We could tell that better if it had a body and legs.   See if you can find some other pieces that would fit."

Sue's problem was so deep that she did not feel that she could modify the pieces that she chose.   "Can I cut out some pieces?" she asked.

Miss Jackson sensed that cut pieces would result in rigid, stereotyped thinking, so she said, "Why don't you try tearing them?   Maybe you will find some fun shapes that way."

Sue finally realized that she could achieve her ends without conscious intellectual thinking.   Her intuitive powers came into play and she began to perceive relationships between shapes and the developing image.   The exercise had developed in her many of the elements on our list.

The power to use analogy in art is strengthened by the ability to use metaphors.   Metaphors can be used to help the strange become familiar and the familiar strange.

Miss Jackson looked at Sue's monster with his gaping jaws and said, "With jaws like that he would be great for cracking nuts.   What should we call him?"   She was using direct analogy.

"Wouldn't it be fun if he could tell us about himself?   He looks like a storyteller from another time."   She was trying to help Sue learn to fantasize through analogies.   With any luck the total artistic and verbal experience will produce a play situation in which the child will feel free enough to move into new areas of understanding and learning.

Through Exploring Space

Learning to control and use space is another art technique that children must feel as well as intellectualize.   Many experiences can be provided to help children develop the concept that space is all around them and that they must set the limits on it.   Little children can experience the use of space in endless ways:

- climbing on jungle gyms
- crawling through tunnels on the playground
- curling themselves into tires or hoops
- seeing how many can fit into a wading pool or a dollhouse
- confining space by putting a rope around a designated area or stringing a rope or ribbon from tree to tree
- fitting one child's body into a carton with the end removed so that all the children can witness the shape the child must assume in order to fit the space
- constructing mobiles so children can see that there can be movement in space
- constructing sand villages, dams, or houses in a space restricted by the four sides of the sandbox

- dramatizing action games such as seeing how many can fit into a space ship, or making yourself as small or as big as you can
- throwing a parachute into the air by grasping the sides, then running under it, and then trying to fill the space below the air-filled chute before it falls over
- dramatizing or acting out such stories as "The Wee Wee Woman" and making yourself fit the Wee Wee environment
- dancing, leaping, running, and jumping in the gymnasium instead of making more restricted movements in the classroom, where the space is more limited

Older children can continue to have specific experiences with space through activities such as the following:

- playing the game of statues, where children are whirled, let go, and hold the pose they fall in—an excellent idea for studying shapes in unrestricted spaces
- freezing at a certain point in a creative dance and noting the various shapes bodies assume in space
- seeing how many children it takes to fit a certain space, such as a large box, a telephone booth, or a Volkswagen, and noting the shapes of individual bodies
- plotting the movement of the shapes the human body assumes in different sports—a football game, a relay race, a swimming race, etc.
- collecting shapes most commonly found in the environment; charting where they are found in rectangles (doors, windows, walls, books, pads, desktops), circles (light fixtures, door knobs, cups, saucers, plates, gas burners, pans), squares (ceiling tiles, floor tiles, hotplates), trapezoids (lamp shades, fitted tabletops, pails), and triangles (ice cream cones, cake decorator sets); and collecting shapes commonly used as symbols, such as the heart, the oval, the peace symbol, the cross, the X, and the leaf
- studying the way cartoonists in comic papers use space to indicate a message (the picture and the cloud above the people in which spoken words are printed)
- relating the vastness of outer space to atmospheric space and then to the limited space of the classroom. (A study of the elements of each type of space indicates that movement in space is controlled by the properties of the space itself. For example, the movements involved in walking in outer space are quite different from those required in the classroom. Movement in any space may assume a variety of shapes and forms.)

FIGURE 6–8.   An experience in exploring space.

Through Perspective

Perspective is actually a kind of perception.   The concept of perspective was discussed briefly on p. 80.   Perspective often becomes a problem for the classroom teacher, however, when she feels that children want to show depth and distance in a painting, in scenery, or in an illustration and cannot work out a way that seems to suit them.   Generally they will invent ways of indicating perspective.   It is not uncommon to find a child making objects that he wants to put in the distance small.   Often this technique results in a good design and suits the need of the child well.   It is better for the teacher to provide experiences with perspective that lead the child to experiment and explore on his own than to intellectualize the process or to show him a technique.

Experiences in perspective may be such as the following:

- drawing families with obvious contrasts in size among mother, father, and children
- drawing streets, circuses, carnivals, zoos, and other places that are discussed in a social studies unit, thus creating a need to show depth

- placing one thing before another in large murals or in scenery for a play to indicate distance
- dramatizing distance and discussing what happens as "Bill moves farther across the gym" or "The train goes farther along the tracks"
- studying airplane photos and noting how "flat" perspective differs from eye-level perspective. For instance, on a bulletin board, place an airplane view of Manhattan and a picture of the same place showing the Manhattan skyline.
- painting scenes and/or designs on foam rubber mats and noting what happens when you stretch and twist the foam rubber (see Chapter 1)
- noting what happens when you use a print (such as a block print or potato print) over another print (a block print in a bold color over a sponge print in a softer color). Note how one tends to recede, how the print comes out as the reverse of the original cut, etc.

Perspective is commonly shown by painting distant objects smaller and farther up and down from the perimeter of the paper than the objects that are nearer to the viewer. Many ancient cultures did not show perspective in this manner, however. Perspective as it is commonly painted is representational, but perspective can also be shown as part of a design. The child will invent his own way of showing depth in his paintings and the teacher should feel no compulsion to "teach" techniques such as perspective. The examples of techniques given here are to help those children who feel a need to know representational perspective in order to solve a particular problem.

SUMMARY

The visual arts are constructed from simple elements: line, color, form, texture, tone, and shape. These are combined in countless ways to depict subjects, which can be categorized simply as man, his creations, and his environment. Art may be nonobjective and consist only of the art elements.

Richness of self-expression in art depends upon full understanding of and meaningful experiences with these elements. Their full use depends to a great extent upon our cultural heritage, and there is evidence to suggest that without sympathetic instruction many students may never develop the ability to use them.

There is also evidence to suggest that an appreciation of art and the development of "taste" can come about through instruction if instruction is planned so the child's tastes, rather than the teacher's tastes, are developed.

Developing the elements of visual instruction, or perception, particularly through linear movement, analogy, space exploration, and perspective, can enhance a child's visual expression to a high degree.

ACTIVITIES

Try these activities yourself and do them with children.

Line

1. Take a large soft crayon and a large sheet of newsprint. Select a phonograph record with a fairly regular rhythm. Conduct to the music until you have mastered the rhythm. Bring the crayon down to the paper and continue the rhythm as a visual expression. Music can be seen as different visual patterns.

2. Explore the distinctive types of lines that a number of different scrap materials can make. The edge of a piece of cardboard dipped in paint can be used to print straight lines. If it is bent it will produce curved ones. String can be dipped in paint and laid on the paper. Twigs or sticks can be used as pens. Put tempera paint thickened with wheat paste into a squeeze bottle and trail lines of paint. Each material should help to increase awareness of and interest in line.

3. Standing at a window with a pencil, trace the lines of things on the glass.

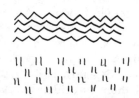

FIGURE 6–9.   Linear patterns.

4. Using linear directions, construct patterns as in Fig. 6–9. (Borders are easier for younger children who cannot handle the concept of repeated patterns.)

5. Make a scrapbook of illustrations using line by itself and in conjunction with the other elements.

6. Procure some light-gauge wire. Thinking of the wire as line, construct three-dimensional objects.

7. To explore line as a letter form, expand a simple monogram with lines, as in Fig. 6–10.

8. To explore line in nature, prepare an exhibition of photos or prints showing such things as wood grain, aerial views of river systems, or grasses.

Texture

1. Make a collection of found objects on the basis of textural interest. Mount them on a card to form a satisfying pattern.

2. Decide how much texture and how much plain surface work best together.

3. Apply tempera paint with a wide variety of materials, such as sponges, weeds, and the end of a 2″ x 4″. See how many different textures result.

4. From the window, discuss the difference between the grass and a tree, both of which are a similar green.

5. Small groups of people must first collect textured materials in paper bags. Then each group guesses the contents of the others' bags by feeling inside the sack.

6. One person is blindfolded and given a "safety guide." Playing the part of blind man, he must identify objects or wall surfaces on the basis of their texture.

FIGURE 6–10. Expanding a monogram.

7. Construct a mosaic by attaching items from a collection of seeds, old jewelry, macaroni shapes, etc. to cardboard with glue. (This can be used to provide experience with other elements of art. Here the interest should come from texture.)

8. Experiment with putting lines together to create visual textures.

9. Using modeling clay and found objects such as nails, screws, and popsicle sticks, emboss a textural pattern. Using small pieces, apply a raised texture. Try combining the two.

10. Make a bulletin board of reproductions of paintings and engravings that rely heavily on surface values or texture: Dutch paintings of the sixteenth century, the paintings of Van Gogh, the engravings of Dürer. If resource materials are available, encourage children to make their own selection.

Color

1. Using wet manila paper and large brushes, experiment with two colored tempera paints and white. Blue, orange, and white provide experience with grays and buffs. Green, red, and white provide a range from pinks and greens to browns and black. Yellow and green confine the experiments to variants of these two colors.

2. Match colors to music. Use records performed in both major and minor keys.

3. Take samplings of color from a given area—leaves, earth, flowers; sand, cement, rock; colors from the kitchen. Then paint a picture suggested by the group of colors that has been chosen. It is helpful if this can be unrelated to the original source of the colors.

4. Using construction paper of assorted colors, put together some pleasant combinations and some unpleasant combinations.

5. Put together "families" of colors from the same source.

6. Divide the colors into those that seem warm and those that seem cold.

7. Paint a warm or cold picture.

8. Make a collection of objects of one color, such as red. Lay out the collection on a neutral background to emphasize the number of variations of one color.

9. Have dress-up days using one color. On yellow Monday, wear or bring something yellow. Find a poem that either

matches the mood or mentions yellow, such as Frost's "The Road Not Taken" where "Two roads diverged in a yellow wood"; "The Magnanimous Sun," by Vachel Lindsay; or "Themes in Yellow," by Carl Sandburg.

Form

1. Using any soft modeling medium, make a fist-sized ball. Using one hand, squeeze a shape. Discuss and compare the forms. Repeat, using two hands. A direct squeeze is preferred over manipulation.
2. To forms produced as suggested in no. 1, add more material to create whatever the original suggests.
3. From bars of soap carve forms based on solids and holes or on natural forms.
4. From the window, see how many different kinds of forms can be seen. How many are related to the following?
   a. A cardboard roll
   b. A cardboard box
   c. A ball
   d. A paper cone
   e. A paper pyramid
   How many things contain more than one basic form?
5. Place some damp sand in a box. Using found objects or your hands, create a series of depressions. Pour plaster of Paris over the depressions. When the plaster dries, raised forms on a plaster background can be lifted from the sand.
6. Using toothpicks and balsa-wood cement, construct a form.
7. Using a ceramic clay such as terra cotta, construct a form that creates large areas of light and shadow when under strong light.
8. Collect driftwood and found objects that have interesting forms.

Shape

1. Play with the concept of families of shapes. A family might consist of shapes that have six straight sides, or one curved and three straight sides. The latter can be cut from colored construction paper and stuck to a second sheet.
2. Cut out large circles from construction paper. A paper plate can be used as a guide. Divide the circle using a limited number of cuts—say five. How many things can

you make from the shapes?   (This helps children see things in terms of simple shapes.)

3. Make constructions with building blocks of various shapes. Building blocks are still one of our best creative toys.
4. Mimeograph shapes and complete the picture.
5. Cut shapes from a simple printing material such as a potato, and print shapes in a pattern.
6. Using the overhead projector, create exciting visual images by hanging shapes cut from paper so that they cast shadows on the translucent screen (see Chapter 8).
7. Make collections of related things that have different shapes, such as leaves or carpenter's nails.
8. Make an exhibit of prints that rely on shapes: Picasso, Braque, Mondrian, Leger, or the contemporary nonobjective painters.

Tone

1. Make a drawing on black paper with white chalk.
2. Take a half sheet of black paper and make one interesting cut through it.   Place the two pieces on a sheet of white paper with a space between them.   See both the positive and negative shapes.   Reverse the process by cutting the white paper.
3. Using the concept of black on white and white on black, cut out decorative shapes from black paper and mount the shapes on white paper; compare the patterns.
4. Make a painting using black and white tempera.
5. Put together a bulletin board or exhibit that emphasizes tone.
6. Lay out pieces of colored and gray construction paper on a table.   Choose the darkest, the lightest, and the ones that fit in between.
7. Using a spotlight, create exaggerated patterns of light and shadow on objects or on other lights and shadows.
8. Standing at the window, decide if nearby things are darker than more distant things.   Repeat the experiment for a week, noting any changes.

Perception

1. Make a checklist to determine how much has been perceived in any experience.   For example, observe an apple.   Then, turning away from the apple, answer the following questions.

An Apple

	Yes	No
Did it have any flat spots?		
Was more of it red than green?		
Was it warm to the touch?		
Was the texture visual?		
Was the texture tactile?		
Was the texture uniform all over?		
Could you smell it from far away?		

2. Remain blindfolded for an extended period of time and try to reorient the senses so that you can operate freely.
3. Make a collection of optical illusions.
4. Sit quietly and try to identify every sound that you hear.
5. Make a collection of objects of similar weights but different sizes for a weight-judging contest.
6. Have one person place a variety of objects on a tray. Cover. Uncover for two minutes. After an additional two minutes of "forgetting," write down the articles seen. Have someone change the position of one or more articles. See if you can determine which ones have been moved.
7. Make a collection of scents for others to identify.
8. Make a drawing of a well-known object and then compare it with the original.
9. Move like an elephant, a small dog, or a gorilla.
10. Express an idea using only body language.

SELECTED BIBLIOGRAPHY

Anderson, Donald M. *Elements of Design.* New York: Holt, Rinehart and Winston, Inc., 1961.

Arnheim, Rudolf. *Art and Visual Perception.* Berkeley, Calif.: University of California Press, 1954.

Broudy, Harry. "Quality Education and Aesthetic Education." *Concepts in Art and Education.* George Pappas, ed. New York: Macmillan Publishing Co., Inc., 1970.

Burnham, Jack. "Systems Esthetics." *Concepts in Art and Education.* George Pappas, ed. New York: Macmillan Publishing Co., Inc., 1970.

Child, Irwin. "Esthetics." *Handbook of Social Psychology*, 2nd ed., Vol. 3. Gardner Murphy and Eliot Aronson, eds. Reading, Mass.: Addison-Wesley Publishing Co., Inc., 1968–1969.

Collier, Graham. *Form, Space, and Vision: Discovering Design through Drawing.* Englewood Cliffs, N.J.: Prentice-Hall, Inc., 1963.

DeLisi, Rita. "An Experiment in Visual Education." *Programs of Promise: Art in the Schools.* Al Hurwitz, ed. New York: Harcourt Brace Jovanovich, Inc., 1972.

Dewey, John. *Art as Experience.* New York: Minton, Balch and Co., 1934.

Faulkner, R., E. Ziegfeld, and G. Hill. *Art Today,* rev. ed. New York: Holt, Rinehart and Winston, Inc., 1963.

Fearing, Kelly, Clyde Martin, and Evelyn Beard. *Our Expanding Vision.* Austin, Tex.: W. S. Benson & Co., 1960.

Feldman, Edmund. *Becoming Human through Art: Aesthetic Experience in School.* Englewood Cliffs, N.J.: Prentice-Hall, Inc., 1970.

Gombrich, G. H. *The Story of Art,* 12th ed. New York: Phaidon Art Books (Praeger), 1972.

Hochberg, Julian. *Perceptions.* Englewood Cliffs, N.J.: Prentice-Hall, Inc., 1964.

Itten, Johannes. *The Art of Color.* New York: Van Nostrand Reinhold Co., 1961.

Jefferson, Blanche. *Teaching Art to Children.* Boston: Allyn and Bacon, Inc., 1969.

Kabol, Martin. *World of Color.* New York: McGraw-Hill Book Co., 1963.

Kellogg, Rhoda. *The Psychology of Children's Art.* New York: CRM Books, 1967.

Kessler, Leonard. *Art Is Everywhere.* New York: Dodd, Mead & Co., 1958.

————. *What's in a Line?* New York: William R. Scott, Inc., 1961.

Lansing, Kenneth. *Art, Artists, and Art Education: Study Guide.* New York: McGraw-Hill Book Co., 1969.

Linderman, Earl W. *Invitation to Vision: Ideas and Imaginations for Art.* Dubuque, Iowa: William C. Brown Co., Publishers, 1967.

————, and Donald W. Herberholz. *Developing Artistic and Perceptual Awareness,* 2nd ed. Dubuque, Iowa: William C. Brown Co., Publishers, 1971.

Lowry, Bates. *The Visual Experience: An Introduction to Art.* Englewood Cliffs, N.J.: Prentice-Hall, Inc., 1961.

Mueller, Robert E. "The Science of Art." *Concepts in Art and Education.* George Pappas, ed. New York: Macmillan Publishing Co., Inc., 1970.

Rader, Melvin. *A Modern Book of Aesthetics,* 3rd ed. New York: Holt, Rinehart and Winston, Inc., 1960.

Salome, R. A. "The Effects of Perceptual Training upon the Two-Dimensional Drawings of Children," *Studies in Art Education,* 7, 1 (1965), 18–33.

Smith, Ralph A., ed. *Aesthetics and Curriculum in Art Education.* Chicago: Rand McNally & Co., 1966.

————. "The Three Modes of Perception," *The Instructor,* April 1969, 57–64.

Wachowiak, Frank, and Theodore Ramsay. *Emphasis: Art.* Scranton, Pa.: Intext Educational Publishers, 1965.

Weismann, Donald L. *The Visual Arts as Human Experience.* Englewood Cliffs, N.J.: Prentice-Hall, Inc., 1970.

White, Burton L., and Peter W. Castle. "Visual Exploratory Behavior Following Postnatal Handling of Human Infants," *Perceptual and Motor Skills,* 18 (1964), 476.

Wilson, Brent G. "An Experimental Study Designed to Alter Fifth and Sixth Grade Students' Perceptions of Paintings," *Studies in Art Education,* 8, 1 (1966), 33–42.

Wolff, Janet, and Bernard Owett. *Let's Imagine Colors.* New York: E. P. Dutton & Co., Inc., 1963.

CHAPTER VII

Teaching Art in the Curriculum

"All passes, Art alone Enduring stays to us."

Henry Austin Dobson[1]

The authors of this text believe that art not only enriches life, but is a way of life. In order for art to be a way of life, however, the knowledge and skills learned in art must become tools for living throughout the day. For a child, the greater part of his living is in school. Art must, therefore, permeate the school day. A school must teach art for art's sake, but it must also teach the practical and everyday uses of art that bring joy to life and creative fulfillment to the individual. In this chapter we show ways this can be done without violating creative or artistic principles.

ART AND OTHER SUBJECTS

The subject matter of the elementary school curriculum becomes the child's life for the greater part of the day. Through incorporation into subject matter, art can relate to a greater portion of his life. The classroom teacher and/or the art teacher can make use of subject matter to:

    1. provide children with experiences that build new knowledge, understanding, skills, and capabilities

    2. provide the opportunity for children to apply their acquired knowledge and skills in new relationships (the testing grounds of creativity)

1. *Ars Victrix*, stanza 2.

Examples of the use of other subjects in developing children's art and creative potential appear throughout this book. In Chapter 1, for instance, Miss Larkin and her students had many life experiences in art through the development of a puppet show. The puppet show evolved originally from a language arts project in creative writing.

The art teacher can help the classroom teacher to identify the art experiences the children should logically and normally have within the context of the subject matter being studied; the classroom teacher can keep the art teacher informed of that subject matter.

Both teachers have to plan the art experiences together—and carefully. *They should set up definite objectives and goals* so each lesson is purposeful and rewarding. Each should operate as best she can with the class and should not covet a few minutes per week as her own while the other is off somewhere not knowing what goes on in her absence. The objectives set by the teacher should be worthy goals that will contribute to the full life experiences of the children in the classroom.

If they are to relate art to subject matter, the art and classroom teachers must understand that subject matter does not have to be sequentially organized particularly for the teaching of art; a child uses whatever he has in his reservoir of experience when he creates. All experiences are absorbed and used according to his own needs and perceptions. The expression of subject matter in various forms is proof of the child's progress in both academic learning and creativity. Teachers normally test their students' learnings through cognitive, convergent means—they see if all children can come up with the same answers. They could very profitably test children through divergent means by asking the child to express his learnings from an experience artistically or creatively. In this case the ideal product will be the one that is so unique it is different from all other products. *It is not the subject matter that makes for artistic expression, but the manner in which it is presented.* The amount of originality in the presentation of an experience is an expression of the degree to which the child related the experience to himself.

The Curriculum as a Tool for Art

The art teacher and the classroom teacher are both interested in developing aesthetic perception in children, and they can use social studies, language arts, science, and other areas of the curriculum to do so. Such experiences may or may not be "art." Because they form the core of the child's thoughts for the greater part of each day, they may serve to motivate him to produce art. In order to produce art, the child must feel *sensuous* values; that is, he must react to a topic with feelings of his own. He must also find *formal* values in the topic; he must see things in relation to each other. Finally he must be aware of *expressive* values; he must feel and identify the quality of the experience itself. These aesthetic values are of concern to the artist, and a classroom teacher working with an art teacher can help to develop them. In this way curriculum areas can be very useful as tools for art teaching.

Eisner says: "In the productive realm of the art curriculum the focus of student attention is on the creation of a visual form having artistically prized qualities." [2]

A group of suburban middle-school children were studying a unit on housing. As part of the unit they visited a slum school and a city slum area. They then saw some films on slums, documentary portrayals which supplemented their own direct experiences.

The films dealt frankly with malnutrition, filth, cockroaches, rats, cold, hunger, disease, and starvation. During these experiences, the team of teachers from the suburban and the slum schools continually helped the children to express their feelings by sharing words, encouraging free discussion, and playing on emotion as well as fact. The study required the teachers to go below the surface of facts to help the children discover cause and effect: Why do slums exist? What happens to people born in these places in terms of getting a job and earning a living? What does it cost them to live in these places? The exploitation of the poor by landlords was discussed. The types of jobs held by the disadvantaged were studied in relation to their salaries, and the salaries in relation to their rent and other living costs. The effect of income on educational opportunities and types of schools was studied. Values were discussed in relation to circumstance, so the children understood the depth of the problem and experienced the bewilderment, the futility, and the despair of the people who lived in these places.

The teachers helped the children to find words to express their feelings, words such as "futility" and "despair." The children expended some of their own despair by forming an ex-

2. Elliot Eisner, *Educating Artistic Vision* (New York: Macmillan Publishing Co., Inc., 1972).

change team—certain children swapped places with children in the slum schools once a month. They wrote endless numbers of creative poems and stories expressing their feelings. They were encouraged to paint and use other art media to give vent to their feelings. The influence of their experiences showed in the colors of their designs and the themes of their poems. These could be classified as real art.

Eisner states that a child's artistic ability is in large measure a function of that which he has learned.[3]

Art as a Tool for the Curriculum

Many products of curriculum integration may not truly be labeled art. Sometimes planned curriculum experiences serve purposes other than that of producing real art; they provide a motivation and/or a practice field for the development of certain art techniques. In these cases, art serves as a tool.

This role is legitimate. The teachers who work with children should be continually aware that producing a real art product requires questioning and strategies above and beyond the teaching techniques that make social studies or science interesting. In supplying subject matter for the children's artwork (through various areas of the curriculum), these teachers can hope that one unit of study will become such a vital, dynamic experience for a child that it will motivate him to produce art.

In some of the illustrations that follow real art is created; in others art is used as a tool. In some, the experience helps children discover and invent new techniques. In all cases, the total creativity of the child is being developed.

ART AND PROJECTS

In the chapters in Part 1 of this book, continual reference was made to the integrated personality of the child. It is unlikely that much progress will be made with projects imposed on children if they are not an integral part of the child's life and he does not establish a personal relationship with them. When projects are imposed on children by a teacher who is driving to "cover" or accomplish a certain unit of work, it is doubtful that the child will grow in art or in personality integration.

3. *Ibid.*, p. 105.

Such projects, especially those designed to teach social studies, can become a sequence of baited traps, where a child becomes embroiled in a succession of activities totally unrelated to his own personality or his own creative expression. He is apt to subdue both his personality and his creativity in order to do whatever pleases the teacher.

Projects can be very valuable both in accomplishing the objective of making learning interesting and in developing art ability. The projects described in this chapter were selected because they avoid teacher imposition and consider the following criteria.

1. The project should be highly motivating to all children. This does not mean that the teacher cannot have many projects in mind. It does mean that she is flexible enough to readily accept children's ideas when they will accomplish the objectives she has in mind.

2. Her objectives should be very clear, both general and specific, immediate and long-range. If she can describe her objectives in behavioral terms, she may wish to do so. However, the writing of behavioral objectives is not especially applicable to goals in developing creativity, so she should set down her objectives in the manner best suited to her mode of teaching.

3. The children should have a part in the planning. This includes the setting up of objectives, the selection of the experiences that make possible the meeting of objectives, and the determination of evaluation techniques to be used in assessing the unit of study. If art means the integration of personality, as we have previously implied, care must be taken to be sure children relate emotionally and intellectually to their classroom experiences so that the subject matter and the experiences they are pursuing become integrated with and absorbed in their personalities. Emphasis should be placed on visual education—the development of perception (see p. 207).

4. In planning objectives and activities many options must be considered. Because children are different and unique and the goal in creative education is to keep them so, each child must be presented with a smorgasbord of experiences from which he selects those that best help him to meet his own personal goals. Work on projects within a project should be on a volunteer basis so children are always engaged in activities with which they identify and which they feel a reason to complete. As part of each project, a teacher should take the time to help each child identify his own objectives.

5. Inasmuch as most units taught in science, social

studies, or the language arts are built around the amassing of knowledge and the learning of skills—especially skills of communication—art, a means of creative communication, should be included in the planning stages of every unit.

The illustrations that follow are taken from actual classroom situations where the teacher and the art teacher worked closely to accomplish carefully set objectives with the overall goal of providing rich learning experiences for children. At the same time they saw these experiences as a means of developing new knowledge and skills in children. They also saw these planned experiences as a means of furnishing an outlet for the child's creative potential—particularly that potential released by his new-found knowledge and skills. The reader is not to assume from these accounts that there are no lessons in the school program dedicated solely to the teaching of art.

Art, like all disciplines, contains a body of knowledge that should be taught. The creative teacher teaches this in meaningful, creative, and child-like ways (see p. 197). Art, like most disciplines, contains a body of skills that must be practiced. The creative teacher provides many open-ended, goal-centered, problem-solving situations for practicing them.

Rather than regarding art as an embellishment as it is regarded in many schools today, the authors feel that it is essential for the following reasons:

1. It contributes through the obvious; children create with the materials at hand, rendering either the process or the product creative.

2. It presents a challenge to creative thinking and creative problem solving simply in the manner in which it is presented. One teacher presents a group of children with a cart full of art materials of all kinds. Another teacher gives her students a piece of white paper and some black paint. Both then pose the problem: using any of these materials, construct an art product that shows fear. In the second situation, the child is restricted in his materials. His mind cannot take flight as the mind of the boy in the first situation can, but both situations are highly tension-producing. In the second situation, the child must be more creative than in the first.

3. It provides an opportunity for open-ended learning situations where skills can be used in divergent ways.

4. It develops those characteristics and traits mentioned in Chapter 3 which are essential for creative development.

5. It contributes to personal fulfillment and adds to the self-realization of the individual.

6. It provides the child with experiences to parallel his development.

7. It provides a manner in which individual differences can be developed in a group process and consequently it promotes the growth of the whole child.

8. It provides a way to develop skills that can be used to enrich the total school curriculum. The total school curriculum becomes a source of developing creative power.

"Art is life" was the theme of the spring festival in the Richmond School. Miss Walker, the art teacher, and Mrs. Dearborn, the elementary school supervisor, worked together at the beginning of the year to plan some units to be developed throughout the school for the major purpose of demonstrating to parents, teachers, and children that: (1) art is an important part of life; (2) art knowledge and skills can enrich one's life a great deal; (3) aesthetic outlets provide a positive means for personality development; and (4) art can be the basis for most learning.

With an outline of their plans and a dittoed copy of their noble objectives for each teacher, Miss Walker and Mrs. Dearborn attended a series of faculty meetings where creative brainstorming resulted in a multitude of ideas for art activities that

FIGURE 7–1.   Art is life: a school festival.

could be the base of a learning experience or that could be integrated into the experience. In the spring, the festival of the arts was held to show the community that, indeed, art is life and that the objectives of the project had been accomplished.

The festival was held outdoors on a beautiful spring afternoon. As the sun set, the audience moved indoors to view the evening program, which was planned and developed by the children in various classes throughout the school.

When one group of children had delved into the origins of current fashions, they had become highly interested in the early nineteen hundreds. They presented the remainder of the school with the idea that the era of the 1920s become the theme of the festival. Consequently, the children who acted as ushers and guides dressed as flappers, gangsters, and other personalities of that era. The expressions of the times were studied in language arts periods, and the slang of the times was revived: whoopee, hot-dog, red-hot mamma, jazz, 28 skidoo, feeling groovy, daddy-o. The programs for the festival were developed around this theme and the decorations and signs at the festival reflected the type of artwork common in that period (Fig. 7–2).

FIGURE 7–2. The program cover provides the opportunity to communicate with aesthetic expression.

The exhibits themselves were planned so they presented a color-ful, well-designed, well-organized concept of the work of the children during the past several months. Art was indeed the basis of life in this school.

There were many instances when the visitor was made aware that art skills were required to teach social studies, as during the evening program when one group of children showed a motion picture on pollution and the problems presented by it in Richmond. It was done partly with animated cartoons and partly with real life photography, all with a complete soundtrack. The children, working in groups with their teachers, had taken field trips to all the places in town where pollution problems existed and had photographed them with a 16mm motion-picture camera. Using the footage along with carefully planned ani-mated cartoons (which the audiovisual man taught them how to make) they presented a very dramatic reel on the power of pollution to bring about the death of beautiful Richmond. To counterbalance the negative and to make for a more dramatic presentation, another committee of children devoted its time to photographing the beautiful places in town. These were used in the film to show what all of Richmond could be like. To make the soundtrack, the children had sought out appropriate music for each scene. One scene showed a small brook sluggishly flowing on, congested with green foam, floating beer cans, and papers; it was accompanied by the music from *Danse Macabre*. For a beautiful scene in Richmond's town park, the children chose "Everything's Beautiful." Against this musical background the children talked in dialogue.

In this production the children learned the art skills involved in artistic motion-picture animation, moving titles, montage, collage, and costuming. Their creative development was enhanced by their practice in fluency (of thinking and speaking), flexibility (in the animation sequences), elaboration (on themes), and originality (in presentation of subject matter). Inherent in the experience was the opportunity to magnify, to minify, to put things to new uses, to reverse, and to adapt—just about every type of creative thought process possible. Chief among them was the constant pressure placed on the children to pass judgments, to make decisions, and to evaluate.

There were also many instances where the visitor was made aware of the fact that social studies knowledge and skills could become a source of art expression and aesthetic satisfac-tion for each child.

One group of primary-school children had been to the zoo

as part of a social studies unit on animals. Because their teacher, Mrs. Scott, sensed that all the children might like to stitch and sew, she taught the children to stitch on burlap with yarn. Each child cut his favorite animal out of cloth from the scrap box and sewed it onto a wall hanging. The result was colorful and very beautiful; it was used at the top of the stair landing to give color and interest to an ugly wall (Fig. 7–3.)

Part of the program consisted of a series of dramatizations. These presentations grew out of the children's studies in literature. Different groups listed the stories they had read that they felt were the most suitable for presentation. After the choices had been listed, children in various groups signed up for the story they would like best to help present.

The teacher then presented the problem, the solution of which called for some creative thinking: "I want you to think of a very unusual way, as different as possible from what all the other groups do, to present your story," she said.

Periods of brainstorming and planning followed. Then

FIGURE 7–3. Art and the social studies: a study of animals results in a cloth and burlap wall hanging.

FIGURE 7–4.   The tortoise from The Tortoise and the Hare.

the children went to work to collect props, construct scenery, make costumes, write scripts, and select or create musical backgrounds.

One group dramatized "The Tortoise and the Hare" by making enormous papier-mâché animals over bent chicken wire (Fig. 7–4). Another group made an exhibit of the characters in *Alice in Wonderland* from papier mâché over old bottles and twigs (Fig. 7–5). One group wrote its own play in poetry form, *The Bookworm and the Librarian*, and produced a puppet show around it.

FIGURE 7–5.   Alice in Wonderland.

Music was integrated into the festival program in many ways. The school band gave a concert in which one of the numbers was written by one of the children in the band. The music teacher helped him to write it down and orchestrate it. Musical backgrounds were planned for all the puppet shows and plays, and soundtracks accompanied the taped presentations and the animated films. Some children used original songs in these presentations. One hit of the evening was an interpretation by a group of boys and girls of the songs of the 1920s through bodily movements. They included steps from the Black Bottom and the Charleston (Fig. 7–6).

Other ways that the festival contributed to the understanding of art is life were as follows:

1. A beautiful outdoor art exhibit demonstrated the use of art in every formal school subject as well as in art projects expressly for the purpose of learning art and art skills.

2. Techniques for obtaining various art effects were demonstrated by the children at various centers.

3. Poems, stories, and plays written by the children were read or exhibited in conspicuous places.

4. A school paper was assembled for sale at the festival (Fig. 7–7).

FIGURE 7–6. Music, art, and physical education.

FIGURE 7–7. The school newspaper contains stories, poems, and artwork by the children.

5. A film entitled *A Child's World* was shown as part of the entertainment. This film was made by the teachers with the help of the children. It was a delightful study of children's faces and children's activities around the school. An appropriate soundtrack was dubbed in, and titles and credits were added.

All these activities, so enthusiastically presented by the children, showed how art is life. They pointed out very specifically how children's school and home studies provide the knowledge and experiences that make it possible for art to exist, and how art, in turn, supplies the aesthetic qualities, the characteristics, and understanding that give the child an aesthetic means of communicating about his world.

ART AND THE SOCIAL STUDIES

Regardless of the particular approach of a specific social studies program, it is designed to make the child aware of his immediate and his remote world.

As the child grows older and his own world boundaries

expand, he draws more and more of the things that interest him. Classroom units, holidays, special occurrences, and exciting events often become subjects of children's paintings. Boys in the intermediate grades draw airplanes, battleships, cowboys, astronauts with fantastic garb, and Martian men. Girls of the same age draw female movie stars with long party dresses, ballet dancers, and handsome men. They also like landscapes and pictures of foreign countries. At all ages they use art to show their growing sense of design, their changing emotions, and their maturing visual skills.

As the subjects of the child's painting change, so do his techniques and his abilities. Clay modeling becomes a popular form of art expression. Large painting, as on friezes or scenery for a play, gives the child a different feeling of space, area, and paint. Sewing, weaving, fresco painting, and puppetmaking all have their place in providing a child with creative outlets using varied media. If these media are available most of the time in the classroom, some day the child will "discover" them and the techniques for using them. His joy at finding new art forms will provide a motivation for his work.

One teacher helped provide new ideas through the following classroom experience.

The horizons of a fifth-grade class were broadened when Shelly came to school. Shelly's father worked for a large American oil company, and every year the family spent December through March in Mexico. Along with many postcards from Mexico, Shelly brought to school a serape, a sombrero, some lovely jewelry and glass, and some dolls.

Immediately she was confronted with a flood of questions. "Why are the hats so widebrimmed? Why are the roofs of the desert-houses flat? What is a serape used for?" Of course, every child was motivated to the point where a unit on Mexico became inevitable. The teacher saw tremendous possibilities for integrating all the children's work into lifelike situations that would incorporate many art experiences. Some of the creative elements of the unit are listed here to illustrate the rich experiences the children had as a result of the Mexican unit.

1. The class read *The Painted Pig* and wrote a play from it.
a. They made costumes for their play.
b. They planned and painted scenery for their play.
c. They made properties for their play (Ramona's tear strings, clay articles, wooden articles, and cardboard articles).

d. They designed program covers and gave the play at a fiesta.
e. They made posters advertising the play.
    2. The class drew and painted many pictures of Mexican life showing their feelings as well as their learnings.
    3. One committee made a large scrapbook for classroom reports and designed the cover.
    4. The children gave a fiesta in the gymnasium to which they invited the entire school.
a. Committes designed and built booths for displaying their material on Mexico.
b. Children planned exhibits of their paintings for the fiesta.
c. Each child made and wore a serape and a sombrero of his own design.
d. The children created a life-sized papier-mâché burro. He was used at the fair in an exhibit of children's handmade wares.
e. The class made Mexican pottery and tin jewelry to sell at the fair.
f. The children tried weaving and other Mexican crafts.
g. They decorated the gymnasium to represent a real Mexican plaza.
    5. The class planned a program for the fiesta.
a. They made Aztec masks and learned an ancient dance.
b. They learned a Mexican hat dance and created costumes to wear while dancing.
c. They learned songs in Spanish and English.
d. They presented their play, *The Painted Pig.*
    6. The class served a Mexican meal.
a. Each child made placemats with Mexican designs.
b. Committees made centerpieces with a Mexican theme for each table.
c. The children made favors using Mexican designs.
    7. The class had a piñata party where the children played Mexican games. One committee designed and made the Mexican piñata and filled it with gifts for all.
    8. They dramatized a Mexican Christmas.
a. The children made costumes and properties.
b. The children created lighting effects for the Mexican procession to the nativity.
    9. They studied Mexican art.
a. A lecturer from Mexico who was visiting a neighboring town talked to the children and showed them many paintings and handicrafts.
b. Children studied Mexican artists and found reproductions of their paintings for bulletin-board exhibits.
c. The children studied Spanish architecture and found buildings in town with Spanish influence.

d. They studied the ancient Aztec Indians and made masks for the Aztec dance at the fiesta.

10. They read many Mexican stories and made hand puppets and marionettes to dramatize the stories.

11. The children studied Mexican music.

a. They learned songs in Spanish.

b. They listened to Spanish recordings.

c. They studied and heard recordings of the opera *Carmen,* which they eventually went to see.

These creative art experiences were possible only because the children were skillfully introduced to a whole new world and were allowed to experience the things connected with this world.

Mr. Crain, the teacher of the group, had planned with the art teacher those art processes and skills that the children would need to be taught or would "discover" before the unit was over. His list looked like this:

1. Making costumes from crepe paper.

a. sewing

b. folding, stretching, and cutting crepe paper

2. Constructing and painting scenery.

a. sponge painting

b. felt painting

c. tempera painting

d. use of colored paper

e. spray painting

3. Making Ramona's tears.

4. Working in clay.

5. Whittling.

6. Constructing from cardboard.

7. Making posters.

8. Printing (for program covers).

9. Cutting tissue paper designs (fiesta).

10. Using papier mâché (burro).

11. Making a piñata.

12. Constructing from wood (booths for fiesta).

13. Arranging exhibits.

14. Making sombrero designs (weaving).

15. Designing tin (jewelry).

16. Making masks.

17. Weaving and painting (placemats).

18. Studying Mexican artists.

19. Studying Mexican paintings and designs.

20. Studying Aztec culture.

21. Creating a puppet show.

Some suggestions for correlating art with social studies are the following:

1. Illustrate phases of history (How did you feel when you won the battle of Yorktown?) and use the illustrations for wall murals, bulletin boards, scroll movies, or scrapbooks.

2. Make get-well cards for students who are ill at home or who have been hospitalized.

3. Make clay maps, salt and flour maps, or papier-mâché maps. They can become art objects when painted and embellished with products of a given area, historical events, or homes of famous people.

4. Make puppets for presenting historical and current social problems (What problems are caused by water pollution?).

5. Build dolls, forts, or models (an adobe hut might be made).

6. Use shadow plays to present current problems (Tell the story of pollution in this country with colored lights and shadows).

7. Make dioramas depicting historical events, countries as they are today, or problems such as slums, pollution, and poverty.

8. Make stuffed toys (What kind of animal would you create to put in our Koo-Koo zoo?).

9. Design holiday decorations (What have you always wanted to put on a Christmas tree that your mother wouldn't let you?).

10. Make masks from as many materials as possible (paper bags, paper plates, papier mâché, tin, aluminum foil, and clay molds).

11. Make mobiles (Show your impressions of ski jumping or swimming at the Olympic games).

12. Construct posters in two or three dimensions for advertising plays, puppet shows, etc.

13. Take photographs for various topics in social studies.

14. Make tabletop mock-ups of social studies projects.

15. Create flannelboard stories or reports.

16. Draw cartoons of political issues.

17. Plan slogans, designs, etc. to promote political issues.

18. Construct kites, models of wigwams, kayaks, etc.

19. Paint scenery for plays and puppet plays.

20. Design silly machines and explain what they do.

21. Make and decorate kites of any shape that will fly.

ART AND THE LANGUAGE ARTS

The language arts are called the communicative arts. Art is also a means of communication—a creative means of communication. When the communicative arts are used creatively, poetry, literature, drama, and creative prose result. Art and the language arts have many elements in common.

The language arts can be creative verbal communication; art is creative figurative or emotional communication. To separate them for instructional purposes is legitimate, for the skills needed to communicate by the two methods are different. To separate them in classroom usage is often artificial.

In the first chapter of this book, many illustrations were given of the use of a combination of language arts and art to develop an effective means of communication. Miss Larkin's class combined verbal and figurative symbols to produce an appealing and informative program for their puppet play *Fractured Fairy Tales;* Miss Hill combined creative writing (by using the story of the bullfrog and the dragon fly) with color interpretation and music for better and more effective communication. The teacher on p. 27 extended the feeling of communication when she had the children interpret *Where the Wild Things Are* with magic chalk and blue light. In the art festival described at the beginning of this chapter pictorial and verbal symbols were combined for communication.

Art experience forms a regular part of the development of the communication skills and can be utilized in many natural ways to develop the creativity of all children. Some of the more obvious ways teachers use art with the language arts are listed below.

Primary Grades

1. Illustrate stories and poems. (What is the author saying to you? How does he make you feel?)
2. Make murals for literature projects.
3. Make clay objects.
4. Try molding with sawdust and papier mâché. (Let's make imaginary animals for our stories.)
5. Make stick, finger, fist, or paper bag puppets.

6. Make dioramas for literature.

7. Make stuffed toys. (What kinds of animals can we make for our indoor circus?)

8. Illustrate original stories and books.

9. Make masks from paper plates, papier mâché, aluminum foil, and paper bags. (Represent your favorite character in our Book Week program.)

10. Sculpt favorite characters in soap.

11. Make montages. (How can we show happiness with these materials?)

12. Paint scenery for plays.

13. Make puppet shows, costumes, and scenery.

14. Paint abstractions such as "happiness," "sadness," etc.

15. Make valentines.

16. Make mobiles. (Let's show everyone all the stories that we have read by Dr. Seuss.)

17. Make posters.

18. Make block prints. (How can we make covers for the programs for our play?)

19. Use art for original chalk talks.

Intermediate Grades

To the above list add such activities as:

1. Do felt-pen drawing and lettering. (How can we show everyone where our room centers are? Who will make charts of the questions for this unit so we can see them from anywhere in the room?)

2. Construct wooden or paper-carton models of types of communication, historical events, scientific inventions, etc.

3. Make dioramas showing historical events or natural resources.

4. Make books.

5. Plan photographic compositions.

6. Draw three-dimensional posters and bulletin boards.

7. Make costumes. (What kind of clothing did Robin Hood and King Richard wear?)

8. Do flannelboard paintings. (Show anger with these colored pieces of flannel on the flannelboard.)

9. Design cartoon strips.

10. Make advertisements, slogans, etc. to publicize school events.

11. Design and print Christmas cards, and then write verses for them.

ART AND PHYSICAL EDUCATION

In recent years a great deal of effort has been expended on the study of bodily movement. This focus of energy has been classified as "the movement movement." Since movement is one of the bases of art (see Chapter 6) and since movement is a natural expression of the energy of man, some mention must be made of the relationship between art and physical education. Physical education can be classified as a study of movement that has been patterned for various purposes.

Just as the motions of drama can be the base and control for the patterning of movement, so can the free or patterned movement of dances, games, and athletic contests become the training ground for the rhythm that will later appear in the child's artwork (Fig. 7–8).

Dance is movement put to a pattern. It is a form of expression, and as such can be employed as a means of developing creativity. In an accepting, permissive atmosphere, dance can be utilized to develop divergent thinking processes. Originality can be fostered, individuality can run rampant, and the

FIGURE 7–8.   Dance is movement put to a pattern.

characteristics and qualities of creative people can be encouraged in a legitimate manner.   Dance also provides a way of expending excess physical energy and emotional tensions.   It provides a foundation for linear movement and the expression of movement in visual art.

The dance program is closely allied to the music program, but in dance, movement and thought are more important than music.   Music accompanies and enriches the creative idea; it is not the dominant factor.   Art can become a visual way of expressing the same idea.

A series of experiences that utilize rhythmical noises rather than music helps the child to concentrate on his own ideas and his own bodily interpretation.   Children discover what they can do with their arms, their legs, and their trunks.   They explore the possibilities of putting these movements into patterns.

It is a logical step from this type of activity to the presentation of specific problems in art that can be solved by the movement of the paint across the paper or the use of contrasts of light and shadow.   The child is free to use any shape or form and any medium.   One ten-year-old, after an exceptionally productive session of creating dance rhythms, went to his classroom and set to work to "make a dance picture," as he told his teacher.   What his product really turned out to be was a group of children in energetic, rhythmical poses all suspended by threads from sticks in a mobile construction.   It was so carefully done that the figures actually moved all the time.

Examples of the types of bodily movement problems that can be solved through art media are:

1. Paint the feeling you get from rock-and-roll dancing, from military marching, or from turning cartwheels.

2. With colored lights and shadows and a wall or sheet, dramatize an Indian harvest festival.

3. Paint the meaning of the words rhythms, balance, racing, dying, happy, and sad.

4. List all the types of dances you know.   Then select one type and make a huge silhouette of it on white paper for the spring dance (Theme: the dance of dances).

5. Use these experiences for a study of linear movement (see p. 211).

The teacher should provide many experiences in all areas of the school curriculum that can be translated into patterned movement.   As in other forms of creative expression, the subject of the dance should be derived basically from current interests of the children.   Almost any experience can be translated into a dance expression: a football game, a holiday, a trip to the zoo, a nursery rhyme, or a piece of popular music. Any subject that appeals to teacher and pupils can be used.

Art can be closely allied to activities in physical education, especially those related to rhythm and dance. The movement program can provide a high incentive for art instruction. At the same time it furnishes a showcase for creative expression.

ART AND SCIENCE

Art and science are sometimes considered to be at opposite ends of a continuum. But art could not exist without science; it has its basis in scientific knowledge.

Much of the science taught in the elementary school can be taught through the art program or at least in close relation to it.

Indirectly a teacher begins to teach solubles to kindergarteners when she tells a child, "Add more water to the paint, Bobby. It is too thick. That's why you can't spread it."

Almost as indirectly a child learns that adding too much water alters the colors of the paint—it "washes it out" and in many cases even makes it totally inadequate for his purpose. He finds himself adding more pigment in order to attempt to rebalance the situation.

Although no kindergarten teacher is going to go into a long discussion at this time about the frequency and intensity of particles of paint pigment floating in water, this experience, which eventually becomes commonplace for the child, is one on which the teacher can readily draw a few years later when the child is mature enough to be learning about solubles. Knowing that all pigment is not soluble in water can lead to a broadening of his concepts and to experimentation. He discovers that certain kinds of pigment, such as enamel paint, are soluble in other liquids, such as gasoline, turpentine, and linseed oil. The difference between acrylic and oil paints becomes much more understandable to a child who knows that one is soluble in water, the other in linseed oil or turpentine. He sees the advantages of the two media rather readily and knows how to clean and care for his art tools.

The possibilities of integrating science with art are manifold at every age level.

In Miss Collins's room, for instance, the children received

several buckets of new clay. Miss Collins wanted the children to know how to care for the clay, so she emphasized the fact that the clay was heavy and wet because it was full of water.

Tying it in with a recent unit on evaporation in which the children had performed many "experiments," she asked, "What did we learn about water when it is left exposed to air?"

Immediately the class concluded the clay would need to be kept damp in the metal buckets in which it came or else it would dry out. To make the clay workable and usable for individual children, the children all cooperated in rolling the clay into balls that could be handled effectively.

Miss Collins felt she could show the children how to throw the clay to cure it of air bubbles. As she started to throw it and cut it on a wire, one of the children asked the inevitable question, "Why?" Instead of answering Maria's question, Miss Collins said, "Let's see what happens when we cure the clay and when we don't."

She encouraged a few children to cure clay and to make some crude object from it. Some others made some crude objects from uncured clay. Then they made a list of the objects and the people who made them and indicated which were made from thrown clay and which from crude clay. Each of the objects made with the crude clay was marked with an X so it was easily identifiable. These were allowed to dry thoroughly for several days. Then they were taken to Mr. Hadlow, the art teacher. One day he arranged the pieces in a kiln with the marked ones on one tier and the cured ones on another. He called the children when the pieces were ready to be brought from the kiln. Most of the uncured ones had blown up when the air in them expanded under heat. A few had not. All of the cured ones had baked.

After discussing this phenomenon, the children checked out the remaining pieces with the chart they had made to be certain that their observations were reliable. It was true. Only two of the ten uncured pieces of clay had survived the heat.

From these observations, Miss Collins launched into a unit on the expansion and contraction of air and metal, which gave the children many rewarding experiences, art experiences among them. For example, they took a trip to a local china factory to see china being made. One of the questions on a list of many was, "Do you have to cure china before you bake it?"

The children in Miss Collins's class never used clay without "throwing" it first. Their understanding of processes not only made art experiences more meaningful to them but also gave them a finer and more respectful relationship with the medium they were using.

Science is taught in the elementary school for several basic reasons. Two of the most important of these are to develop in children an inquiring mind and to develop in childen a working knowledge of the scientific method.

The scientific method is modern man's system or process for searching for truth. In elementary school texts it is defined by steps: (1) a problem is identified, (2) data are collected about the problem, (3) a hypothesis is formulated, (4) the hypothesis is tested, (5) a conclusion is drawn, and (6) the conclusion is applied.

Art teaching and creative teaching can promote the accomplishment of the two objectives of science. Miss Collins did not follow these steps exactly, but she paralleled them very closely in the lesson described above. The learnings of science were very meaningful when applied directly to practice in art.

Mr. Hadlow, on another occasion, did follow the scientific method very closely with equally effective results. He was preparing the children to understand various "resist" processes. His objective was to teach the children to see that certain materials, like people, are not compatible and may reject each other. The other objective was to teach them to use this fact to identify materials that resist each other and use them to good advantage in creating art objects.

One day when he was working as a consultant in the classroom he told the children that he wanted them to help him in planning some of the art activities for the coming weeks. "First of all," he stated, "I would like you to discover something new so you can work with new facts and new techniques. I have some problems with materials here, and I want to get your ideas about them."

The children crowded around. "All I'm going to ask today," said Mr. Hadlow, "is 'Why?' You think about these things for a couple of days, and then I'll come in and you tell me why you think they happen."

He proceeded at this point to take a piece of paper from his box of materials. Over it he poured a small stream of water. The paper wilted immediately as it absorbed the water. Mr. Hadlow took a piece of wax paper. He poured water over it, and the water ran off. He looked at the children, raised his eyebrows, and asked, "Why?"

The children immediately began to talk about their answers. Mr. Hadlow held up his hand for silence and then said,

"Not today—think carefully about it, then give me all the reasons you can think of next time I come. Now watch this."

This time he took a cup of turpentine, which he allowed the children to identify through smell. Next they identified a cup of gasoline. Mr. Hadlow then proceeded to drop water with an eye dropper onto the surface of the turpentine and then the gasoline. The drops of water congealed in large drops on the surface of each liquid. Even when Mr. Hadlow stirred the materials in the cup, the water came to the top in large globules. Mr. Hadlow looked at the children, raised his eyebrows, and asked, "Why?"

Under the table where he was working, Mr. Hadlow had plugged in a novelty lamp. By now the mass of wax compound in the lamp was hot and was rising and falling in unusual free forms. Mr. Hadlow reached down under the desk, brought the lamp into view, and asked again, with the same raise of his eyebrows, "Why?"

His last demonstration was to take a piece of white cotton cloth in one hand and a piece of white polyester cloth, which he identified for the children, in the other. He told the children that the pan on the table before him contained a cold-water dye which some of the students had mixed for him just before class. Mr. Hadlow placed both the pieces of cloth in the dye, chatted a while with the children, and then said, "Well, let's see what's happening here." He fished the cloth from the dye. The white cotton cloth was now a stunning fuchsia, whereas the white polyester cloth was still white. Mr. Hadlow, with a twinkle in his eye, said, "Why?"

"Boys and girls," he continued, "there is something common to each of the four things I did this morning. If you think about each of them, perhaps you will be able to tell me what that common element is when I come next time. I'll leave these materials here so you can experiment and prepare to tell me why each happened."

Off he went, leaving the children to discuss, experiment, and think. The first three steps of the scientific method had been done: a problem had been posed, data collected, and a hypothesis drawn.

When Mr. Hadlow returned to Miss Collins's room, the reasons for the phenomena were listed on the chalkboard. The list looked like this:

Wax and water do not mix.
Gasoline and water do not mix.
Turpentine and water do not mix.

The red stuff in the lamp does not mix with the clear stuff in the lamp.
Cotton absorbs water.
Polyesters do not absorb water.

And the generalization that had resulted from a long discussion was also written on the chalkboard: some materials do not absorb other materials; some materials resist other materials.

"A truth," said Mr. Hadlow, "is a fact that remains constant when put to test again and again. I have made a chart here so we can check out our statement. For the next few minutes and then for a few days, let's see if your statement remains constant under test. In each of these tables, Miss Collins and I have listed some materials. You are to try them out and fill out the chart with as many examples as you can. Let's do a couple together so you will understand what we are doing.

Some Materials Resist Other Materials

This Material	Resists	This Material
Wax paper	RESISTS	Water
Gasoline	RESISTS	Water
Turpentine	RESISTS	Water
Polyester	RESISTS	Water

The students experimented on the piles of materials on the various tables, and the following items had been added to the chart at the end of fifteen minutes.

This Material	Resists	This Material
Oil	RESISTS	Water
Crayon	RESISTS	Water
Nylon	RESISTS	Water
Dacron	RESISTS	Water
Wood stain	RESISTS	Water
Floor wax	RESISTS	Water
Furniture polish	RESISTS	Water
Enamel	RESISTS	Water

Using Miss Collins's previous lesson on solubles, Mr. Hadlow led the children into a discussion of water bases. They concluded that some paints and dyes were water soluble and that water could be changed in color by the addition of these materials. Basically, however, it was still water, so all the words on the right side of the chart could be changed to read water paints or water dyes.

After a while Mr. Hadlow introduced a new chart and asked the children to work on both charts until the following day when he would return. At the end of the day the new chart looked like Fig. 7–9.

Mr. Hadlow and Miss Collins had completed the first four steps of the scientific method: the children had identified a problem, collected a body of facts, tested their hypothesis, and recorded the results of their work. Mr. Hadlow then took these facts one at a time and probed the children into discovering the art processes that were possible as a result of this knowledge. Working with Miss Collins, he carefully planned the experiences so they tied in with the subjects being taught in the classroom; each process was taught to meet a specific objective. Some of the "discoveries" and products resulting from this experience are recounted below:

1. Using the knowledge that enamel paint is soluble in

SOME MATERIALS ARE COMPATIBLE		
THIS MATERIAL ⟶	ABSORBS OR MIXES WITH ⟶	THIS MATERIAL
cotton	"	water
paper	"	water
enamel paint	"	turpentine
enamel paint	"	gasoline
tempera	"	water
powder paint	"	water
latex	"	water
acrylic	"	water
oil paints	mix with	linseed oil
oil paints	mix with	turpentine
oil paints	mix with	gasoline
paper	absorbs	enamel paint

FIGURE 7–9.   A chart of compatible materials.

gasoline and water resists enamel paint, the children brought partially used cans of paint from home workshops and attics, thinned them with turpentine, and dropped them on top of water, where they spread and mingled in fascinating patterns. Mr. Hadlow encouraged the children to "pick up" the designs with a paper that would absorb both the enamel paint and the water. Some children later experimented with the process using colored paper, glass, boxes, and three-dimensional objects. The process of "marbleizing" was literally discovered by these children through the application of the scientific method. The children later used marbleized paper for backing for bulletin-board displays, for covers for notebooks and scrapbooks, for the fly leaf of books (when they explored bookbinding), and for freshening up old, worn paperclip holders and other small containers used in the classroom.

2. Using the knowledge that paper absorbs water (or water paint) and that wax and wax crayons resist water (or water paint), the children experimented by coloring on manila paper with wax crayons and then washing the whole business with colored water paint. This activity was carried out in relation to a field trip where the class went to collect and study the shapes, colors, and smells of various spring flowers. Some of the very beautiful designs that resulted were used for framing and for notebook and scrapbook covers.

3. Using the knowledge that wax resists water dye and that cloth absorbs water, Mr. Hadlow introduced the ancient art of batik one day when the children were involved in a study of the Orient. Discovering that wax melted at one hundred degrees Farenheit and that it could be spread like paint was a new experience for the children.

Care was taken to instruct the children in the hazards of hot wax. It was concluded that six people would work at a time around a table where two cupcake tins were sitting on a hot plate. In some of the sections of the cupcake tins clear paraffin and beeswax were melted (a good science lesson came out of an exploration of the reasons for combining these two types of wax). Other sections contained various kinds of melted wax materials—melted crayons, melted candles, and heated commercial wax. The children asked such questions as, "Why can't we paint our designs on the cloth with liquid wax like our mothers put on their floors?" Mr. Hadlow's response was, "Why not?" He warned the children, of course, that their idea might not work, but he also pointed out the fact that risk-taking and adventuring were part of the process of creating and so they should feel free to try with the understanding that their idea might fail and that they should not be disappointed.

The work with melted wax crayons was also an experiment. One smart child had observed that the crayons were colored through some process, and that, whatever it was, that color might color the material like a dye. So some children experimented with batik by putting colored wax crayon directly onto the material before dyeing it; others applied melted colored wax crayons to the material before dyeing it. There were some fascinating results, and the children really discovered a new resist process.

Batik was so interesting to these children that they all made scarves, ties, and smocks (from men's old shirts). Many of the products were given to mothers for Christmas gifts. The children also saw practical use for batik in making special curtains for their puppet show, *The Five Chinese Brothers,* and regular scenery for their puppet play. A few used batik to make wall hangings, bookmarks, sweatshirt designs, dollhouse curtains, bedroom curtains, napkins, and placemats.

Science lessons came from the fact that gasoline dissolved wax, so the materials could be rinsed in gasoline to remove the wax from the materials. When some of the material remained stiff after the rinsing, Mr. Hadlow reminded them that by heating the wax they could get paper to absorb it. Consequently, when the dyed material was placed between two sheets of newsprint and pressed with a hot iron, the remaining wax was drawn from the material into the paper.

4. Using the knowledge that string, like cloth, absorbs water dye, Mr. Hadlow introduced tie-dyeing. He showed that areas that were tied off with string would be unaffected by dye because the string absorbed all the dye before it reached the material. The children realized that they could add another item to their chart when Miss Collins introduced the fact that rubber bands could be used instead of string, because rubber resists water. All sorts of experiments resulted—folding the cloth in various ways for different effects, tying and dyeing in a variety of ways, making a variety of knots in the material to see what would happen, and tying various objects such as nuts, bolts, chunks of wood, paperclips, scissors, and a host of other water-resistant items into the cloth for a variety of shapes. The children had a great many opportunities to explore and create with their new-found skill. They made backdrop curtains for a puppet show and front curtains for an assembly program dramatization.

They made gifts such as placemats, scarves, neckties, and cloth book covers. Some of the children made curtains for their bedrooms or articles of clothing to wear. But the most fun of all was when everyone brought a cotton undershirt to school, dyed it to suit his own taste, and then, a few days later, wore it to school with a matching skirt or pair of slacks for a tie-dye party held by the class. At this party the placemats were tie-dyed, the entertainment was given before the tie-dyed curtains, and the programs had tie-dyed cloth covers. Needless to say, Mr. Hadlow and Miss Collins also wore T-shirts that they had tie-dyed along with the children.

The experiences that Mr. Hadlow and Miss Collins planned from the science lessons above were manifold. Only some of them have been described here. Lack of space prohibits more detailed descriptions of how the children learned how to "crackle" by covering cloth with wax and squeezing it so dye ran into the cracks in the cloth to create a fascinating background for block prints and other batik designs, or how the children were led to discover that scratching wax off a surface can create a very different effect when the surface below is exposed in a variety of ways. This resulted in some fascinating designs on a Halloween bulletin board.

Enough has been said of this unit, however, for the reader to see the tremendous possibilities of fusing science and art when two teachers plan carefully together so that art has meaning, processes are understood, and scientific principles are practiced.

We have discussed at great length the need to develop perception and visual skills in children and to provide experiences related to all the senses. Many experiences can be provided in the science curriculum to develop perceptive and sensory skills. For instance, in the primary grades, teachers often hatch chickens in their classrooms. Children are taught to observe and record the progress of the eggs daily. As small differences in height, weight, color, temperature, and size are noted, the child's perceptions develop.

In the middle grades, children carry out such activities as making a time-lapse film of a flower opening or taking pictures of a plant growing. They sharpen their perceptions as they view the films and pictures for small differences taking place from frame to frame.

The type of observation required in observing the process of all scientific experimentation sharpens children's perception.

ART AND MATHEMATICS

Not long ago, art exemplified the free, the open-ended, the flexible, the fluid, and the creative in the minds of men, and mathematics represented the law-bound, the closed, the rigid, the frozen, and the uncreative in the minds of men. A more modern belief allows for a much less rigid version of mathematics. The new math in the elementary school has shown that although the products of mathematics are generally precise and predetermined, the processes of mathematics can be very creative.

Does art bear enough relationship to mathematics at the elementary school level to allow the type of integration we have been talking about to take place with any sort of meaning to the young child?

When we consider the strategies employed by the classroom teacher in teaching math, we can see that math affords considerable opportunities for art experience, and art ability can greatly enhance the mathematical experience.

Consider the number of times a teacher tells a child, "Draw ten Indians" or "Draw four apples." Consider the frequency with which a modern math teacher uses a bulletin board to demonstrate a number concept or to develop a number fact. The creative use of these materials can develop art abilities in children considerably. And, if creatively used, they can develop his creativity as well. Westcott and Smith show how this can be done.[4] In the creation and construction of mathematical games, for instance, creativity can be promoted to a great extent.

Many of the exercises in mathematics workbooks are a block to creative development. In an attempt to test whether or not children know the cardinal value of numbers, for instance, one workbook says, "Draw four apples like this one" and a simple drawing of an apple is given. A creative teacher recognizes that exercises such as these merely call for memorization skills and do not contribute to the child's perceptual, sensory, or creative development. She can make the assignment more creative, more open-ended, more challenging, and yet test the same learning by rewording it as follows: "On a piece of paper draw four boxes and in each one draw something you saw on your way to school this morning" or "Draw six boxes and in each one draw something you heard on your way to school this morning."

4. Alvin M. Westcott and James A. Smith, *Creative Teaching of Mathematics in the Elementary School* (Boston: Allyn and Bacon, Inc., 1967).

Art, like math, is based on the relationship of elements. In Miss Nowell's classroom the children made a collection of all the places they could find circles in their environment. Their exhibit included tires, hub caps, gears, a pie plate, a gas burner, a plate, a saucer, a cake plate, a clock, measuring spoons, a bubble blower, a butterfly-net frame, a doorknob, samples of money, a lifesaver, a candy lifesaver, a pan, a piece of hose, a battery, a bottle, a vase, a milk-bottle top, a button, an earring, a set of "granny" eyeglasses, a television dial, a wastebasket, a buckle, and a steering wheel. The children, for an activity, made composite paintings using only circles. These were very effective and showed unusual ability in creative thinking.

Research has shown us that children who are allowed to manipulate and explore materials and objects at an early age are more creative when they mature. In a kindergarten or primary grade where art materials are a common part of a child's environment, manipulation of these materials can contribute a great deal to the child's background of mathematics experience. Seeing tempera paint in half-pint jars or seeing paint in quart cans over and over makes possible the understanding of the concept of quart and half pint at a later date, when some teacher attempts to tie an arithmetic experience to the child's experiential background. In many classrooms such experiences are so numerous (and so obvious) that they are often taken for granted and not used at a teachable moment. Consider, for instance, the degree to which measures can be taught in cutting paper from a roll for scenery or a bulletin board in measuring powdered paint for mixing, or in measuring liquid or powered dyes for doing tie-dyeing or batik. The teaching of fractional parts can be related to making papier mâché, glue, or fingerpaint from a recipe. The teaching of ordinal values ties in naturally with placing paintings in order on a mural, in a roll movie, or at an exhibit, and with figuring of frames per foot of film in developing an animated cartoon. Addition, subtraction, multiplication, and division exercises are a part of figuring the cost, distribution, and inventory of class materials (How many scissors are still missing from the scissors holder?).

Mathematics are needed to accomplish certain art projects, such as measuring space for a frieze or mural, making certain architectural or mechanical drawings, and constructing models (especially to scale).

It appears that mathematics is a tool for certain kinds of art expression. Conversely, there are times when art can become a tool for mathematics. A classroom teacher can make art serve

both purposes by using it in both capacities in her class curriculum.

ART AND MUSIC

In Chapter 1 Miss Hill used art and music together to teach
musical facts and to provide the opportunity for children to show
their creative ability.   Many related music and art projects grew
out of this lesson.   In the account of Miss Larkin's puppet show,
music was an integral part of the entire project.

At the festival of the arts described in this chapter, music
was enjoyed in many ways—through a band concert by the children, through solos played by individuals on their instruments,
and through recordings played as background music for various
exhibits.   The music and art teachers worked independently of
each other in developing and perfecting those activities that fell
logically under their jurisdiction.   But a project such as an arts
festival requires a great deal of team planning among the art
teacher, the music teacher, the physical education teacher, and
the classroom teachers.   Such planning was evident in the products that resulted: the puppet show, the dance numbers, and the
skits, all built around the theme of the flapper era; the production
of the two motion-picture films with soundtracks; the animal
parade (Fig. 7–10) utilizing music created by the children themselves; and the many musical accompaniments to the individual
presentations of the entertainment.

It is virtually impossible to separate music from art for a
very long period of time in the elementary school.   One seems
eventually to lead the other, probably because they blend and
complement each other so well.   Art is the most common *visual*
form of man's expression of his creativity, and music is his most
common *audio* form; combined they make creative expression
richer and more exciting.

In most of the accounts of art projects and activities in
this book, music is eventually utilized in one way or another.
Some teachers deliberately pose open-ended problems to children using art and music together.   The most common of these is
perhaps the one where the teacher puts several media (with
which the children have already had experience) on a table
before the children and says, "I am going to play a recording.
Select any medium you wish from the table and use it the way
the music tells you to."

FIGURE 7–10.   The parade of the animals.

Although some art teachers frown on this activity, the authors have seen children become very responsive in their approach to media through the use of this technique. Freedom and enjoyment come to many children.

The danger of using a strategy like this comes in over-using it, in expecting all children to react to it, or in limiting the media to one choice. Obviously, the teacher's objectives must be clear, although they can be manifold. In the above illustration, for instance, one teacher was using the technique described because she felt her students were very inhibited. They drew or painted only real things—factual representations—and she felt this particular type of motivation would free them to use design and color more. With about eighty percent of the children it worked.

Other objectives for employing this strategy might be as follows:

1. To help children understand that "feeling" or "mood" can be expressed visually.
2. To help children feel the rhythm of music and a corresponding rhythm to painting.

3. To help children feel a variety of rhythms in music (by playing several recordings).
4. To help children visualize music.
5. To show children that a variety of interpretations of music with a variety of media are logical.

Mr. Thompson brought some copies of great paintings into his classroom and asked the children to gather in groups around the painting that, for any reason, they enjoyed most. Each group was then asked to search through the school record collection (or their home collection if one was available) to select a record suggested by the painting. The selections were shared and evaluated simply by having the other children react to them. No attempt was made to impose any group's choice on another group. For the next several days, one painting was displayed in the beauty center in the room and the record chosen by the group was played before school and during study periods.

Some teachers have children interpret paintings (especially abstract paintings) with music, props, or dancing.

One creative teacher asked older brothers and sisters from the high school to come in and play their musical instruments for her class. At the close of the demonstration she had the children choose a medium and paint the sound of the instrument, that is, the squeak of the violin, the boom of the drum, the wailing of the saxophone, etc. The results of these explorations in color, line, intensity, and sound were most remarkable.

Children enjoy dramatizing their favorite songs, especially holiday songs such as "Frosty, the Snowman" and "Rudolph, the Rednosed Reindeer." When these are adapted to "polished" dramatizations or to puppet shows many art experiences can be included.

Mr. Burke used music from *Swan Lake, Nutcracker Suite,* and *The Firefly* to develop some dance interpretations. The results were so enjoyable that the children went on to polish one into a "mini-ballet," which they presented at a school assembly. The artwork that went into the making of the costumes and background was especially creative. The children tie-dyed sheets to give the effect of flames. To add to the effect, flashing lights behind the sheets silhouetted the dancers at times. The costumes for the production were all individually made from crepe paper; the entire group first explored the many things that could be done with crepe paper, then each child was left to his own resources to create his own costume.

Art and music become partners when the children read

about the lives of the composers and present them through the use of the flannelboard, shadow plays, puppet dramatizations, or musical skits.

Mrs. Wilkins was working with dramatics. She used open-ended situations to develop the children's creative-thinking ability. One day she had the children dramatize forms. This worked so successfully that she tried it with music. On cards which she placed before the class, she put a green triangle, two blue squiggles, a yellow oval, a red free form, and an orange trapezoid. She asked any child who had an idea to select music that would go with any card. The children could choose a recording, suggest a known song which the class would sing, play an instrument from the box of percussion instruments in the room, or create a piece of music. For the blue squiggles, Brenda chose "The Blue Danube." For the red form, Ron played "The Sabre Dance." For the orange trapezoid Marcia wrote her own poem and played it on the metallophone to her own music:

Words

You're just a shape
By day—But night
Makes you a lampshade
Shining bright.

Buddy said the green triangle made him think of Joyce Kilmer's *Trees*, so the class sang it together.

In the elementary school curriculum music and art appear to be natural companions for the development of each child's creativity.

SUMMARY

Art is life. It is inconceivable, then, to teach or practice art in isolation from those experiences that constitute life.

A child spends over half of his waking hours at school. Consequently, the experiences he encounters there (including the study of his major subjects) make up at least half of his life and constitute the largest segment of the reservoir of resources from which he draws in order to create, especially in art.

A conscientious attempt should be made in all school programs to integrate art with the subjects studied in school and create a cyclic role. Other subjects provide skills and content for art expression, and art expression provides an outlet for communicating learning in a creative manner.

Art teaching relates to each of the subjects in a unique manner.   Consequently, a union of art with any other curriculum area is not a difficult task.   The social studies are areas selected from the social sciences that explore the problems of man socially, historically, economically, anthropologically, geographically, and politically.   They delve into topics with which man has been confronted through the ages: food, clothing, courtesies, shelter, values, economics, politics, history, geography, transportation, and communication.   Through the ages specific problems have changed, but they can still be classified under the same general headings.

Art is, in all fairness, a social study.   It has its history, and man's relations to man has been depicted in its geography. Art has provided a manner of record keeping, a means of expressing a man's aesthetic qualities throughout the ages.   It is related to clothing, food, values, perception, transportation, communication, politics, economics, education, and life styles, especially as they relate to perception, sensitivity, and empathy.   But it goes beyond this: it is a study of the soul of man, his dreams and aspirations, an outward means of expressing his inward beauty.   It is his creativity expressed at all stages of his individual development.   Most of all, whereas social studies deal largely in generalities with due homage paid to individual men of great ideas, all art speaks for the individual man: it is a record of the individual's contribution to each culture.   It is, indeed, an umbrella that overhangs all the areas of the social studies curriculum.

Art is also a means of communication.   The language arts curriculum in today's elementary school is concerned with developing standard and effective means of communication in each student.   Thus art and language arts have a common goal, for art in any form is effective communication.   Their difference lies in the fact that one deals with verbal and the other with nonverbal communication.

Inasmuch as other areas of the curriculum attempt to accomplish objectives similar to those objectives defined for the art program, these areas can become closely allied to art and each can contribute to the development of the child's creativity.   Each can also contribute to the other in developing creative expression. These areas include dramatics, movement education, and music.

Mathematics and science are curriculum areas that have roots in art history and that may be taught along with art experiences.   Conversely, art experience can become a highly motivating aid in teaching math and science.

Even though art forms an umbrella area under which all subjects may be grouped, because of its great contribution to the affective and cognitive learnings of man, it also stands alone. Many experiences should be provided in the school curriculum where art is taught in relation to other subjects, but many experiences should also be planned where art is taught for art's sake. Planning for such experiences means setting conditions in the classroom that make possible the expression of creative thinking in art forms.   Art is a manifestation of creativity.

ACTIVITIES

1. Visit a classroom or study your own.   Note all the ways children express themselves visually.   In how many instances are these visual forms inspired by some area of the curriculum other than art?
2. Take a modern social studies unit on a topic such as drugs and see how many real art experiences you can plan from it.
3. Following is an excerpt that presents a point of view different from the one expressed in this chapter.   Discuss it in relation to what you have just read.
   Eisner states:
   Art education, I believe, has unique contributions to make to education.   Although it might be necessary at various times to use art for other purposes in education, those other purposes should be conceived of as short-term goals that are necessary for the achievement of those aims that only art can provide.[5]
4. Examine some children's paintings and then discuss the following statements.   Which one do you feel is true?
   a. Children paint what they know, not what they see.
   b. Children can only paint what they see, not what they know.
5. Recall a childhood experience that you have remembered over the years.   To what degree were your senses involved in this experience?   Do you feel your memory was affected by the degree of sensory involvement?

5. Reprinted with permission of Macmillan Publishing Co., Inc. from *Educating Artistic Vision* by Elliot W. Eisner. Copyright © 1972, by Elliot W. Eisner.

6. Try your hand at the following:
   a. Paint joy, mirth, revenge, hate, bitterness, and fear.
   b. Paint the linear movement of the steps of the Watusi and the waltz.
   c. Paint while a rock-and-roll record is playing.
   d. Paint a painting entitled *Red* without using red, *Blue* with no blues, etc.
7. Working in a group, experiment with making a film on "the children's art world" to be used to explain your art program to parents at a PTA meeting. Plan titles, soundtrack, music, and dialogue. Explore the possibilities of using animation and puppets in the film. Let yourself go—any 8mm camera will allow you to have many exciting art experiences.
8. Take a theme from one of the following:
   a. Pollution is ruining the country.
   b. Make love, not war.
   c. Here comes the judge.
   d. I never thought I'd eat the whole thing.
   e. Play it again, Sam.
   f. Winter sports.
      Working in groups, have half the group write about the topic and the other half paint about it. Compare results: which were the more communicative and what were the differences in the methods of communication?
9. Brainstorm all the ways you could use a dance pattern to motivate children to art activities.
10. Make a painting or crayon drawing that shows the magic of numbers.

SELECTED BIBLIOGRAPHY

Baranski, Matthew. *Graphic Design.* Scranton, Pa.: Intext Educational Publishers, 1960.

Barron, Frank. *Creativity and Psychological Health.* New York: Van Nostrand Reinhold Co., 1963.

Bassett, Richard, ed. *The Open Eye in Learning: The Role of Art in General Education.* Cambridge, Mass.: The M.I.T. Press, 1969.

Bereiter, C., and S. Englemann. *Teaching Disadvantaged Children in the Preschool.* Englewood Cliffs, N.J.: Prentice-Hall, Inc., 1966.

Bland, Jane C. *Art and the Young Child.* New York: Museum of Modern Art, 1968.

Canaday, John. *Keys to Art.* New York: Tudor Publishing Co., 1963.

Capers, Roberta M., and Jerrold Maddox. *Images and Imagination: An Introduction to Art.* New York: The Ronald Press Co., 1965.

Chase, Alice Elizabeth. *Famous Paintings.* New York: Platt & Munk, 1962.

Conant, Howard, and Arne Randall. *Art in Education.* Peoria, Ill.: Chas. A. Bennett Co., Inc., 1963.

Culbert, Samuel A., and Jerry Fisher. "The Medium of Art as an Adjunct to Learning in Sensitivity Training," *Journal of Creative Behavior,* 3, 1 (1969), 26–40.

Doerner, Max. *The Materials of the Artist,* rev. ed. Trans. by Eugene Neuhaus. New York: Harcourt Brace Jovanovich, Inc., 1969.

Feldman, Edmund. "Engaging Art in Dialogue." *Concepts in Art and Education.* George Pappas, ed. New York: Macmillan Publishing Co., Inc., 1970.

Greene, Marie Zoe. *Gallery Book for Children.* Chicago: Department of Education, Art Institute of Chicago.

Hastie, M. Reid, ed. *Art Education. Sixty-fourth Yearbook of the National Society for the Study of Education.* Chicago: University of Chicago Press, 1965.

Horn, George. *Art for Today's Schools.* Worcester, Mass.: Davis Publications, Inc., 1969.

———. *Bulletin Boards.* New York: Van Nostrand Reinhold Co., 1962.

Jameson, Kenneth. *Art and the Young Child.* New York: The Viking Press, Inc., 1968.

Johnson, Charlotte Buel. *Contemporary Art: Exploring Its Roots and Development.* Worcester, Mass.: Davis Publications, Inc., 1972.

Lacey, Richard. *Seeing with Feeling.* Philadelphia: W. B. Saunders Co., 1972.

Levi, Julian. *Modern Art: An Introduction.* New York: Pitman Publishing Corp., 1961.

Lewis, Hilda P. *Child Art, The Beginnings of Self-Affirmation.* Berkeley, Calif.: Diablo Press, 1966.

Loughran, Bernice. *Art Experiences.* New York: Harcourt Brace Jovanovich, Inc., 1963.

Luca, Mark, and Robert Kent. *Art Education: Strategies of Teaching.* Englewood Cliffs, N.J.: Prentice-Hall, Inc., 1968.

McFee, June King. *Preparation for Art.* Belmont, Calif.: Wadsworth Publishing Co., Inc., 1961.

McIlvain, Dorothy S. *Art for the Primary Grades.* New York: G. P. Putnam's Sons, 1961.

Montgomery, Chandler. *Art for Teachers of Children.* Columbus, Ohio: Charles E. Merrill Publishing Co., 1968.

Munro, Eleanor C. *The Golden Encyclopedia of Art.* New York: Golden Press (Western Publishing Co.), 1961.

Randall, Arne W., and Ruth Elsie Halvorsen. *Painting in the Classroom.* Belmont, Calif.: Fearon Publishers, 1970.

Rueschoff, Phil, and Evelyn Swartz. *Teaching Art in the Elementary School.* New York: The Ronald Press Co., 1970.

Seiden, Don. "The Metro Experience." *Programs of Promise: Art in the Schools.* Al Hurwitz, ed. New York: Harcourt Brace Jovanovich, Inc., 1972.

Smith, Ralph A. "The Liberal Tradition and Art Education." *Concepts in Art and Education.* George Pappas, ed. New York: Macmillan Publishing Co., 1970.

Taylor, Calvin W., and Frank E. Williams. *Instructional Media and Creativity.* New York: John Wiley & Sons, Inc., 1966.

Yochim, Louise Dunn. *Perceptual Growth in Creativity.* Scranton, Pa.: Intext Educational Publishers, 1967.

CHAPTER VIII

Media, Materials, and Tools

But my children wander wondering among tummocks
of junk
like stunted starvelings cruelly set free
at a heaped banquet of food too rich to eat.

JOHN UPDIKE[1]

This chapter is planned to be of special help to the teacher who is largely responsible for teaching art in the classroom and to the art team responsible for ordering supplies and setting up art centers.

John Updike's quotation is a stunning statement about the availability of art resources. We often hear teachers say that they cannot carry on a respectable program because they have so few art supplies. Almost any environment offers an unlimited number of supplies—but not always the right ones. Some supplies are basic, such as scissors, paint, and paper, but, at times, substitutes can even be found for these.

In Chapter 4 we discussed various viewpoints regarding the introduction and use of media. In this chapter we would like to alert the reader to the many types of media and tools available and to some ideas for their use. Because many supplies can be salvaged from the environment, a teacher should give careful consideration to her expenditures when limited funds are available for media and materials.

The first criterion for the use of any art material is that it

1. Reprinted with permission of Alfred A. Knopf, Inc. from John Updike, "My Children at the Dump," *Midpoint & Other Poems* (New York: Alfred A. Knopf, Inc., 1969). Copyright 1969 by John Updike.

facilitate the self-expression of children and not serve as a stumbling block. A second criterion closely allied to the first one is that the art material afford the child the opportunity to experience mastery or self-assurance. Otherwise it is a poor choice for that particular developmental age.

Remember that in art expression a child is solving a personal problem with the media available. He will select the one that best helps him to solve it.

MEDIA FOR CREATIVE EXPRESSION

Paints

Tempera Paint. Tempera paint is without a doubt the most useful of all the paints. It now comes packaged in squeeze-bottle containers, which make it easier to handle. Pints seem to be the most economical size for a variety of reasons. If the jar is broken, you only lose a pint and not half your supply. The size is easier for young children to handle, and the smaller container makes it easier to keep the paint mixed. If you are forced to accept glass jars with the built-in problem of removing stuck lids, take the lids off the jars that you are using and replace the lids with watercolor cups or large jam-jar covers that will sit on the top. This means that the paint can be spilled, but at least the children can get at it without the intervention of the strongest custodian. Most tempera paints now come in plastic jars, which remove the hazard of breakage.

It is surprising how few colors are vitally necessary for an art program. Light blue, red, yellow, black, and white can be combined to make practically any color desired. The addition of a green and an orange speeds up the mixing process and extends the range somewhat. Browns are extremely easy to mix from these colors and are usually much more pleasing than the ready-mixed colors. All of this presupposes that the children are going to have the freedom to mix their own colors.

Fingerpaint. Fingerpaint is a far more flexible material than is generally realized. In addition to its normal function, it makes a good printing ink. It can be applied in a number of ways and, unlike tempera color, is transparent. It is not manufactured in as many colors as tempera paint.

Watercolors. Watercolors are supplied in pans or tubes in an ink-like consistency. Soft brushes are required for their use and water is needed to soften them. They are difficult for young children to control and manipulate. They are of value with older groups of children, especially when painting outdoors or in some situation where paints need to be transported.

Paper

Manila Paper. One of the cheapest and most useful of all papers is manila. It has a creamy color and usually has a slight tooth to it. It is good for use with tempera and other water-based paints because it has a tendency to dry flat and to resist wrinkling. It works well as a printing paper and folds well. It should not be stored for longer than one year. Many papers become extremely brittle when stored for any length of time; it does not pay to buy large quantities unless the paper is to be used within a reasonable amount of time.

Ditto Paper. Ditto paper, which in the past has been one of the few plentiful supplies in schools, is ideal for printing because of its slightly absorbent surface.

Newsprint. Newsprint, which is identical to the material on which the daily paper is printed, is great for working with paint at an easel, but it is not nearly as good with crayons, for it tends to tear too easily. It is a relatively inexpensive paper.

Art Paper. Art paper is packaged in multiples of a 9 inch by 12 inch format (the next size up is 12 inches by 18 inches, and so on). The larger sizes, which are in many cases more desirable, are difficult to store since they must be kept flat. Large folders are one solution; tie tapes keep the paper tight and prevent it from falling to the bottom of the folder.

Construction Paper. Construction paper, another basic, is again one of those papers with a limited shelf life. It will fade very rapidly if exposed to sunlight. Poster paper is the same material, but it is approximately half as thick. This is much better for younger children, because they are able to cut it much more easily when it is folded. Many art activities depend upon the child's ability to cut folded paper. Poster paper also works well for such things as paste-ups, where the heavier construction paper is not needed.

Cardboard. Chipboard is an inexpensive, heavy cardboard that is useful in almost any situation. It is almost too heavy for young children to cut, but an ordinary papercutter makes short work of it. Cardboard is also available in many other different and decorative finishes. It is nice to have them available, but if you are on a limited budget chipboard is enough for basic needs.

Tagboard. Tagboard is a thin cardboard that comes in colored or plain sheets. It is more durable and stronger than construction paper and thus is suitable for paper construction projects, book covers, shadow puppets, greeting cards, and the like.

White Drawing Paper. White drawing paper is one of the few "musts" for the effective art program. It comes in all sizes and weights and can be used with nearly all art media.

Fingerpaint Paper. Fingerpaint paper has a smooth side and a dull side; the smooth, shiny side absorbs so little it almost resists paint. Consequently it is easy to move thick paint about on the surface by blowing or pushing. Children can work on the paper for a while before the materials dry out.

Bogus Paper. Bogus paper is a heavy, gray, rough-textured paper. It is relatively inexpensive. Because it is highly absorbent, it is used for special projects with tempera and other water-based paints. Its rough texture makes possible unusual effects with crayons, chalk, pencil, and charcoal.

Matt Board. Matt board is smooth on one side and a pebbled tan on the other. It is heavy and strong. It is used for mounting and displaying paintings or prints and as a base for constructing collages.

Rice Paper. Rice paper is a thin, almost transparent, tough paper. It is absorbent and is generally used for printing.

Watercolor Paper. A firm, heavy, slightly textured paper that comes in various grades, watercolor paper, as the name implies, is designed for watercolor paints, although it is also effective for ink, pencil, and charcoal.

Tissue Paper. A very thin paper, tissue paper is used commercially for wrapping, but it has many other exciting uses in art. It is used in collages, crafts, printing, and making pictures with polymer. It comes in breathtaking colors.

Crepe Paper. Crepe paper has unusual stretching qualities. It, too, can be purchased in stunning colors and color combinations. Its soft qualities allow it to fold and fall in ways similar to cloth. It can be pulled, wetted, stretched, crushed, cut, and twisted. It is excellent for making displays, costumes, and decorations.

Chalk

Regular white blackboard chalk (especially the soft type) comes in exciting colors and can be used wet or dry on almost any surface. It can be used especially effectively on dark-colored construction or bogus paper. It is useful for murals, scenery, coloring large areas, or stenciling. It requires a fixative.

Crayons

Crayons are perhaps the most versatile of all the art materials available; it is worthwhile buying the best grade possible. If possible, every child should have his own to use whenever he desires. Although there are special thick ones for kindergarteners, it has been the authors' experience that many children in kindergarten find the thick crayons too cumbersome. Soft wax crayons, although they have a tendency to break more readily, are much more useful than the harder-pressed varieties. They are usually packed eight or sixteen to a box.

Pastes and Glues

Regular school paste is usually available in most schools. It has its uses, but it can be a very real source of frustration for children. It takes a fair amount of technique to get things to stick together; applying it with the fingers usually results in a coating over everything. Wallpaper paste is a great all-purpose material. It works well where material is to be stuck down or mounted, and it has the great advantage that one can apply it with a brush. An easel brush works as well as anything. Wallpaper paste can be made to any consistency desired—just remember to add the paste to water, because adding water to the paste spells disaster and results in nothing but lumps. When constructions need to be joined together, a rubber cement is ideal. It rubs off the hands as soon as it is dry, and it may be used as contact cement— glue is applied to the two surfaces that are to be joined, the surfaces are left to dry for a moment, and then they are brought together. The bond is immediate and very strong. White glue, which is a vinyl product, has a wide range of uses, but tends to be too expensive for general use in the classroom.

Airplane Cement. Airplane cement is excellent for light construction work, such as construction with toothpicks, popsicle sticks, balsa wood, drinking straws, and light plastics. It dries rapidly. Some schools no longer use it because its fumes, if sniffed over a period of time, can have ill effects on children.

Clays

Clay of some sort should be included as a basic material. The easiest type to handle is the oilbound nonhardening type, which goes under many trade names. The better quality products do not become hard and difficult for young children to manipulate after storage. Whether or not to buy it in different colors is a matter of preference. Using one color has the advantage of help-

FIGURE 8–1.   A clay pot by a middle-school child.

FIGURE 8–2.   Grandmother in Clay *by a middle-school child.*

ing the child to recognize form as distinct from color. Even though this type of clay does not dry out, it works best if it is kept in an airtight container. Clays that need firing can be bought in powder or moist form. Moist clay makes life a great deal easier. If a large, covered crock is not available, it can be kept in plastic bags. Ceramics is a specialized activity that is well within the reach of anyone; however, the teacher must have a good deal of background knowledge before she can use it with young children. Moist clays that can be hardened by drying or baking in a cooking oven make a good substitute. In the primary grades, where the manipulation of materials is very important, Play-doh often provides a good substitute for clay. Play-doh can be purchased or easily made by the teacher (see p. 315). It comes in a variety of colors, and its advantage over clay is that it does not set up.

Plasticene. When permanent form is not as important to the child as manipulation, Plasticene is the ideal medium. It is much like clay, but it has an oil base so that it can be molded and will not set up. Plasticene does not harden, so the child can enjoy a Plasticene shape for a period of time and then reshape it when he feels a need to change it.

Inks

Printing is not only a favorite pastime among young children, it is also one of the most valuable in terms of learning experiences. Materials can be very simple; the only supplies that are really necessary are brayers and printing ink. Printing ink is usually oil-based, which makes for difficulties in clean-up. Preferable are the water-based inks, which can be rolled out onto almost any surface without the risk of staining and which can be readily cleaned up with a wet sponge.

TOOLS FOR CREATIVE EXPRESSION

Palettes

Old cafeteria trays are ideal as palettes, for they keep the paint within bounds and serve many other useful purposes. If the paints are placed in a central location, the children can bring their trays up and help themselves to the needed color. A tea-spoon left in each jar helps to keep the colors clean. This makes far less mess than having a limited number of jars and people darting about with brushes dripping paint.

Brushes

One of the golden rules of painting is to use the largest possible brush that will do the job. Flat-bristled brushes are by far the most useful and are capable of making a wide variety of strokes. The most useful size is one-half inch, although it is a good idea to have some larger sizes available. Smaller, pointed watercolor brushes are nice to have around when there is a need for fine detail, but they are not a good tool for the young child. Painting techniques are discussed in Chapter 5.

For stenciling, a stiff brush with flat ends is needed.

Knives

Children can quite safely use knives under supervision. In a busy classroom a knife is almost indispensable. Utility knives, which have a relatively thick handle, are much easier for the younger child to hold than X-acto knives. These blades are extremely sharp, which means that material can be cut with a minimum of effort. This is one of the factors that makes them comparatively safe, for the child is better able to control their action.

Scissors

Many primary classrooms are equipped with blunt-ended scissors as a safety precaution. This limits their usefulness as a tool, and it is doubtful if there is a greater safety factor. Scissors are the ideal tool to make holes in things, and blunt-ended scissors just will not do the job. It is important to have several pairs of left-handed scissors available. Many left-handed children are able to learn to use the normal scissors, but they are hampered by not being able to do so well.

Brayers

Brayers, rubber rollers mounted on wooden handles, are made in several widths and are often supplied in sets. They are indispensable for making prints and provide another means of applying paint.

Carpentry Tools

The best carpentry tools for your purpose are the smallest professional tools that the hardware store carries. Beware of the children's variety; they work poorly, require more effort, and on this score are more dangerous. A basic kit consists of a small saw with fine teeth (a cross-cut saw), a light hammer with a claw at one end for removing nails, a pair of pliers with a jaw that also cuts wire, a large and small screwdriver, and some C clamps. These are essential to hold the work to the table and minimize the risk of injury. Children should be taught never to work on wood unless it is secure; it is always the hand that is doing the holding that gets into trouble. Additional tools that extend the possibilities are a plane and some chisels. These are not as dangerous as they sound if they are always driven in with a mallet or a small block of wood. It has been the authors' experience that quite young children can be taught to use tools safely and well.   If you have an industrial arts department, the staff will without doubt be glad to help you select tools and provide information about fastening, gluing, and constructing.

NEW HORIZONS IN ART MEDIA

Inventions and Discoveries of the Technological Age

Paints.   Art has always been with us, but the means that we use to carry out our artistic intentions are changing.   This very often makes profound changes in our perception of art.   The development of oilbound paints in the fifteenth century by Flemish artists made widespread changes in the painting of the period. Paintings with the new medium were characterized by glowing light, deep tonality, and enamel-like surfaces.   These were quite different from paintings produced using opaque pigments bound with the whites and yolks of eggs.

In our century, the development of polymer paints, the acrylics, has produced a new range of effects that are being exploited by contemporary artists.   It is now possible to model onto the canvas heavy forms that would never have dried if they were produced with oil paint.   The many media now available to the painter have weakened old definitions of painting.   In many cases it is difficult to determine the boundary line between painting and sculpture.

Techniques.   Many techniques are now gathered together under the broad heading of fine art.   Both color and black-and-white photography are now well established as art forms and not merely mechanical means of capturing an image.   Industrial techniques are now being used to extend the artist's creative vision; the artist utilizes the skills of workers in metals, plastics, and electronics.   In the past, sculptors often made use of the skills of bronze workers who would cast the sculpture from the original clay model.   Today there is a complete symbiosis of artist and craftsman in some areas.   The artist produces the concept in drawings and plans; the craftsman produces the finished work.

Our modern technology has produced other unique art forms composed of transient images—for example, the motion picture.   Images can be produced electronically on cathode ray tubes. Projection equipment can be used to create images by techniques other than photography. The laser beam is now capable of producing "holograms," three-dimensional images in space.

New materials are becoming available every day; many of them are merely being used to create traditional art forms. Acceptance of some of the new things to come out of experimentation with these materials is slow and requires a constant redefinition of the content of art.

Architecture. Architecture, often called the mother of the arts, has a profound effect upon what we produce and how we produce it. One of the factors in the development of oil paints was the fact that Gothic architecture aimed at the elimination of the wall. There was no wall space for the huge frescoes that made up much of Italian art during this period. Artists turned to producing the kind of portable paintings that we are familiar with today. The reduction in scale required an increase in detail and a change in medium. Oil painting was the result.

Civilization is impossible without architecture. It is interesting to keep an accurate record of the actual time spent within a building during a twenty-four-hour period. For most of us, this far exceeds the time that we spend in the open. It is not surprising then that our perceptions, feelings, and total development are greatly determined by this shield of architecture that we draw around us.

Changes in architectural form are accepted only very slowly. Wooden houses have changed very little in form or construction throughout the history of this country. Even when we are able to accept radical departures for our commercial buildings or our churches, we insist on colonial styles for our homes. New materials and methods are capable of solving housing problems in revolutionary ways: mass-produced modules could be fitted together in an infinite number of plans; plastics could be used to produce structurally strong, weather-resistant exteriors and interiors that could be finished in one piece; buildings could be constructed that would not require traditional foundations or heating methods; houses could be designed that would not conform to the concept that rooms have to be rectangular. But humans resist change. The rectangle may have become dominant because of the ease with which it could be constructed with available materials, but, whatever the reason, it is the form that is universally demanded today.

This reluctance to make changes in our basic environment is reflected in much of the stereotyped thinking that takes place in other areas. It is difficult to think about art without thinking about the setting that we provide for it. We know that color can have some profound psychological effects on the viewer. Color associations are so strong that such things as mood, alertness, and the ability to function in various ways can be directly attributed to the color of the environment. In the same way, architecture exerts a profound influence. This is obvious in church architecture. We do not see the movie-theatre type of enclosure as suitable for worship. There are so many similarities between schools and other forms of architecture that we have to begin to question the effect that this might have on learning. There is a direct comparison between the long corridors and closed-doored rooms of our schools and the cell blocks of jails. Add visual clues such as fences, trucks, and materials and it is hard to decide if one is looking at a school or a factory. If the forms that our schools take is a direct offshoot of the function that we expect them to perform, then we should perhaps begin to question that function.

Application of New Media in the Classroom

Light.   Nearly every classroom teacher has access to overhead and slide projectors. These are seldom seen as an opportunity to involve the children in creative experiences. Their use depends upon a supply of available teaching material. The fact that they are not often used may be because they merely duplicate the use of books or chalkboards.

Projection techniques can provide a unique method of allowing the child to examine a reality that has already become fixed and is expressed only in clichés. Toys have a fixed size and are usually viewed from the same level and in the same context. Creative children try to vary the point of view by putting their heads to the ground to look up at the toy. It is difficult to imagine the toy soldier several feet high set in another world where distances are scarcely perceived. Projection makes it possible for him to create such an image.

If one believes that the process is as important as the image in the production of art, then found objects are a legitimate way of starting the process. One needs a transparent screen, which can be purchased or easily constructed. One also needs an overhead projector and a box of colored acetates or cellophane. This again can be purchased, but a great deal of

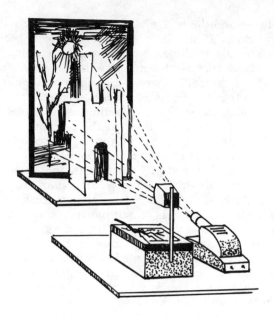

FIGURE 8-3. An excellent set-up for experimentation with light, color, and form.

cellophane can be salvaged from wrappings and packaging. One also needs a scrap box full of small toys and found objects such as bottletops, pieces of card, toothpicks, dried grass, and plastic flowers. The collection will grow quite naturally from the activity of the children.

The projector needs to be situated so that everything placed on the stage appears on the screen. It should not be necessary to turn out the lights; other activities can continue while a small group works with the projector.

By placing the found object on the overhead stage the child is able to magnify it, to give it a new importance and a new relationship to its environment. He has a ready-made method of dealing with exaggeration and distortion. At the new scale he is able to view his image without the inhibitions of previously conceived ideas.

Place a small model of a palomino horse on the overhead projector and project it onto the rear of the translucent screen. The image is dark and bears no relation to the original color of the model. Visual clues have been changed and the silhouette assumes a much greater importance. Place a sheet of red acetate under the horse and the image is changed to a dark red horse on a red background.   If blue is substituted, the horse becomes blue and as such is unquestioned as a perfectly acceptable version of a horse.   Now that we have a blue horse what else can we combine with the image?   There is a temptation to follow normal associations, to think in terms of fences or horse stalls.   Instead, let's consider other possibilities.   Adding more horses results in an overlapping of images.   Although the new image still maintains the character of a horse, it displays none of the easily identifiable visual clues that cliché-thinking demands.

In his search for things to add to the horse the child learns a great deal about the creative process of combining one thing with another.   Dissimilar objects change their connotations when combined.   The knife is one thing when it appears with the fork and something else again when it appears with a gun or a piece of wood.   Putting together is one of the most satisfying of creative experiences.   Happy is the child who has a box of junk, a few tools, and the space to put them together according to his own creative leanings.   This is why the littered lot is preferred to the sterile playground.   In the classroom the projector can be an excellent extension of these activities.

In his search for other things to add to the horse the child may try such things as pieces of cardboard or matchsticks.   From these he will discover for himself another means of creative expression, the use of adaptations.   The pieces of cardboard become buildings on the screen, matches become fences, and a sponge becomes a tree.

At this point the child is also investigating another important aspect of the creative process, what Arthur Koestler calls the bisociative process.[2]   It is fun to engage in a creative activity or problem-solving situation and trace the process for oneself.

The child has a problem—he wants to complete his image of the horse.   His mind is dealing with two planes of reference.   The first plane consists of all the accumulated experiences that come to mind about horses: farms, fields, country fairs, and early fears and impressions.   The second plane is made up of the materials on hand: cardboard, bottletops, toothpicks, colored cellophane.   As with all creativity, there is a period in which the child simply packs these two planes with impressions and ideas.   According to Koestler's theory, the creative insight takes place when an idea on the plane of the horses and their environment joins forces with ideas on the plane of the

2. Arthur Koestler, *The Art of Creation* (New York: Macmillan Publishing Co., Inc., 1964).

media to form a new idea. Bottletops project circular images; horses pull carriages; carriages have wheels; wheels are circular. Cardboard projects a rectangular image, which fits with the circular image to provide the body of the carriage. Toothpicks are soon perceived to be not only a thin shape, but a shape related to the shape of the shafts or tynes that connect the horse to the wagon.

Using the overhead projector in this way has many advantages over other forms of art production. The initial skills required are not great, a commitment to creative activity is a must. Results can be achieved fairly quickly, at which point the child can make an evaluation; if he is not satisfied with the result, he is ready to try radical alterations because he knows that it is only the work of a moment to recapture the original image. He is forced to reexamine concepts that have grown up around the normal way of doing things. Many of the old solutions do not help in this new situation. The image is transitory, which gives it its own type of freedom; if he wants to preserve the image it is relatively easy to do so with a photographic slide.

This method of using projection equipment can be extended to provide an infinite range of variables by adding either a second overhead or a slide projector. The two projectors should be set fairly close together. The overhead projector is used in the manner described; the slide projector is used to add a second color or image.

Figure 8–4 was produced in the following manner. Transparent things were being placed on the overhead stage. When one of the students contributed a drinking glass, another said that it looked like the view through the telescopic sight on his father's rifle. The second student then added two thin threads to give the illusion of cross hairs. They then attempted to add through the overhead a bird that had been used as part of a shadow puppet show, but it blotted out the whole image. The answer to this was to hang the cardboard cut-out of the bird behind the screen, adjusting the distance until it reached the correct proportion. At this stage the image was discussed with the teacher, and it was generally agreed that it could be given greater dramatic effect. A piece of blue cellophane was added. This was not enough, so a red piece was added from the slide projector. The lens was left in place so the projector cast a circular image which everyone liked but agreed was too large. This problem was eventually solved by punching a hole in a piece of cardboard and placing this in the slot provided for the slides in the projector. The antics of one of the boys trying to get

FIGURE 8–4.   A light picture.

into the act were capitalized on—his hands, or rather the shadows of them, were incorporated into the image.   At this stage the students felt that the image had something to say and were very impressed with their efforts.   This is why it was recorded on a slide.

Projectors can be used in many other fascinating ways. Movement of both color and subject matter can be achieved.

16mm Films.   The value of filmmaking has been widely recognized in recent years, but very few schools have the equipment or the funds to run an adequate program.   There is one very useful alternative that merely requires a movie projector and some old film.

If old film is soaked in a strong solution of bleach, the old image can be easily removed, leaving a perfectly clear piece of film.   Or a "leader" film, which is clear and not exposed, can be purchased.   This film can now be drawn on with felt pens.   Some designs move slowly down the film; others, particularly marks that move across in unconnected ways, become a momentary flash when projected.   The resultant film has its own rhythm, which can often be matched to the musical rhythm of a phonograph record to provide a soundtrack.   One teacher projected such a moving color background from the rear and had the children dance before it. Their bodies, of course, were in silhouette.

Videotape. Videotape equipment is not expensive and it is no more difficult to operate than other audiovisual items; many schools are now purchasing portable units. Once the initial purchase of videotape equipment has been made, videotape can provide many of the learning situations inherent in filmmaking without the expense. The tape may be used over and over again, just like recording tape. The use of videotape is well within the capabilities of elementary school children. Once some of the problems inherent in the medium are understood, it can be used as an effective addition to the art program.

One of the most fundamental things to be learned from making a tape is composition. It quickly becomes obvious that what one points the camera at is not the same thing as what appears in the viewfinder. When the camera is pointed at James, only his head and shoulders appear. If the cameraman wants two people to appear together in the same film segment, he must have them stand quite close together. The medium imposes its own rules on the artist and he must learn what the rules are if he is to be successful. Another concept to be learned from work with videotape is that we see things only in relationship to other things and we can play all sorts of tricks by arranging these relationships. If we make a short piece of film that shows a boy running, another that shows a speeding car, and finally a piece that shows the boy lying down, the response will be that the boy has been hit by the car. The same principle can be applied to painting.

Magic Chalk and Black Light. Art suppliers now carry a wide selection of fluorescent chalks, crayons, and paints. These all glow in the presence of black light, which is usually supplied by a fluorescent light tube. Bulbs much like the regular incandescent light bulbs are now available.

Many of the chalks are invisible until the black light is turned on. This suggests one range of activities. The total effect is very different from other media; it has its own unique qualities. This in turn suggests another range of possibilities.

A group of practice teachers were shown the material, and these unique characteristics were pointed out. They were asked to find a creative way of using it with a group of third graders. It was Halloween and they were looking for ways in which the holiday could be used to stimulate creative ideas for parties and decorations.   The material excited both children and teachers.

To begin with, the children were shown the materials and encouraged to experiment without feeling that they had to provide ideas about Halloween.   Experimentation with any medium is more productive when it is pure research.   So many children wanted to see what the experimenters were doing that there was a traffic jam around the light.   One of the teachers started to carry the light fixture from child to child, and from this was developed the concept of a Halloween story.   Other experiments might have resulted in a scolding if the teachers had not been perceptive; some of the children applied the chalk to themselves. Once it was discovered that found objects could be made to fluoresce, experimentation was turned in this direction.   After a break, the problem was brainstormed and the results carefully pulled together.

The final production, which the class presented to other grades, was theater in the round.   The story dealt with the happenings in a village on Halloween night.   Cartons had been opened up to suggest the interior of houses.   Puppets had been constructed from cardboard jointed with paper fasteners and decorated with fluorescent chalk.   Similarly treated string was used to give the illusion of a spider web on which appeared a monstrous, glowing spider.   Glowing human hands appeared with no bodies attached.   As the story was being told to the accompaniment of music from a tape recorder and sound effects from everyone, the light was moved from scene to scene.   As soon as the light was moved, the previous scene became invisible.

It is interesting to note that although many of the stereotyped images connected with Halloween appeared, there were many new images resulting from the involvement with the new medium.   The novelty of the approach demanded new solutions.

Television productions using fluorescent materials can stimulate creative thinking not only in the arts, but in the formation of ideas, concepts, and fluency in speech and writing.

Have the children agree upon a broad storyline; then have each child illustrate a part of it on a piece of paper.   The papers need to be of a standard size.   When all is complete, the sheets are taped to a continuous roll that can be cranked in front of a cut-out in a cardboard box to simulate the TV screen.   Each child can tell his part of the story as his picture appears, or he can record it onto a tape to make a real talking picture.   The fact that the room is darkened and the picture glows should stimulate the creative abilities of even the most reticent child.

Polymer Gloss Medium. Polymer gloss medium is a relatively new material used to thin the new polymer paints. It has many of the same qualities and uses as traditional varnish. It differs in that it dries rapidly, is very transparent, adheres to most surfaces, and will hold quite heavy things together (which makes it ideal for collage or montage). It is completely waterproof when dry. Its disadvantages for the classroom teacher are price and the fact that if the brushes are not carefully washed immediately after use, they are ruined. You will find liquid starch makes a very good substitute for polymer gloss in most cases.

The polymer medium and tissue paper can be used to produce broad painting-like images that require full use of the student's ability to think intuitively. The tissue can be torn or cut and then laid in place. If the polymer medium is then brushed over the top, it will penetrate the tissue and fasten it down under a transparent coating. The image can be built up in layers; other materials such as magazine illustrations or printed material can be added. These materials, which resist the penetrating action of the polymer, only need a coat of polymer gloss on the back.

This is an ideal way to finish a piece made from papier mâché. The final coat of paper should be smooth and white. Small pieces are the easiest to apply. In planning the final effect, the student must make use of and accept the changes in tone and color produced by overlapping the pieces. If starch is substituted, the piece will not be water-resistant and will lack some of the gloss. This gloss can be achieved quickly by spraying the piece with a can of lacquer.

Plastics. One of the most useful and easily available plastics is polystyrene. This is the material used by the supermarket for meat trays. It makes an almost ideal printing medium for use in the elementary grades. The material is available in sheets from art supply houses. If funds are limited, it is comparatively easy to collect the meat trays, so expense is not a factor in the use of the material.

The trays can be trimmed with scissors to provide a flat surface. The child can proceed with a pencil much as he does with any other drawing. The indentations need to be clear and reasonably deep. Felt pens of the spirit-ink type not only indent the material, but dissolve it.   This makes it possible to lower large areas.   The disadvantage of using colors is that they lead the child to think that the colored areas will print.   In actual fact the reverse is true, because they are now below the printing plane.   The blocks are inked in the usual manner with a brayer and some water-soluble ink rolled out on a sheet of glass or a plastic-topped table.   The best results are achieved if the ink is built up on the block slowly by successive rollings.   If the ink is too thick, it will fill up the indentations.

The most satisfactory way of taking a print is also the simplest.   Turn the block face up and lay the paper on top.   Rub the back of the paper with a spoon or smooth object that glides over the paper.   Lift the paper occasionally to make sure that the whole area is being covered, and keep the paper free from one corner.

If the block is to be used to print wrapping paper, choose a paper that is soft like tissue paper.   Lay down a soft pad of newspapers and print by pressing the block onto the paper.   This allows you to see where you are going and to appreciate the possibilities of combining two printings to make a new image.

If printing ink is not available, fingerpaint can be substituted.   Alternative methods of applying the ink are to dab it on with a flat cloth pad or to soak several layers of blotting paper with tempera color and use this in the same way that pads are used to print rubber stamps.   Ditto paper makes the ideal printing paper, so all the materials for this activity are readily available.

Styrofoam.   Styrofoam has a fine granular surface.   It is supplied in all manner of shapes and sizes, and it is easily worked with simple tools.   Sculpture can achieve new dimensions with this material.   Cutting out pieces is simplified if a small hand-held jig saw is available (Fig. 8–5).   Cutting with a knife is more difficult, for the material tends to grip the blade.   Scoring and breaking is another solution to the problem.   Special tools that cut with a hot wire are available.

Once the basic shape has been cut, the material can be worked with a piece of sandpaper.   Tools can be fashioned from sandpaper by rolling it and pasting it into a cylinder.   The cylinder is then pasted onto popsicle sticks.   Two pieces can be folded and pasted together to make a double-sided cutting tool.

Glue is all that is needed to fasten pieces of styrofoam together.   It is a good idea to hold pieces in place (while the glue is setting) with common pins.   If color is to be applied, make

FIGURE 8–5.   Sawing styrofoam.

sure that the paint that you use does not dissolve the material. Many of the spray paints will act as solvents.

Styrofoam makes an excellent armature for use with other materials such as papier mâché. It provides structural strength and bulk and is lightweight.

CRAFTS FOR CREATIVE EXPRESSION

Crafts have always been thought of as exercises in the development of skills and dexterity. There has been a tendency to see crafts as the point at which art becomes useful and applicable to our daily lives. Crafts may have to do with the utilitarian—ceramics, wood crafts, metal, weaving—or the decorative—jewelry, mosaics. In the days of master craftsmen it was not only the skills that were valued, but the creative uses to which they were put. The industrial revolution led to a separation of the two; craftsmen merely carried out a set of instructions. An awareness of the value of crafts has been carried down to the present day. Art programs at camps are often based on craft kits. Manufacture of these kits is a million-dollar business today. It is this use of crafts that has tended to encourage the image of art as a frill—an attempt to reinstate the values of cottage industries—rather than as a contemporary and vital part of the child's education.

Skills are an important human objective; we take great delight in developing them. The success of a skill is seen in the finished product, so in this form of creativity the product and process assume equal values. When we think of crafts as a means of developing the child's creativity, one major question arises. What is the relationship between skills and creativity? We know that not all skillful people are creative; many are merely productive. If we teach the child a set of skills, will he always operate within the limit of these skills? How much does he need to know in order to make a beginning, and what means can we use to help him perceive the need for new skills and ways to develop them?

We used to believe that to excel in a skill one had to learn an ideal way of doing things. The sports world reminds us that records are being broken by people with unorthodox styles. The achievement of a skill can be as individual as the product that results from it. This is not meant to imply that all that is necessary is to provide the children with materials and tools. We are fortunate in possessing a vast amount of inherited knowledge accumulated over thousands of years; it is unreasonable to insist that the child rediscover it all for himself. What we are talking about, then, is the careful balance so familiar to elementary school teachers. Vital information is given when there is a need for it so that the student's creative drive is not hampered by technicalities.

Bill was constructing a model fort from stiff cardboard. He had a very clear idea of the kind of fort that he wanted, but the idea was floundering because he was unable to fasten the pieces together. The teacher was tempted to suggest that they explore the ways in which this might be achieved, but realized that the time spent doing this would merely delay the creative exploration of the concept of a fort. She showed Bill how to use rubber cement as a contact glue. The rubber was spread on both surfaces and allowed to dry. When the two parts were brought together, they adhered immediately. One result of receiving this piece of information was Bill's discovery that he could now add pieces in positions that he had considered impossible before. The final product took on an entirely new form.

It saves a lot of time if the child who is working with tools is shown how they can be used both effectively and safely. Children can be introduced to tools at an early age. A young child is often given a hammer and nails to play with; the fact is that a hammer improperly used can do as much damage as a saw. Under proper supervision children who have acquired enough coordination might 'well begin using tools seriously in kindergarten. The authors have provided power tools for second-grade children to use and had a perfect safety record. Children who come to kindergarten never having been allowed to use scissors or other tools because their parents were afraid they would hurt themselves start out under a handicap.

Weaving

Weaving is enjoyed by both boys and girls. The fundamental concept can be taught by weaving with paper. To make the form, a sheet of paper should be folded in two and cut as in Figure 8–6. It is important to end up with an odd number of strips. If the worst happens and you come out with an even number, cut one off.

Weaving strips can then be cut quickly on a papercutter from paper that is the same width as the paper used for the form. Initially the child needs to see that if the piece is to hold together, he must plan on an over-under procedure. The second row should start under-over. Once this has been established, he is free to find ways to create his own patterns. The material can be given greater variety by cutting the strips in different widths, by punching holes in the paper, or by using old fingerpaintings or any other materials that work conveniently to make the strips.

Woven Paper Baskets. A large paper cup is cut as shown in Figure 8–7, again into an uneven number of strips. Children

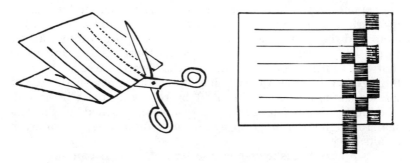

FIGURE 8–6. Cut the form, then open it out to weave the cross strips.

FIGURE 8–7.   Woven paper baskets.

must work hard at developing the concept of uneven numbers. In the authors' classes we developed the technique of holding one strip and counting the others. If it came out even we knew that the one we were holding was the odd one. Flatten the cup on a table and weave into it whatever you have available. The secret for getting a good wide shape is not to pull the weaving strips too tight. It may be necessary to fasten the last row with staples. The method is given, but how the child uses it depends upon his own creativity.

The Box Loom. The box loom is shown in Figure 8–8. It is relatively simple to construct; the construction of a loom might be a joint project run by the classroom teacher and the shop teacher. An uneven number of strings are wrapped around the loom and the ends joined. Every other one goes through a hole in the heddle, which is used to separate these "warp" threads so that the shuttle containing the cross or "weft" threads can pass through. When the weaving has been completed on the top of the loom, the tension is taken off by removing the tension rod. The cloth is moved around by pressure on the heddle, the tension rod tightens things up again, and another length of warp awaits the weaver.

Figure 8–9 shows how the legs of a chair can substitute for the loom and some popsicle sticks for the heddle. Woven belts can be produced or, if the heddle is made wide enough and

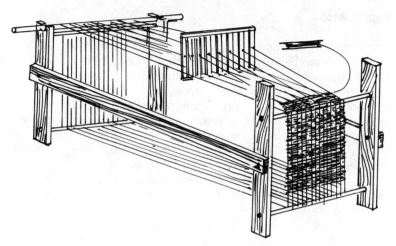

FIGURE 8–8.   The box loom.

fairly coarse materials are used, small mats can be woven quite quickly.   One of the problems encountered most often is a tendency to pull the cross threads too tight, which narrows the material.

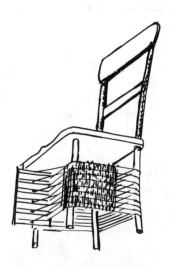

FIGURE 8–9.   A chair can be used to make a loom.

Papier Mâché

Papier mâché is one of the least expensive and most useful of all the art media available.   All that is required is newsprint and wallpaper paste.   The paste should be added to water and whisked until it is about the consistency of heavy cream.   For three-dimensional work an armature is needed—rolled paper works well and is always available.   Three rolls taped together as shown in Fig. 8–10 can be bent to form an armature for a wide variety of forms.   Short lengths of wire in the center of the rolls help them to retain their shape when they are bent.

Bulk is best added by taping wadded paper into place before the paste and paper are added.   Practically any object can be incorporated—plastic bottles, styrofoam, paper cups, and pieces of egg cartons all help to give bulk and form.   Newspaper can be torn into very even strips if it is torn from top to bottom. Strips are the easiest shape to apply; they can be used much like

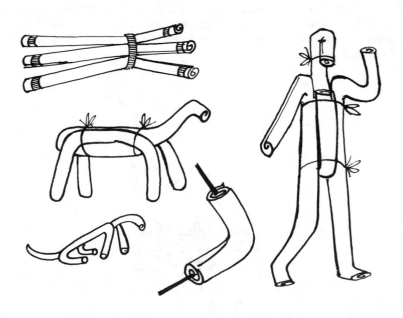

FIGURE 8–10.   Basic shapes for papier mâché.

bandages to hold things together.   Cut-down bleach bottles make ideal containers for paste, because the paste does not stick to them.   The strips are dipped in the paste and then removed by dragging them against the side of the containers.   If the paste is the right consistency, the strips emerge with just the right load of paste (Fig. 8–11).

Four or five layers of paper are usually needed; they need to be well smoothed together to make a strong, cohesive layer. Alternate layers of newspaper and white paper towels help the child to see areas that he has missed and ensure an even coating. A final coat of white paper will go on more smoothly if it is applied in small pieces like fish scales.

Modeling of small detail is easily accomplished with a modeling paste made by dipping a facial tissue in the paste and squeezing it dry.

If it is necessary to remove the papier mâché from the support of a product such as a bowl, a separating layer is required.   The support is given a coat of a grease like petroleum jelly or cooking fat.   The first layer of paper is applied to this coating without any paste.   The object is then laid up in the usual way.   Once dry, the support can be easily removed and the initial layer of paper peeled away.

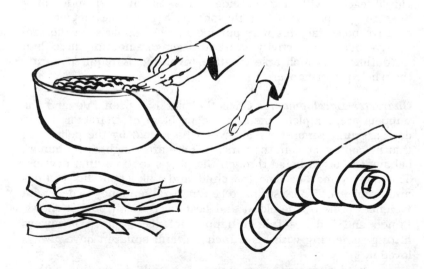

FIGURE 8–11.   Papier-mâché strips.

Puppets

It is a pity that so many puppet shows that start out with a rush of joyous enthusiasm end with a pile of unfinished puppets and little incentive to try again.   The difficulty with young children is that the mechanics of a puppet show exceed their attention span. For this reason puppets are not as widely used as they might be. This is unfortunate, because puppets are an ideal way of "getting it all together."   A puppet show can be delightful entertainment, but it can also be a way of involving children in a wide range of skills and learning experiences.   (See the story of Miss Larkin on p. 10.)

The Plot.   Every puppet show requires a story and a script.   The characters can be derived from the story, or the story can be based on the characters.   The puppets can be made first, and then the story can grow from the need to include them in a situation.   The story can be written down or, if this slows the creative process down too much, it can be recorded on tape.   This has the added advantage that once the story is out of the way the players can concentrate on the action of the puppets.   The individual teacher will have to decide if there is any merit in learning lines for puppet plays.   If the objective is the development of creative potential, this may put too much emphasis on the productive side of the activity.   The story may be nothing more than an outline, in which case creative invention is required during the whole performance.

Character Development.   Once the plot has been laid and the puppets are complete, there is the problem of character.   How does a grumpy monster react when he is told by the policeman that he cannot sleep in the park?   There are insights into human behavior to be gathered through the play situations that develop. The puppet may become the child and talk about his feelings and problems.   There seems to be a natural tendency to deal with violence.   One of the oldest and best-loved of all puppet shows, Punch and Judy, is full of happy violence.   Punch is always hitting something with his truncheon, and children have always loved it.

In dealing with the puppet the child is dealing with a complex world of feelings, relationships, emotions, and concepts.

Group Organization. When children are allowed to play together freely and creatively, one of the first things that they do is set up the ground rules. This period can be identified by a good deal of noise. The rules, when they emerge, are often far more tightly drawn than those that the adult would have laid down. Setting up the rules seems to be a necessary and valuable part of the learning experience. If the rules are always imposed by the adults, a feeling of dependency and regimentation is developed. The children learn from this process the necessity of giving up some individual rights and freedoms; otherwise, the show never gets on the road. The groups need to be flexible enough so that children can move to one with which they are compatible. This in turn demands a certain flexibility in the use of the puppets.

Development of Skills. Activities concerned with the creating of the puppets, the scenery, the special effects, and the theater involve almost every aspect of the fine arts. It is difficult to think of an artistic skill that does not have some application in the puppet theater. Painting, sculpture (using all types of materials), design, printing, wood and metal crafts, and photography all find a place. Finally and perhaps most important of all, the puppet show places a premium on all those creative traits that together make up the creative personality.

Integration with Other Disciplines. A puppet show needs music to set the mood and carry the audience along. If the children can make their own, fine. If not, then they can choose music that fits their need. From the act of making selections will come a better understanding of the power of music to evoke moods and communicate ideas and feelings.

Puppets can be used as an intermediary to teach almost anything from social studies to physics. The content of the show can represent an entirely different area of learning from those involved in the production itself.

Puppets provide a means of "getting it all together" in the sense that all the disciplines can be related to this one endeavor so that the child can perceive the unity of what he is learning. Children constructing parts for the theater can be helped to appreciate the value of math in solving the problems of fitting things together. Story ideas become part of the reading program. Music becomes more than repetition of songs from song books. Relationships among all the aspects of art can be seen. Libraries become a valued resource.

Glove Puppets.   To be effective with the young child, puppets must be easy to manipulate and easy to make.   Marionettes with their intricate joints and strings are too difficult.   Glove puppets like the ancient Punch and Judy can be made simply by pushing a paper cup to the bottom of a sock to give structure to the head and then adding all manner of things from the scrap box (Fig. 8– 12).   The plastic eggs that are used for packaging pantyhose are ideal for this purpose; one half egg is all that is needed.   If the sock is a long one and a hole is cut for the insertion of the hand in the middle, it is easy to make animal forms.   In the case of the dragon in Figure 8–13, the tail was stuffed with a roll of paper and small rubber bands helped to make it taper.   This type of puppet works well with a table as a stage since it must be operated from below (Fig. 8–14).

Puppet Heads.   Puppet heads can be constructed from papier mâché.   This is good for children who want to expand their interest in puppets.   For young children it takes too long and delays the involvement with the puppet theater.   To construct a head some type of armature is needed.   Paper can be taped to a small cardboard roll and papier mâché added (Fig. 8– 15).   If the head is for a rod puppet, there is no need to remove the armature since no space is needed for the fingers.   Light

FIGURE 8–12.   A glove puppet.

FIGURE 8–13.   A dragon puppet.

bulbs can be completely enclosed so there is little danger of breakage. If the head is for a glove puppet, a small balloon can be used, although the paper covering needs to be dry and strong before the balloon goes down or it will collapse the paper with it. Using paper and paste as a form of modeling clay, the features

FIGURE 8–14.   A table stage.

FIGURE 8–15.   A papier-mâché puppet head.

can be built up. Many young children find this concept hard to handle and prefer to add the details with styrofoam balls and pieces of styrofoam.

Paper Bag Puppets. Luncheon-sized bags are ideal for paper bag puppets. When folded they provide a flap into which the fingers can be inserted to give the illusion of a mouth. Details can be cut from construction paper and pasted on (Fig. 8–16). For the very young this kind of puppet is easy to make and to operate.

Rod Puppets. Rod puppets too are operated from below. They have the advantage of being very simple to make. The ideal materials are some light dowels and a collection of styrofoam balls. The balls are impaled on the top of the rods to form the base for the head. Details of the face can be made simply from cut paper or buttons. Hair might be an old piece of fur. All of these materials can be attached easily with straight pins. Costumes can be created by draping and tying pieces of cloth to the stick. Arms are best attached loosely so that the movement of the stick gives the figure some motion. Stick puppets can be put together in a matter of minutes so that a puppet show can be conceived, put together, and performed in the same afternoon. A refinement of this type of puppet uses rods to create special movements, such as the opening of an animal's jaw or the move-

FIGURE 8–16.   Paper bag puppets.

ment of an arm.   The rods may be pieces of coat hangers (Fig. 8–17).

The puppet can be given legs in the same way that the arms are attached.   A stiff wire is then attached to the head so that it can be operated from above.

Shadow Puppets.   The shadow puppet is an ancient puppet form. There are records of shadow puppets in ancient China and Egypt.   In Southeast Asia the highly developed art still flourishes today.   In this chapter we discussed the potential of overhead projection as an art medium.   The same system makes a very exciting method of presenting shadow puppets.

The scenery can be assembled quickly on the overhead stage from old toys, pieces of cellophane, and colored acetate. These are projected onto the rear of a translucent screen.   Children may prefer to prepare the scenery by drawing it with felt pens on clear acetate; a roll of the material is usually attached to the machine.

The puppets can be made from almost anything.   A paper towel and a piece of rod can become a puppet in short

FIGURE 8–17.   Rod puppets.

order.   Drape the towel around the rod, gather it in to form a head, and hold it in place with a piece of tape.   A system of trial and error will show where the towel needs tearing to suggest arms and legs.

The children are often able to fill in missing details with their imagination and perceive even rudimentary shadows as definite characters.   Since we are interested in puppets for the learning that can come out of them, as well as for their capacity to provide a joyous experience for the students, there is no real point on insisting on a higher degree of craftsmanship.   The fact that the children are able to become involved rapidly and easily in a puppet world is one of the biggest advantages of the system.

Children have a tendency to watch the puppet rather than the shadow.   A mirror placed so that they can see the front of the screen helps them to more fully appreciate the properties of the shadows that they are making.

Children playing with this system make many discoveries related to the education of vision.   They discover, for instance, that they are often unable to recognize an object from its shadow. Shadows often suggest one thing and turn out to be another. Things that have soft edges appear to be more distant; soft edges occur when the object is held further from the screen; two objects of recognizable shape make a third that cannot be recognized when the shadows are brought together.

After the children have had some experience in making puppets, the creativity of the children can be developed by encouraging them to decide on their own creations. A teacher may show the children how to make papier mâché for puppets, but the children themselves can discover many ways to construct the puppets and their own puppets will vary in structure and design.

One class held a discussion on ways they could make marionette legs and bodies. Several methods were suggested:

rolling paper and pasting it
wetting and rolling masking tape
using papier mâché
cutting puppets from wood
sewing cloth forms and stuffing them
using plastic wood

Each child proceeded to make his puppet in his own way. Approximate size was determined by the class and then the children were left to their own resources. There was great variation in the finished puppets—each child experimented with the use of many materials from the scrap box. They made hair with paint, cut crepe paper, and unbraided rope, yarn, steel wool, string, loopers, artificial hair, and braided cloth. They made eyes from paint, buttons, beads, tacks, glitter, cut paper, and enamel. Each aspect of the building of the puppets called for creative thinking on the part of the children and the results were unique and individual. Children learned from each other and challenged each other to new creative efforts.

Puppet Theaters. Sooner or later most children want to construct and have a puppet theater of their own. For convenient storing, it is best to make a folding theater. Plans for a simple one are given below. Three pieces of cardboard are cut to shape and the joints taped on both sides with a heavy wrapping or masking tape. The proscenium arch is wider than the back of the stage and is attached by cutting simple half joints or slots, as shown in Fig. 8–18. Curtains are a nicety; they can be arranged on a rod resting on the sides behind the arch. A sheet of cardboard that can be lifted like a fire curtain in a regular theater when the performance begins is generally simpler than drawn

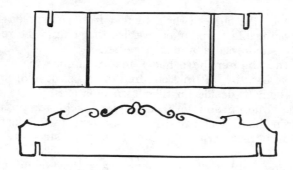

FIGURE 8-18.   A puppet theater.

curtains.   This type of theater works best with puppets that are operated from above.

For hand puppets, an arch similar to the one above may be constructed with the cardboard bent in the opposite direction to provide wings to hide the actors.   The arch can simply be placed on a table near a wall, and then the scenery can easily be taped to the wall.

Printmaking

Printmaking, which was once tied to the concept of cutting a lino block, has often been regarded as too difficult and dangerous for the young child.   There are, however, many ways in which young people can produce prints that are both safe and inexpensive.

As a creative activity, printmaking allows for a great deal of experimentation with a process. Between the artist and the image lies a magical area in which all sorts of unexpected things happen. All kinds of opportunities present themselves; new directions appear. The solution of one problem becomes the pointer to yet another.

Learning takes place in several different areas. One is the ability to develop techniques that make the creative expression possible. In experimenting with the process the child learns to be more flexible. He learns to make use of the ability to see new relationships between his needs and the materials at hand. He is able to use the ability to see things in unusual contexts and to use materials in unusual ways. He needs to be able to think intuitively. Printing provides a way to examine the contribution that production and evaluation make to the creative idea. It helps to develop aesthetic perception.

It is easy to become involved with the teaching of print-making and never be aware of what is taking place in these areas. The product can become more important than the process; the emphasis on skills can outweigh the other things that might be learned. In order to avoid leaving the child with the idea that there is a set way of making a print, it is necessary to be careful how much demonstrating one does. If the teacher merely inks up his brayer with printing ink and then transfers the print to the paper, she has practically covered the basic skills. The child is aware of the basic equipment that is available, the brayer and the inks, and has enough procedural information to get him started. The next step is to have the children consider all the other things that they could use to make a print. A junk box is invaluable at this point. Learning can be speeded up if materials known to be useful are included. See the opening story in Chapter 1 of this book.

For all of this experimentation the concept of repetition needs to be grasped. Printmaking allows us the freedom to produce more than one copy. Although we might enjoy printing a line from a piece of ink-soaked string, we would have only dealt with part of the problem—we would be unable to repeat the image.

This concept leads to experiments in ways to put some of the interesting things that have been used together so that a number of prints can be made. This in turn leads to the understanding that prints can be made either by an additive process or a subtractive one. We can glue cardboard shapes down onto

PART 2   The Nurture and Use of Art in the Elementary School

another piece of cardboard, or we can take some modeling clay and cut away the pieces that we do not need. When we approach printmaking from this point of view we are much less apt to fall into the trap of teaching it as a skill or a gimmick. If the teacher brings in a bag of potatoes and some knives and teaches the children how to make potato prints, a whole area of learning is left out. The next time that printing is introduced the child will rightfully expect to be given another method.

Experimentation by the child can be helped by the kinds of questions that the teacher asks. The success of the project depends upon knowing the right questions to ask. If the child has made a print from a piece of clay the teacher might ask him all the ways that he could think of to change the shape of the clay and the resultant print. If he decides that he could cut shapes into it the teacher might ask him to consider all the other materials that he could easily cut. Her objective is to help him see the possibilities of such things as vegetables. It is the discovery of unusual uses of dissimilar materials that the teacher perceives as important rather than the ability to make wrapping paper using a potato.

Basic information is best handed over as a free gift. There is no point in having the child rediscover the wheel; it is better that he be shown the wheel and left to discover his own uses for it. Methods of applying materials to printing surfaces can be given when the need for them arises without interfering with the creative process. If the materials are to be printed with water-based ink, then they need to be waterproof; this can simply be demonstrated.

To say that we are teaching the children to do print-making can mean very many different things. The teacher has a very definite place in the process, but she needs to perceive her part as the ability to liberate the creative potential of the children and to help them to develop skills that will fill their individual needs. In order to do these things she needs to be aware of all the possibilities—what there is to be learned and how prints can be made.

Monoprinting. Monoprinting is a good place to begin print-making, because the technique involves many things with which the child is already familiar. We have already discussed mono-printing with fingerpaint in Chapter 2. This can be extended in various ways. Materials needed are a plastic-topped table or some old trays on which to spread the paint. Effects will vary with the kind of paper used.

Try fingerpaint paper to begin with. The paint is manipulated on the tabletop until a satisfactory arrangement is arrived
at. The paper is then placed face down on the paint and rubbed
with the side of the hand. Much of the final effect will depend
upon the direction in which the paper is removed.

For a variation of this technique, proceed in exactly the
same way initially, but after the paper is in place draw on the
back of it with anything you choose. Do not smooth the paper
into place. The result will be an image etched in dark lines with
the imprint of the ink in the background.

Another alternative is to spread the ink and then do the
drawing directly upon the ink. The image is then printed by
applying the paper. Cut paper shapes placed on the ink will
print as negative shapes when paper is placed over them to make
a print. Although only one image is produced, as in painting,
there is a distinctly different quality to the result, and it is
possible to see in this simple procedure ways in which printing
experiments might progress.

All of these alternatives involve fingerpaint, which invariably leaves the paper wrinkled when it dries. If the print is
to be mounted, it may be flattened by ironing the reverse side
under some damp newspapers. There is much to be said in favor
of mounting artwork. It gives the object a value and separates it
from other things so that it can be seen and appreciated. Children should be encouraged to do it themselves; it is often enough
to trim the print and carefully place it on a sheet of construction
paper.

Printing with any other inks requires a means of applying ink to the printing surface. This is most commonly done
with a rubber-covered roller. Inexpensive ones can be so irregu-
lar and ineffective that they frustrate the most persistent student.
The rubber needs to be thick and soft enough to make even
contact with the ink and the print. A little of the ink is squeezed
out onto a smooth surface and rolled out as thinly as possible
with the brayer. If there is too much ink, the brayer will skid on
the surface. Oilbound inks are transparent, thin, and intense;
they produce a superior print. They also require turpentine to
clean up. Waterbound inks make a good substitute, for they are
easily cleaned up with a sponge and do not stain. Fingerpaint
can also be used in the same way, but the pigmentation is not as
intense. Tempera paint is too thin to roll satisfactorily, but it
works well if it is used with a pad on which the block can be
dabbed. Waterbound materials have more bulk than the oilbound varieties and have a tendency to clog the indentations of

the block. If a large number of prints are to be made, it may be necessary to wash the surface periodically.

Additive methods are sometimes used to make collage prints. One of the simplest procedures is to paste cardboard shapes onto a second sheet of cardboard. The block is now inked with a brayer and printed in the usual way. All kinds of exciting materials from the scrap box can be used instead of cardboard. Pieces of cloth and materials such as lace, string, burlap, toothpicks, and packaging material can be used for their texture or shape. When everything has been glued firmly into place (Elmer's glue works well), the piece should be given a coat of shellac to waterproof the materials and prevent them from picking up on the inking roller.

Blocks that have a well-defined, raised surface can be printed in reverse by placing the paper on the uninked block and working the inked brayer over the back of the paper. This same idea can be used with crayons. This is technically a rubbing. It works best if the paper covering is taken off the crayon and the crayon is held flat.

Practically anything that can be cut into can be adapted to a subtractive process. About the only requirement is that the surface be reasonably smooth and even, since what remains of this surface is what prints.

Lino Cuts. The lino cut is probably the best-known printing method in the schools. It is only really suitable for children of about fourth grade and above since it requires a fair degree of strength and coordination. The lino, or linoleum, is usually mounted on plywood so that the block can be used on a commerical printing press. A carefully used lino cut can produce several hundred copies.

The block should be held in a special tray, as shown in Fig. 8–19. If both hands are free so that they can be kept on the tools, this assures a minimal chance of injury. The tools (shown in Fig. 8–20) are usually of the interchangeable nib variety. Two handles are supplied, so that the most commonly used shapes are always at hand. Small carving tools are even better and can be kept sharp. The nibs are disposable.

The successful use of lino cuts depends to great extent upon the fluency with which the student can manipulate the basic elements of art. The child's first attempt is likely to consist of a definition of the image formed by placing a line around it. He has not considered all the other means at his disposal to separate one object from another. These skills and perceptions

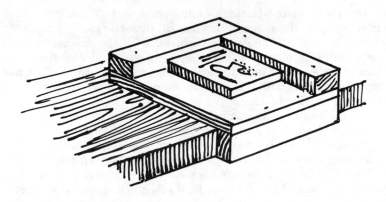

FIGURE 8–19.   A simple block cut to hold a lino cut.

need to be built up in a more direct medium where the problems can be rapidly identified and dealt with.   It takes too long to do this on a cut.   From his work in other areas the child will have observed that one of the things that helps to identify an object when such clues as color are not present is texture.   A section of cloth and a section of lawn may have identical colors.   We depend upon environmental clues in making our identification, but

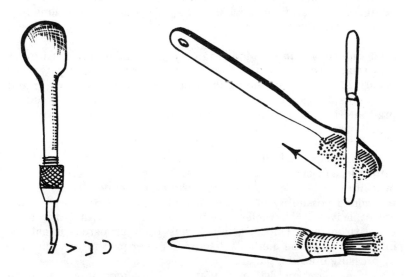

FIGURE 8–20.   Block cutting tools.

we also do it on the textures of the materials themselves. The initial lino cut does not make use of this knowledge, probably because the child is so deeply involved with the development of new skills. He also misses the opportunity to define things in terms of tone—light on dark and dark on light. Even if he has used these means with other media he must discover new ways to adapt them to lino cutting.

The sky is lighter than the bank of trees in front of it, but it is not white. The problem is how to indicate that the sky is gray when all that is available is pure black and white. It becomes necessary to invent a visual symbol or convention that will be identified as gray by the viewer. The invention of such a symbol by the child represents a significant creative breakthrough. It is important that he be allowed to make it for himself with whatever help you can give him. It is far less important that he learn techniques. It would be very easy to demonstrate to the child that by engraving lines across the block he can remove enough material so that the area is read visually as gray. This would simply result in the child operating in terms of the given skill, and the creative potential of the exercise would be missed.

The lino cut is a sophisticated concept requiring its own visual language. For this reason it is most valuable when the child is helped to think in new and original ways, rather than being left to operate on the basis of symbols and conventions that he brings from other media.

Modeling Clay Prints. Modeling clay is available in almost every classroom. In helping the child to use it for printing, the teacher is carrying out one of the basic principles of creative thought and problem solving. The child is familiar with the clay as a sculpting material. Seeing these sculptural forms in terms of printing is making the familiar strange.

The clay can be used as it comes in the package. The student has several surfaces on which he can carve so that the same piece of clay can be used to make several prints. Any kind of knife can be used to remove parts of the clay. There is also the added possibility of impressing objects into the clay. Each object leaves a characteristic impression that will print as a negative space. Once the block has been prepared, it can be inked by any of the methods discussed under printing and printed by pressing onto the paper.

A more sophisticated way of using modeling clay is to spread it to a uniform thickness between two thin pieces of wood, such as rulers, and then to carve into this surface. The print in this case is best taken by placing the paper on the block and rubbing the back. Care must be taken not to apply too much pressure during printing or the block will be flattened.

Vegetable Prints. Many vegetables if cut in half provide a ready-made and distinctive image. An orange cut across the quarters gives a very clear print. However, there are many cheaper vegetables to work with. Potatoes are an old standby. Many children find it difficult to cut the potato in half smoothly enough. The surface can be worked with almost any implement. The prepared block can easily be printed by dipping it into a pad of tempera, watercolor, colored ink, or even vegetable coloring. Young children make random dabs; it is only when they are more mature that they are able to organize their motifs into the mathematical arrangements found in adult art. Children normally reach the fourth grade before they are able to deal with this concept easily.

Found-object Prints. If one can print with the end of a carrot, then one can print with anything that presents a flat surface—sticks, cardboard rolls (the ends make perfect circles), pieces of sponge, leaves, the ends of pencils. The list is endless. Printing can be combined with other media to produce distinctive results. The print can be made on paper that has been colored in various ways. Washes of paint can be applied, or the paint can be sponged on to give a textural effect. The print can be made on tissue paper that has been pasted down. The child should be encouraged to consider all the possibilities. Watercolor printing inks make it difficult to apply color to the print, for the water smears the image. A related way to apply a second color before printing is with the brayer. Lightly inked, the brayer can be rolled over the paper to form bands in several directions.

Roller Prints. Roller printing allows the child to make multiple impressions and to see the possibilities of organized, repeated patterns. All that you need are some small-diameter mailing tubes cut into short lengths. The material that is to form the image is glued to the pieces of tubing. It is important to make sure that everything is about the same height. When the glue is dry, it is best to shellac the surface (this improves the print, but can be omitted if necessary). The roller is inked in the same way that the brayer was and the impression is rolled out onto the paper. It helps to have a soft pad under the paper to be printed on; an old blanket or several thicknesses of newspaper will serve the purpose. This is a great way of producing colorful wrapping paper.

Stenciling

Stenciling is a simple technique whereby color is forced through a hole cut in a masking material onto the paper below it. The masking material might be paper or metal. Heavy waxed paper is ideal because it does not absorb watercolor paints. The paint is commonly applied with a stencil brush which has short bristles ending in a flat surface. Young children find this hard to manage; the stencil becomes too wet and the paint creeps underneath the mask to spoil the image. An alternative to paint is crayon, which can be moved across the hole onto the mask and back again. The main difficulty here is tearing the masking paper. Perhaps the easiest method for young children is to spatter the paint on with a toothbrush and the back of a knife. This removes the problem of holding the stencil long enough to color it. Another simple material is chalk; the child rubs his finger over the chalk and onto the stencil.

The technique alone will fascinate the child and make him want to try it for himself. One of the problems is to demonstrate enough of the technique to enable the student to perceive the possibilities without locking him into the method shown. There are many found objects with holes in them through which color can be forced. The scrap box might provide old computer cards, plastic vegetable containers, doilies, etc. Once the process is understood, the students can be encouraged to suggest all the ways they can think of to produce their own holes. Have the children save the pieces that they cut out. If they do not discover the possibility for themselves, lead them to the discovery that they can use these pieces to shield the first image while they apply a second color around it or to produce a negative image.

Once again the student is involved in the process of finding unusual uses for familiar materials. Exploring the process is as important as the result. What he says with the medium will be influenced by the limitations and the advantages that it offers. These are unique enough to make many of his old concepts about the way in which things can be done of little use to him. He is forced to examine new possibilities.

Flexibility is encouraged by the possibility of using the

stencil in reverse.   If a dry medium is being used, the child is much more likely to discover that he can turn the stencil over and reverse the image.   If it is wet with paint, he is too concerned with making a mess on the paper.   One horse can be repeated in a number of different positions and reversed to make a herd of horses.   Accidental overlapping can be turned to advantage; the student can be helped to see the possibility of using overlappings to express concepts of space and the relationship of one object to another.

It is only when one has become involved in printing that one is able to fully appreciate the part that it has played in the development of the human race.   There is a feeling of kinship with the cave painter of 20,000 years ago who placed his hand against the wall and made a stencil by blowing a mixture of fat and pigment against it through a hollow instrument, probably a bone.   Such stencils have been found at Lascaux.   In our own country we have stenciled furniture, walls, and even floors; stenciling used to be substituted for wallpaper and carpeting. There are charming prints from the fourteenth and fifteenth century in Europe that match very closely the simple, innocent approach of today's child.

An understanding of and feeling for the process can become a means of seeing history as the business of people exactly like ourselves.

DO-IT-YOURSELF MEDIA

Below are some of the recipes the authors have found successful in creating respectable substitutes for expensive art supplies. New worlds of exploration and expression were opened to the children in our classrooms when these materials were introduced.

Paints and Varnishes

Fingerpaint Base No. 1

1½ cup laundry starch
1 cup soap flakes
1 quart boiling water

Mix starch with a small amount of boiling water.   Add the rest of the boiling water; stir in soap flakes.

Fingerpaint Base No. 2

1 package wallpaper paste
1 cup soap flakes
boiling water

Mix wallpaper paste, soap flakes, and enough boiling water to make a thick, creamy mixture. Add food coloring or tempera paint to color.

Silk Screen Liquid Starch Paint

liquid starch
powder paint

Add liquid starch to powder paint until the mixture is the consistency of light paste.

Silk Screen Tempera Paint

tempera paint
soap flakes
water

Add a small quantity of soap flakes to the tempera paint to give it viscosity and to deter drying. Add water only if necessary. Fingerpaint of a creamy consistency can also be used.

Varnish Base

3 parts powder paint
1 part varnish

Mix ingredients with a palette knife on glass. Using a brayer or printing roller, roll mixture back and forth until it is tacky. Then apply it to the block. This varnish base will dry more quickly than oil-based ink. It is suitable for use on nonabsorbent, smoothly finished paper.

Water Soluble Varnish

When working with tissue, use Argo gloss starch as a varnish.

Clay Substitutes

Crepe Clay

1 fold of white crepe paper
1 tablespoon of salt
1 cup of flour
water

Cut the crepe paper into tiny pieces. Place in a large bowl; add only enough water to cover the paper. Allow the mixture to soak for 15 minutes and then pour off the excess water. Mix the salt and flour; add enough of the flour-salt mixture to make a stiff dough. Knead well until it is blended with the crepe paper.

Flour Clay

1 cup flour
1 cup salt
1 rounded teaspoon powdered alum

Add water slowly and knead until a clay-like consistency is reached.

Cornstarch Clay

½ cup cornstarch
1 cup salt
1 cup boiling water

Boil mixed ingredients to the soft-ball stage and knead on waxed paper until malleable.

These substitutes can be handled exactly like clay. They can be pressed on maps to make a relief, and, when dry, they can be painted. They retain shape without crumbling. For a colored mixture, add powdered paint to the water when mixing it. Wrap the clay in a wet cloth if you want to keep it a few days.

Modeling Media

Crepe Papier Mâché

1 cup crepe paper
4 or 5 tablespoons flour
2 tablespoons salt
water

To make crepe papier mâché, prepare a packed cupful of crepe paper cut in small pieces. Add enough water to wet the paper thoroughly and soak overnight. Then mix and rub the wet paper into a very fine pulp. Next add 4 or 5 tablespoons of flour and 2 tablespoons of salt. Work this mixture thoroughly until it is the consistency of clay. Library paste can be added if desired. Mix a batch for each color to be used.

Salt and Flour Modeling Medium No. 1

1 cup salt
½ cup cornstarch
1 cup flour
4 cups water

Let water reach boiling point and add salt. Mix flour and cornstarch with a little cold water; add the mixture to the boiling water and salt. Let this boil until clear, then cool. Knead for a time. Let dry. When ready to use, soften with water. This mixture can be reused.

Salt and Flour Modeling Medium No. 2

4 parts flour
5 parts salt
water

Sift four parts of flour with five parts of table salt. Set aside about one-eighth of the dry mixture and moisten the rest with just enough water to make a smooth, doughy mass. As the salt melts, the dough sometimes becomes too soft, in which case knead into it enough of the remaining dry mixture to get the desired consistency. After modeling this mixture will become hard and can be painted.

Inks and Pastes

Oil-Based Printing Ink for Block Printing

2 parts powder paint
1 part linseed oil
1 part varnish

Mix ingredients to the consistency of a smooth paste. This ink spreads on evenly but will not dry quickly. It is good for paper with a rough, textured surface.

Paste

1 cup flour
1 quart boiling water
1 tablespoon sugar
1 teaspoon powdered alum

Mix the flour in a small amount of warm water until smooth and creamy. Dissolve sugar in the boiling water and pour over the flour mixture, stirring until it clears and jells. Add alum after cooling.

SUMMARY

Supplements to the supply reservoirs of a school art program can be found in almost any environment. Teams of teachers can greatly expand their art resources if they purchase supplies judiciously with the thought in mind that each community and each school can offer substitutes for expensive materials. Children need not be deprived of rich experiences in art because funds are not available for all the newest media, devices, tools, and gimmicks.

A few basic supplies are necessary; these have been reviewed in this chapter. One way to save on supplies is to make certain that the proper medium is used for the proper purpose and that tools are used for the purposes for which they were made and are not wasted or destroyed by serving a purpose alien to their construction.

Many new and exciting media being used in art are of no expense at all: light, styrofoam, and sound, all of which provide children with tools of their generation which they understand and enjoy.

Crafts play a substantial role in the development of creativity and the fostering of artistic expression. Crafts can provide children with the incentive to become skilled workmen and to learn special techniques.

Printmaking is one craft that exemplifies the benefits of

working with any craft.   The printing block, for instance, is an intermediary between the child and his artistic expression.   It provides the child with the gratification that we all feel when we get something for nothing.   There is always the element of magic and surprise.   There is always an added bonus for our efforts— the block and the process make a contribution.

We know from experience that not all children express themselves freely in art; they have already developed fears and inhibitions that cut them off.   Printing can be the means of reaching many of these children, in the same way that an uncommunicative child will use a puppet to talk about himself. The final result is not entirely his responsibility; it does not bare his imagined deficiencies.

Printing is both process and product.   It provides a wide range of creative problem-solving opportunities that call for flexibility, the ability to see familiar things in strange ways.   The powers of intuitive thinking are encouraged and rewarded by the resulting product.   The student is continually involved in evaluation and aesthetic perception.

The teacher can make the exploration of a new medium a joyous and satisfying experience for the child by being aware of all the possibilities available to him and by helping him to discover them for himself.

ACTIVITIES

1. You should work with art media so you will better understand the creative process in children.   Here are some practical situations in which you can try your creative abilities.
    a. List all the uses you can think of for a tin can.
    b. Design a file box to hold the materials you are collecting for use in your classroom (or for student teaching if you are a student).   Make it functional but attractive.
    c. Think of all the materials you can that you might use to represent sheep on a mural your students are making.
    d. Buy a cheap straw purse and decorate it.   Consider all the possible materials you might use.
    e. Design a card for an ill classmate.
2. List all the companies in your town and identify their waste products.   Then brainstorm ways these products could be used in the art program.   Examples: A large box company was happy to supply large sheets of cardboard (which had slight flaws on one side) to a school rather than to burn them.   A

tin can company gave the scrap metal from which cans were punched to a teacher who used them for designs, collages, jewelry, mobiles, and decorations.

3. Try out the recipes beginning on page 313, and test the qualities of the products you make by using them with children.

4. Discuss this statement: Any discussion of color in the elementary school should concern results of experiences with color rather than "correct" or "incorrect" uses of it. The teaching of color wheels and color plans has no place in the elementary school, for such lessons would most certainly cut off the child's own spontaneity and prevent him from discovering meaningfully and joyously that which someone else is telling him. Premature imposition of such knowledge on a child may well cause him to lose his own sense of adventure and risk-taking and to become dependent on the teacher for his decisions or insecure in his approach to art expression.

5. Following is a list of suggestions for you to try yourself with puppets or to try out with children:
   a. Choose a piece of music with some obviously broad divisions, such as changes in tempo or instrumentation. Using whatever puppets are available, translate the music.
   b. Using a styrofoam ball on a stick, pin on accessories to create a variety of characters.
   c. Have the puppet conduct show and tell sessions.
   d. Have the shy or hesitant child use his puppet to present his show and tell.
   e. Experiment with animation of inanimate objects such as food packages or eggs to teach health and nutrition.
   f. Experiment with tape-recorded soundtracks for puppet plays. Record at one speed and play back at another speed.

6. Peanut shells can be turned into finger puppets. Make caps for each finger from peanut shells. Draw faces with a felt-tipped pen. Have your children work in twos or in small groups and present mini-puppet shows while seated at their own desks. If you are a college student, let go of your inhibitions and prepare "mini-dialogue" shows with someone in your class. Use such topics as "The Generation Gap," "Booze in College," "Curfews," "Dorm Food," "Dorm Living," "Love Story," or "Rock and Roll," and present them to each other.

7. For your college class, or, if you are a teacher, for a faculty show or party, plan a light show based on some of the principles and ideas discussed on pp. 280–284. Explore with light and music, thinking of all the experiences you can have. Then think through the art objectives you could accomplish and the skills and techniques you could teach in such a project with children.

FIGURE 8–21.   Children hang life-sized puppets of their teachers.

8. One type of puppet not mentioned here is the life-sized puppet. Children can make life-sized puppets from garbage bags or paper bags. Then, Japanese fashion, they can put loops around the puppets' wrists, ankles, and forehead and fasten them to their own bodies so they can make the puppets move.

One group of children made life-sized puppets of their teachers. When asked later how they would like to see the puppets displayed, one child jokingly said, "Hang them." So the puppets of the teachers (and the principal) were hanged (Fig. 8–21).

Take plastic garbage bags. Blow them up. Decorate them to make them life-sized puppets. Create a puppet show for class presentation or for a faculty party from your puppets.

9. Play some honky-tonk piano music. While it is playing, paint with felt pens on a strip of motion-picture film as described

on p. 284. If you can do this with a group, have half the group write phrases, words, ideas, a poem, or a piece of prose —anything that comes to mind as they listen to the music. Then make a soundtrack for the film by playing the music at low volume while each person reads what he has written into a microphone. Be sure to raise the volume between each person's reading so the music plays a part in the soundtrack. Now play the film and the soundtrack together: you have reacted to the stimuli in your environment with music, sight, words, color, and motion.

10. Try experimenting with prints—print with materials not mentioned here. By teasing your own creative thinking powers, you may invent a new process.

11. Take each medium in turn and list unusual uses for it: fingerpaint, printing ink, crayons, fabric dyes.

12. List substitutes for various media. Examples: paste—starch; paint—food coloring.

13. Experiment with media that can best help children learn perception, spacial relationships, intuitive thinking, and divergent thinking.

14. Try to arrange for children to deal with the same motivating experience using different media.

15. Invent art experiences with materials not usually considered art media, such as peas, beans, macaroni, or soap.

SELECTED BIBLIOGRAPHY

Albert, Calvin, and Dorothy Seckler. *Figure Drawing Comes to Life.* New York: Van Nostrand Reinhold Co., 1962.

Aller, Doris, and Diane Aller. *Mosaics.* Menlo Park, Calif.: Lanc Magazine & Book Co., 1960.

Andrews, Michael. *Creative Printmaking.* Englewood Cliffs, N.J.: Prentice-Hall, Inc., 1963.

———. *Sculpture and Ideas.* Englewood Cliffs, N.J.: Prentice-Hall, Inc., 1966.

Argiro, Larry. *Mosaic Art Today.* Scranton, Pa.: Intext Educational Publishers, 1968.

Barford, George. *Clay in the Classroom.* Worcester, Mass.: Davis Publications, Inc., 1963.

Batchelor, Marjorie. *The Puppet Theater Handbook.* New York: Harper & Row, Publishers, 1956.

Beitler, Ethel Jane. *Create with Yarn.* Scranton, Pa.: Intext Educational Publishers, 1964.

Belfer, Nancy. *Designing in Batik and Tie Dye.* Worcester, Mass.: Davis Publications, Inc., 1967.

————. *Designing in Stitching and Applique.* Worcester, Mass.: Davis Publications, Inc., 1970.

Betts, Victoria. *Exploring Papier-Mâché.* Worcester, Mass.: Davis Publications, Inc., 1955.

Brommer, Gerald F. *Wire Sculpture.* Worcester, Mass.: Davis Publications, Inc., 1964.

Brow, Francis. *Collage.* New York: Pitman Publishing Corp., 1963.

Cataldo, John W. *Lettering: A Guide for Teachers.* Worcester, Mass.: Davis Publications, Inc., 1958.

Cooke, Robert W. *Designing with Light on Paper and Film.* Worcester, Mass.: Davis Publications, Inc., 1969.

Cox, Doris, and Barbara Warren. *Creative Hands.* New York: John Wiley & Sons, Inc., 1945.

Daingerfield, Marjorie. *Fun and Fundamentals of Sculpture.* New York: Charles Scribner's Sons, 1963.

Foley, Doris. *Art Recipes.* Dansville, N.Y.: F. A. Owen, Publisher, 1960.

Frankson, Carl, and Kenneth Benson. *Crafts Activities: Featuring 65 Holiday Ideas.* Englewood Cliffs, N.J.: Prentice-Hall, Inc., 1970.

Friend, David. *The Creative Way to Paint.* New York: Watson-Guptill Publications, 1966.

Greenberg, Pearl. *Children's Experiences in Art.* New York: Van Nostrand Reinhold Co., 1966.

Guild, Vera P. *Creative Use of Stitches.* Worcester, Mass.: Davis Publications, Inc., 1964.

Haupt, Charlotte. *Beginning Clay Modeling: An Approach for Teaching Elementary School Children.* Belmont, Calif.: Fearon Publishers, 1970.

Hooper, Grizella. *Puppet Making through the Grades.* Worcester, Mass.: Davis Publications, Inc., 1966.

Hoover, F. Louis. *Art Activities for the Very Young.* Worcester, Mass.: Davis Publications, Inc., 1961.

Horn, George F. *Crafts for Today's Schools.* Worcester, Mass.: Davis Publications, Inc., 1972.

Horne, Joicey. *Young Artists.* Toronto: Longmans Green, 1961.

Hornung, Clarence P. *Lettering from A to Z.* New York: William Penn Publishing Corp. (Tudor Publishing Co.), 1954.

Hunt, W. Ben. *Crafts and Hobbies.* New York: Golden Press (Western Publishing Co.), 1964.

Hutchison, Harold F. *The Poster.* New York: The Viking Press, Inc., 1968.

Janson, H. W., and P. J. Janson. *The Story of Painting for Young People.* New York: Harry N. Abrams, Inc., 1963.

Johnson, Lillian. *Papier Mâché.* New York: David McKay Co., Inc., 1958.

Johnson, Pauline. *Creating with Paper.* Seattle: University of Washington Press, 1958.

Kampman, Lothar. *Creating with Colored Paper.* New York: Van Nostrand Reinhold Co., 1967.

——. *Creating with Crayons.* New York: Van Nostrand Reinhold Co., 1967.

——. *Creating with Poster Paints.* New York: Van Nostrand Reinhold Co., 1967.

Kenny, John B. *Ceramic Design.* Philadelphia: Chilton Book Co., 1963.

Kepes, Byorgy. "Light as a Creative Medium." *Concepts in Art and Education.* George Pappas, ed. New York: Macmillan Publishing Co., Inc., 1970.

Krevitsky, Nik. *Batik—Art and Craft.* New York: Van Nostrand Reinhold Co., 1964.

Kuwabara, Minoru, Kenzo Hayashi, and Takanori Kumamoto. *Cut and Paste.* New York: Ivan Obolensky, Inc., 1961.

Lanier, Vincent. "Newer Media and the Teaching of Art." *Concepts in Art and Education.* George Pappas, ed. New York: Macmillan Publishing Co., Inc., 1970.

Linse, Barbara Bucher. *Elementary Art Activities.* Belmont, Calif.: Fearon Publishers, 1970.

Malcolm, Dorothea C. *Design: Elements and Principles.* Worcester, Mass.: Davis Publications, Inc., 1972.

Manley, Seon. *Adventures in the Making: The Romance of Crafts around the World.* New York. Vanguard Press, Inc., 1959.

Marks, Mickey Klav. *Sand Sculpturing.* New York: The Dial Press, 1962.

Mattil, Edward. "Meaning of Crafts." *Concepts in Art and Education.* George Pappas, ed. New York: Macmillan Publishing Co., Inc., 1970.

Morey, Anne, and Chris Morey. *Making Mobiles.* New York: Watson-Guptill Publications, 1966.

Moseley, Spencer, Pauline Johnson, and Hazel Koenig. *Crafts Design.* Belmont, Calif.: Wadsworth Publishing Co., Inc., 1962.

Nelson, Glenn C. *Ceramics.* New York: Holt, Rinehart and Winston, Inc., 1960.

Pattemore, Arnel W. *Printmaking Activities for the Classroom.* Worcester, Mass.: Davis Publications, Inc., 1966.

Peck, Ruth L., and Robert Aniello. *Art Lessons on a Shoestring.* Englewood Cliffs, N.J.: Parker Publishing Co., 1968.

Rainey, Sarita R. *Weaving without a Loom.* Worcester, Mass.: Davis Publications, Inc., 1960.

Randall, Arne W. *Murals for the Schools.* Worcester, Mass.: Davis Publications, Inc., 1956.

Robertson, Seonaid, M. *Creative Crafts in Education.* Boston: Routledge & Kegan Paul, 1952.

Roettger, Ernst. *Creative Clay Design.* New York: Van Nostrand Reinhold Co., 1963.

————. *Creative Paper Design.* New York: Van Nostrand Reinhold Co., 1959.

Roukes, Nicholas. *Classroom Craft Manual.* Belmont, Calif.: Fearon Publishers, 1970.

Schlein, Miriam. *Shapes.* New York: Young Scott Books (Addison-Wesley), 1958.

Schultz, Lloyd. "Light Media: A Course in Expression and Communication." *Programs in Progress: Art in the School.* Al Hurwitz, ed. New York: Harcourt Brace Jovanovich, Inc., 1972.

Sheaks, Barclay. *Painting with Acrylics.* Worcester, Mass.: Davis Publications, Inc., 1968.

Sternberg, Harry. *Woodcut.* New York: Pitman Publishing Corp., 1962.

Timmons, Virginia Gayheart. *Designing and Making Mosaics.* Worcester, Mass.: Davis Publications, Inc., 1964.

Untracht, Oppi. *Enameling on Metal.* New York: Greenberg Publishers, 1971.

Wankelman, Willard. *Arts and Crafts for Elementary Teachers.* Dubuque, Iowa: William C. Brown Co., Publishers, 1972.

Weiss, Harvey. *Clay, Wood and Wire.* New York: Young Scott Books (Addison-Wesley), 1956.

————. *Paper, Ink and Roller.* New York: Young Scott Books (Addison-Wesley), 1958.

————. *Pencil, Pen and Brush.* New York: Young Scott Books (Addison-Wesley), 1961.

————. *Sticks, Spools and Feathers.* New York: Young Scott Books (Addison-Wesley), 1962.

Whitman, A. *Paper Art. Creative Art Book.* Racine, Wis.: Whitman Publishing Co., 1966.

————. *Print Art. Creative Art Book.* Racine, Wis.: Whitman Publishing Co., 1966.

Winter, Ed. *Enameling for Beginners.* Worcester, Mass.: Creative Hands Bookshop, 1962.

CHAPTER IX

Art Resources

Art is a human activity having for its purpose the transmission to others of the highest and best feelings to which men have risen.

COUNT LEV NIKOLAEVITCH TOLSTOI[1]

There are many resources available to the art team other than those mentioned in the last chapter. In this chapter, the authors explore the need for art resources and then list those that have been of help to them in their teaching.

The art team needs to have at its fingertips the names and addresses that make possible the attainment of art resources other than supplies. The authors have tried here to compile workable lists and to express thoughts on the use of community and home resources.

Every community has resources in common which may be used: parks, libraries, buildings with unique architecture, museums, cultural events, fairs, holiday decorations, store windows, renewal projects, and the like. Each of these can be used to advantage by creative teachers in promoting the art program.

Almost every community also has unique resources that can provide materials and/or inspiration for the school art program: a local artist or commercial illustrator, a town publishing house, a paper factory with carloads of elegant scraps, a tin can company with pieces of scrap metal, a fabric company with beautiful swatches of cloth.

1. Count Lev Nikolaevitch Tolstoi, *The Kingdom of God*, chap. 8.

In one school, the authors found a PTA group that had taken, as their responsibility, the task of compiling a resource file: every parent was asked to put on a file card his occupation, his hobbies, the materials that might be available from his job, and whether or not he would be willing to come to school to tell about his work or his hobbies.   This file proved to be very useful for social studies and art experiences.   Each teacher can develop files of her own at very little cost for a variety of purposes.

PICTURE RESOURCES

Over the years teachers build up files of materials to help them teach social studies, health, and other subjects.   It is equally important to have readily available a similar file to help with the teaching of art.   The extent of the collection will depend upon available space and the interest of the teacher.   There are, however, some guidelines to collecting a useful resource file.

Most resources, whatever their nature and extent, should be available to the children.   If the children help create the resources they will use them with greater frequency and care.

Classification of Picture Resources

The first problem is one of classification.   A print filed under historical costume may be a valuable example of the use of texture.   If there are too many classifications, children find it difficult to find what they want.   In the younger grades reading the title on the file can be a problem.   This can be offset by pasting a representative picture on the face of the card.   If there are too few classifications, files become a mixture of too many things.

Here are some examples for broad areas of classification. Materials can be gathered from magazines and newspapers.

1. People—types, nationalities
2. Historical people—costumes, settings, transportation, weapons, architecture
3. Sports—football, baseball, basketball, soccer, cars, hockey, the Olympics
4. Animals—prehistoric, wild, domestic, circus
5. Trees—single and in groups, leaves, fruits, type of bark
6. Flowers

7. Birds—nests, habitats
8. Transportation—boats, cars, planes, bicycles, airports, docks, railroad depots
9. Buildings—churches, houses, fire houses, stores, skyscrapers
10. Fish—tropical, fresh and salt water, habitats
11. Modern man—aquanauts, astronauts, machinery

These files will provide most of the visual information that the child demands. If the class has supplied most of the material one can be fairly certain that it is of the kind that fits their concept levels. They will choose those visual images that have meaning for them.

Vertical Files. Vertical file pockets that expand to about two inches and fit a standard filing cabinet can be filled to about half their capacity with mimeograph paper. As material is brought in, it can be trimmed and mounted to a sheet with rubber cement. Reproductions too large to fit can be folded; one half is stuck down and the other is folded over it.

Scrapbooks. An alternative is to use the large, old-fashioned scrapbook or the modern ring-leaf binder. These can be kept on a shelf; they are useful where file space is at a premium. The scrapbook limits the use of the material to one student at a time. Many children like to keep scrapbooks of their own and should be encouraged to do so.

Displays of Three-Dimensional Material. Children's art is an expression of their personal experiences. The type of reference material displayed can often create an experience that the child can interconnect with others to produce a painting: a deserted bird's nest with eggs; the skull of a small animal; a rock with interesting colors and markings; a plaster cast of an animal footprint; an old rusty padlock; a horse show; a model boat. The list is endless. The artist's studio is traditionally cluttered with such found objects. Their value lies in the fact that the artist concerned with visual expression looks at them in much the same way the musician listens to sounds and music.

The place where children create their artwork needs to be visually stimulating. The objects displayed are best chosen for their visual interest rather than merely for reference.

Use of Picture Resources

Generally speaking, it is wise to have the children use the references away from the artwork that they are involved with. At all age levels there is a tendency to try to merely copy the material rather than use it for information.   The best time to use the references is before the art activity begins so that there is no interruption of the drive toward self-expression.

When Frank decided to paint an underwater scene, Miss Barclay reminded him of the file on fish.

"There are all sorts of fish here, and they all look so different.   Can you see the things that they all have in common?" Frank mentioned heads and tails.

"Look how many different shapes a tail can have." Miss Barclay traced the shapes with her pencil.   "What else do they all have?"

"Fins."

"Sure.   And if you look carefully they all have them at the same places."

"They are all different shapes too," offered Frank.   "Can I go and see the ones in Miss Jenkins's room?"

By the time Frank was ready to create his underwater scene he had finished with the reference file.   When his painting was finished it was distinctively his own, but his symbols for fish and water had been noticeably affected by his reference work.

Sometimes students feel the need for references while the work is in progress, but again the same procedure can apply.

Sources of Picture Resources

Each month popular magazines like *Time* run features on contemporary artists or rediscovered classical painters.   The reproductions of these men's paintings are of high quality and can be used in many ways to promote the art program in the classroom. Children can bring in the magazines after they have been read at home, cut them up, and file the articles and pictures in the classroom reference file.   Other sources of beautiful reproductions of famous paintings are discussed below.

Prints.   A list of suppliers of prints is included at the end of this section.   In many ways it is better to choose the prints on the basis of their appeal to children rather than as examples of famous paintings.   The following is a list of painters whose works have been found to have considerable appeal for young children: Vincent Van Gogh, Frederic Remington, Winslow Homer, Paul Klee, Pablo Picasso, Pierre Bonnard, Henri Matisse.

To a great extent, the aesthetic development of the child

will depend upon the paintings and art objects that surround him during his formative years. It is unfortunate that we make such strong distinctions between what we consider art to be enjoyed by children and art to be enjoyed by adults. A great deal of what we offer children in the name of fantasy is phony sentimentality. Prints or illustrations for children show an extreme anthropomorphism that denies the child any worthwhile insights or understandings. Animals are depicted with human characteristics that do not do justice to man or beast.

Children allowed to choose their own prints will do so on the basis of standards that they have already acquired. It takes good judgment on the part of the teacher to provide prints that will both capture the child's interest and raise his aesthetic perception. Here is a short list of prints involving various media that have appealed to children.

Mosaics with tile, paper, seeds, or found objects:

* *Empress Theodora,* sixth century, Church of San Vitale Ravenna
* *Emperor Justinian and Followers,* sixth century, Church of San Vitale Ravenna
* *Battle Scene between Alexander and Darius,* from the floor of the House of the Faun, Pompeii, 100 B.C., Museo Nationale Napoli
* *Merz Picture 19,* collage by Kurt Schwitters, Société anonyme Collection, Yale University Art Gallery

Painting with limited palette:

* *Auvers, Vue de Village,* Van Gogh, Dutch, 1853–1890, all greens
* *Starlight over the Rhône,* Van Gogh, Dutch, 1853–1890, all blues
* *The Herring Net,* Winslow Homer, 1836–1910, Art Institute, Chicago, all greys
* *Number 27,* Jackson Pollock, 1950, Whitney Museum, New York, textures
* *Apparition of Face and Fruit Dish on a Beach,* Salvador Dali, 1938, Wadsworth Museum, fantasy

Clay:

* *Recumbent Figure,* 1938, Henry Moore, Tate Gallery, London

Catalogues. Catalogues on art and art supplies can almost be regarded as ready-made scrapbooks. The ones from large mail-order houses contain a broad spectrum of information. For the younger child the information is too scattered and hard to find.

For the older child the use of the index becomes an additional educational bonus.

Specialized catalogues or brochures dealing with such things as cars, camping gear, boats, and snowmobiles are useful just as they are, but they need to be classified.

ADDRESSES FOR ART CATALOGUES

American Art Clay Co., Inc.
4717 W. 16th St.
Indianapolis, Ind.

American Crayon Co.
Joseph Dixon Crucible Co.
1706 Hayes Ave.
Sandusky, Ohio

American Handicrafts Co.
1101 Foch St.
Fort Worth, Tex.

Atlas Equipment and Supply Co., Inc.
2652 Wood St.
Muskegon Heights, Mich.

Bergen Arts and Crafts
Box 689
Salem, Mass.

Berstea's Hobby Craft, Inc.
Box 40
Monmouth, Ill.

Binney and Smith Inc.
380 Madison Ave.
New York, N.Y.

Brewster Corp.
50 River St.
Saybrook, Conn.

Bro-Dart Inc.
1609 Memorial Ave.
Williamsport, Pa.

Economy Handcrafts
47–11 Francis Lewis Blvd.
Flushing, N.Y. 11361

Glidden-Durkee Div.
SCM Corp.
900 Union Commerce Bldg.
Cleveland, Ohio

M. Grumbacher Inc.
460 W. 34th St.
New York, N.Y.

Handcrafters, Inc.
1–99 W. Brown St.
Waupun, Wis.

Hunt Manufacturing Co.
1405 Locust St.
Philadelphia, Pa.

Industrial Arts Supply Co.
5724 W. 36th St.
Minneapolis, Minn.

Milton-Bradley Co.
Springfield, Mass.

NASCO
901 Jamesville Ave.
Fort Atkinson, Wis.

Rich Art Color Co.
31 W. 21st St.
New York, N.Y.

F. Weber Co.
Div. Visual Art Industries
Wayne Ave. & Windrim Ave.
Philadelphia, Pa.

ADDRESSES FOR PRINTS

Harry N. Abrams
110 E. 59th St.
New York, N.Y. 10022

Art Education, Inc.
Blauvelt, N.Y. 10913

Artext Prints, Inc.
Westport, Conn. 06880

Associated American
Artists, Inc.
663 Fifth Ave.
New York, N.Y. 10022

Catalda Fine Arts, Inc.
225 Fifth Ave.
New York, N.Y. 10010

Far Gallery
746 Madison Ave.
New York, N.Y. 10004

Metropolitan Museum of Art
Book and Art Shop
Fifth Ave. & 82nd St.
New York, N.Y. 10028

Museum of Modern Art
11 W. 53rd St.
New York, N.Y. 10019

New York Graphic Society
140 Greenwich Ave.
Greenwich, Conn. 06830

Oestreicher's Prints, Inc.
43 W. 46th St.
New York, N.Y. 10036

Penn Print Co.
572 Fifth Ave.
New York, N.Y. 10036

Dr. Konrad Prothman
2378 Soper Ave.
Baldwin, N.Y. 11510

Raymond and Raymond, Inc.
1071 Madison Ave.
New York, N.Y. 10028

Reinhold Publishing Co.
420 Park Ave.
New York, N.Y. 10022

Shorewood Reproductions, Inc.
Dept. S
724 Fifth Ave.
New York, N.Y. 10019

UNESCO Catalogues
Columbia University Press
440 W. 110th St.
New York, N.Y. 10025

University Prints
15 Brattle St.
Harvard Square
Cambridge, Mass. 02138

E. Weyhe
794 Lexington Ave.
New York, N.Y. 10021

LITERARY RESOURCES

The supply of books related to art education and to art teaching is
ample.   Each book has a contribution to make.

Books on Art

The authors have compiled a selection of books on topics related to the chapter headings at the end of each chapter of this text. The lists have been selected with one of three criteria in mind: (1) the book promotes the philosophy discussed in this text— that art is a means of creative visual expression, or (2) the book presents opposing or new viewpoints and developments in art education, or (3) the book will help the teacher to have new experiences with tools and techniques or to develop new skills. The reader is referred to these lists for help.

Books Related to Art

There are many books available that relate to art even though they are not directly about art. One such book is *The Family of Man*, a photographic essay by Edward Steinchen.[2] It relates the photographer as journalist to the photographer as artist.

It is ideal if each classroom can have this type of book readily available in its own resource area. If it means a trip to the library on another floor to find the book, the chances are it will not be used. If art is being taught creatively, the need for a particular book or reference is hard to predict. Each reference may be needed for only a very short time and it must be found quickly before the child's interest evaporates. Many books of this nature are listed in the selected bibliographies at the end of each chapter.

Art Periodicals

A subscription to an art journal is one way the teacher can keep up on new techniques, new ideas in art, and art resources.

Currently available periodicals are listed below.

2. Edward Steinchen, *The Family of Man* (New York: Museum of Modern Art), 1955.

ADDRESSES FOR ART PERIODICALS

Artist Junior
Artist Junior Publishers
New Haven, Conn.

Arts and Activities
Publishers Development
Corp.
8150 N. C. Park Ave.
Skokie, Ill.

Ceramics Monthly
Professional
Publications, Inc.
4175 N. High St.
Columbus, Ohio

Craft Horizons
American
Craftsmen's Council
44 W. 53rd St.
New York, N.Y. 10019

Creative Crafts
Oxford Press
6015 Santa Monica Blvd.
Los Angeles, Calif.

Design Quarterly
Walker Art Gallery
Minneapolis, Minn.

Everyday Art
American Crayon Co.
Sandusky, Ohio

Journal of Creative Behavior
The Creative Education
Foundation
1300 Elmwood Ave.
State University College
Buffalo, N.Y. 14222

School Arts
The Davis Press
Worcester, Mass.

COMMUNITY RESOURCES

Museums

The role of the museum is changing from that of a fixed collection to that of a teaching facility with continually changing content and emphasis. Museums often have separate workshops and instructional facilities for children with classes and films. If you are fortunate enough to teach within reach of a museum and can arrange school visits, they can provide a vital learning situation. To be effective, such visits need careful planning. It may well be that the exhibit can be seen as an extension of something that has already been touched on in the classroom. The children need a guide to "seeing." There has to be some personal involvement. The child must reach some emotional and intellectual contact with what he sees. Seeing a collection of Indian clothing and weapons becomes significant when it follows a study of the Indian culture of one's own district. One author can remember being highly excited as a child by an exhibition of ornate hinges that he might have passed by but for a previous visit to a black-smith's shop.

Art Leagues

Art leagues can prove to be a valuable resource for the interested teacher and student. Many receive outside funds that allow them to run special children's classes after school hours and on weekends. They not only present exhibitions of members' work, but also that of professional artists. They present the teacher with an opportunity to develop her own skills by working with others with similar interests.

Art league membership can provide a pool of visiting artists. Many members have considerable ability in a wide range of art-related occupations, such as photography, architecture, or town planning.

Libraries

Libraries, like museums, are undergoing a change of image. The institution with the silent, dusty atmosphere is being replaced by a more lively place where the lending of books is only one of the functions. Attempts are being made to expand activities in specialized areas, such as story reading for the young child. Study groups can utilize the total holdings of the library, which include many beautiful books in the field of art with perfect reproductions of works of art. Many of these books are not available in children's sections, but are available to the teacher. Other materials, such as phonograph records, tapes, filmstrips, and color slides, are now becoming a part of library resources. The new concept of the school library as a learning resource center is a great step forward. If adequately staffed, the new library can provide a great deal of help in the areas of art history and art appreciation.

Field Trips

If art is seen as a part of the total learning situation, any field trip can contribute to artistic awareness. It has been the authors' experience that schools have frowned upon field trips because they take time from what is considered more valuable work.

There has been a tendency to regard them as a day off and a break in the monotony of the daily routine.

If we believe that practical experience is one of the best ways to learn, then we need to provide all the practical experiences we can. If learning and art are to be seen as an integral part of life, they cannot be practiced solely in the isolation of the classroom.

A visit to a newspaper may provide some unforeseen stimulation in the field of art. There are impressions of noise, movement, and mechanical shapes. There are the people, many of whom are dressed to suit their occupations. There is the printing process itself. Printing fascinates children, for there is always the element of the unexpected and the challenge to discover new methods. The visit can point out the extent to which we depend upon graphic communication. The methods by which photographs and advertisements are reproduced can awaken a much keener perception of effective use of line and tone.

There are many field trips that might have art education and appreciation as their central intent: visits to old homes, historic buildings, theaters, galleries, flower gardens, nurseries, museums, or antique shows. There are endless possibilities. The value of the trip will, in great measure, depend upon the perceptive nature of the teacher and the extent to which she is able to plan the trip as a part of a total process.

Films

Many commercial films that come to the local movie houses have great potential for use as art lessons. In many communities, matinees can be arranged with the local manager, so classes can go to the movies as part of a field trip. Good films for children include *The Yellow Submarine, 2001: A Space Odyssey, Fantasia, Willie Wonka and the Chocolate Factory,* and *Mary Poppins.* Keeping an eye on the local movie advertisements may reveal some worthy material.

CLASSROOM FILMS AND FILMSTRIPS

Films

Films are most valuable when they are used within a total learning situation. A film designed to teach concepts about the use of color is most valuable at a time when children have had an opportunity to experiment themselves. We know that no two people see the same things in the same way. The things that attract the students' attention the first time the film is shown may have little to do with the true intent of the film. Having children discuss what they have seen and then showing the film again often produces insights that were missed the first time. Films that deal with specific ways of doing things are not nearly as valuable as those that enable the child to see ways in which he might achieve things himself. Some films are designed merely to stimulate creative thinking in certain areas.

Films ordered from distributors should be shown for the purpose of accomplishing specific objectives in the art program. Films that serve a specific purpose are best suited to the needs of children. The authors list below those they have used in elementary or college classes that have been highly motivating and successful.

FILMS FOR CLASSROOM USE

Source of film is indicated and addresses for film companies follow the film listing. c indicates color; b/w is black and white. The key is G—general use; P—primary grades; I—intermediate grades; C—college level.

Adventures in the Arts, c
22 min.
Girls Scouts of America, G

Animules, c
11 min.
International Film Bureau, G

Around My Way, c
11 min.
Contemporary Films, Inc., G

Art in Action with Doug
Kinman, c
Harmon Foundation, I,C

Art in Motion, c
17 min.
Encyclopaedia Britannica
Films, I,C

Art in Our World, c
11 min.
Bailey Films, I,C

Artist and Nature, c
11 min.
International Film
Bureau, I,C

Begone Dull Care, c
9 min.
International Film Bureau, G

Behind the Scenes of a
Museum, b/w
24 min.
International Film
Bureau, I,C

Boogie Woogie, c
4 min.
Syracuse Univ., G

Care of Art Materials, b/w
11 min.
Young America
Films, I,C

Children Are Creative, c
16 min.
Bailey Films, Inc., C

Children Who Draw,
b/w with c
38 min.
Wanami Films, Japan
Brandon Films, USA, C

Copper Enameling, c
15 min.
International Film Bureau, I,C

Crayon Resist, c
6 min.
American
Handicrafts Co., I,C

Design to Music, c,
5½ min.
International Film
Bureau, G

Discovering Color.
Discovering Texture, c
15 min.
Film Associates of
California, I,C

Discovering Ideas for Art, c
14 min.
Film Associates of
California, G,I,C

Eskimo Arts and Crafts, c
22 min.
International
Film Bureau, I,C

Face of Lincoln, b/w
22 min.
Syracuse Univ., I,C

Fiddle Dee Dee, c
4 min.
International
Film Bureau, G

Have I Told You Lately That
I Love You?, b/w
40 min.
Los Angeles, Univ. of S.
Calif., AV Dept., C

Insects and Painting, c
5 min.
Bailey Films, G

Keys to Brainstorming, b/w
20 min.
Univ. of Buffalo,
Creative Education
Foundation, C
moderator: Gary Moore

Little Blue and Little Yellow, c
10 min.
Contemporary Films, Inc., G

The Loon's Necklace, c
15 min.
Encyclopaedia Britannica
Films, G

The Magician, b/w
3 min.
Sterling Films
Syracuse Univ., Mass Media
Min., I,C

Making a Mask, c
6 min.
International
Film Bureau, I,C

Making a Mobile, c
11 min.
International
Film Bureau, I,C

Maurice Sendak, c
20 min.
Weston Woods Studios, I,C

Mrs. and Mr. Peacock, c
10 min.
Syracuse University, G

Peter and the Potter, c
21 min.
International Film Bureau, G

Picture in Your Mind, c
  16 min.
  International
  Film Bureau, G

Report in Primary Colors, c
  20 min.
  Film Production Service, I,C

Rhythm in Paint, c
  20 min.
  Encyclopaedia Britannica
  Films, G

Robert McCloskey, c
  20 min.
  Weston Woods Studio, G

The Sumi Artist, c
  15 min.
  Lobett Productions, I,C

Torn Paper, c
  6 min.
  International Film Bureau, G

Totems, c
  11 min.
  International
  Film Bureau, I,C

A Trip to the Moon, c
  14 min.
  Brandom Films, Inc., I,C

What Is Art?, c
  15 min.
  Encyclopaedia Britannica
  Films, I,C

What Shall We Paint? c
  10 min.
  Film Associates
  of California, I,C

Why Man Creates, c
  25 min.
  Pyramid Films, I,C

ADDRESSES FOR FILMS

American Handicrafts Co.
  83 W. Van Buren St.
  Chicago, Ill. 60605

Bailey Film Associates
  11559 Santa Monica Blvd.
  Los Angeles, Calif. 90025

Brandom Films
  221 W. 57th St.
  New York, N.Y. 10019

British Information Services
  30 Rockefeller Plaza
  New York, N.Y. 10020

Churchill Films
  662 N. Robertson Blvd.
  Los Angeles, Calif. 90069

Coast Visual Ed. Co.
  5620 Hollywood Blvd.
  Los Angeles, Calif. 90028

Contemporary Films, Inc.
  330 W. 42nd St.
  New York, N.Y. 10036

Jeff Dell Film Service, Inc.
  1150 Ave. of the Americas.
  New York, N.Y. 10036

Walt Disney Productions
  Educational Film Division
  350 S. Buena Vista Ave.
  Burbank, Calif. 91503

Encyclopaedia Britannica
  Films
  1140 Willmette Ave.
  Willmette, Ill. 60091

Films Classics Exchange
  1645 N. La Brea Ave.
  Los Angeles, Calif. 90028

Girl Scouts of America
  Film Library
  830 Third Ave.
  New York, N.Y. 10022

Homer Groening
301 Executive Bldg.
Portland, Oregon

Harmon Foundation
Division of Visual
Experiments
140 Nassau St.
New York, N.Y. 10038

Indiana University
Bloomington, Ind. 47401

International Film Bureau
332 S. Michigan Ave.
Chicago, Ill. 60604

Johnson Hunt Productions
6509 De Longpre Ave.
Hollywood, Calif. 90028

Carl Mahnke Productions
215 E. 3rd St.
Des Moines, Iowa 50300

McGraw-Hill Text Films
330 W. 42nd St.
New York, N.Y. 10018

National Film Board
of Canada
680 Fifth Ave.
New York, N.Y. 10019

Portafilms
4180 Dixie Highway
Drayton Plains, Mich.
48020

Santa Fe Film Bureau
80 E. Jackson Blvd.
Chicago, Ill. 60604

Sigma Educational Films
P.O. Box 1235
Studio City, Calif. 91604

Sterling Movies
375 Park Ave.
New York, N.Y. 10022

Sturgis Grant Productions, Inc.
238 E. 44th St.
New York, N.Y. 10017

John Sutherland
Educational Films, Inc.
201 N. Occidental Blvd.
Los Angeles, Calif. 90028

Francis Thompson
Productions
935 Second Ave.
New York, N.Y. 10022

University of California
University Extension
Education
Film Sales Department
Los Angeles, Calif. 90007

Weston Woods Studios
Weston, Conn. 06880

Filmstrips

Filmstrips serve many purposes in the classroom. They should be used when the teacher finds they meet a specific objective. The advantage of filmstrips over film is that the teacher can involve the children in discussion and in activities during the showing of the filmstrip, whereas in a film the simultaneous sound and picture make the presentation an audience situation.

The authors have listed below some filmstrips that they have used successfully in their classrooms to accomplish certain objectives. The distributors' addresses follow.

FILMSTRIPS FOR CLASSROOM USE

The Art of Seeing, c, s
six filmstrips on visual
perception and expression
Warren Schloat Productions,
Inc., C

Children Paint Their World, c
Art Council Aids, G

Emotion Takes Form, c
Art Council Aids, G

Famous Artists at Work, c, s
Set of 7
Set 1: Elsa Schmid, music;
Seymour Lipton, sculpture
Set 2: Richard Lyte, Esteban
Vincent, collage
Set 3: Hank Ketcham, car-
toon; Alton Tobey, mural;
Peter Hurd, watercolor; Ugo
Mochi, outline
Set 4: Marisol, wood sculp-
ture; Robert Sowers, stained
glass
Set 6: Bernard Rosenthal,
metal sculpture; the Atelier
Mourlot, lithography
Set 7: Jacques Lipchitz,
bronze casting; Hui Ka
Kwong, ceramics
Warren Schloat Productions,
Inc., I,C

History through Art, c, s
Set of 3
the Renaissance
the Baroque
the Enlightment
Warren Schloat Productions,
Inc., I,C

Junior Museum, c, s
six filmstrips
Educational Dimensions
Corporation, P,I

Little Adventures in Art, s
4 filmstrips
Warren Schloat Productions,
Inc., P,I

Lives of Old Masters, c, s
4 filmstrips
Michelangelo
El Greco
Francisco Goya
Van Gogh
Warren Schloat Productions,
Inc., I,C

Museum Tours, c, s
6 filmstrips
What Is a Museum?
The Egyptian Room
Ancient Greece and Rome
Knights in Armour
The Age of Exploration
Life in Colonial America
Warren Schloat Productions,
Inc., G

The Sea, c, s
#804, 2 filmstrips
Educational Dimensions
Corp., G

UNICEF Art, c, s
4 filmstrips
Warren Schloat Productions,
Inc., G

The West, c, s
#805, 2 filmstrips
Educational Dimensions
Corp., G

ADDRESSES FOR FILMSTRIPS

You can write to the following places for a catalogue.

American Council on
  Education
1785 Massachusetts Ave.
  N.W.
Washington, D.C. 20036

Art Council Aids
  Box 641
  Beverly Hills, Calif. 90213

Bailey Film Associates
  11559 Santa Monica Blvd.
  Los Angeles, Calif. 90025

Stanley Bowman Co., Inc.
  4 Broadway
  Valhalla, N.Y. 10595

Carnegie-Mellon University
  College of Fine Arts
  Schenley Park
  Pittsburgh, Pa. 15213

Curriculum Materials Corp.
  1319 Vine St.
  Philadelphia, Pa. 19100

Encyclopaedia Britannica
  Educational Corp.
  425 N. Michigan Ave.
  Chicago, Ill. 60611

Eye Gate House, Inc.
  146-01 Archer Avenue
  Jamaica, N.Y. 11435

Grolier Educational Corp.
  845 Third Ave.
  New York, N.Y. 10022

Jam Handy Organization
  2021 E. Grand Blvd.
  Detroit, Mich. 62332

Learning Arts
  P. O. Box 917
  Wichita, Kan. 67201

Life Filmstrips
  Time-Life Building
  Rockefeller Center
  New York, N.Y. 10020

Museum of Modern Art Library
  11 W. 53rd St.
  New York, N.Y. 10019

National Gallery of Art
  Constitution Ave. & Sixth St.
  N.W.
  Washington, D.C. 20001

Philadelphia Museum of Art
  Division of Education
  25th St. & Benjamin Franklin
  Pkwy.
  Philadelphia, Pa. 19130

Sandak, Inc.
  4 E. 48th St.
  New York, N.Y. 10017

Warren Schloat Productions
  Pleasantville, N.Y. 10570

School of the Art Institute of
  Chicago
  S. Michigan Ave. & E. Adams
  St.
  Chicago, Ill. 60603

Society for Visual Education,
  Inc.
  1345 Diversey Pkwy.
  Chicago, Ill. 60614

Thorne Films, Inc.
  1229 University Ave.
  Boulder, Col. 80302

HOME RESOURCES

Parents

A child brings much to school from home—often more than we take the time to find out.   Parents with talent or with unusual hobbies can provide excellent resource material for children. Homes may be the resting place of beautiful paintings, furniture, quilts, weather vanes, hooked rugs, antiques, candle makers, costumed dolls, printers, and clothes designers.   It would be a boon to the art program if each teacher would take the time to find out from the parents about their talents or artifacts that might be used in the school program.

Television

We tend to think of the negative parts of our culture more than the positive elements.   We hear much about violence and death on television, but rarely do people write articles telling of the good that comes from television or how it can be used in positive ways in the classroom.

Television is an instrument of the "now" generation. Children understand it and know more about it, generally, than the teachers do.   Some television shows can be used in school: if the teacher has a *TV Guide* she can make some viewing assignments from it.   Many programs can be used as assignments, such as a recent program on the life of Michelangelo.   It can be argued that TV has increased the child's vicarious experiences to a degree never before possible.   All important events are made visible to all children everywhere.

There are also some debits to be set against TV.   It provides things on a platter, so to speak.   The child is robbed of the necessity of using his powers of visualization which are so necessary for the enjoyment of reading.   A selection of specific portions of the total image has already been made and only these are offered for mass consumption.

One of the most beneficial uses of TV is in teaching art for art's sake.   It is now possible to carry children's experiences with TV over to school in the form of videotapes.   (See the discussion of videotapes in Chapter 8.)

SUMMARY

Art resources abound. The art team has only to look around the school and community to find resources for use in the art program. With a little imagination almost every aspect of art can be taught with materials at hand: color in the changing leaves of nature; movement in the patterns of the wind, rain, and snow; balance in the construction of a snowman; harmony in the peaceful landscape; skills and techniques in the occupations and hobbies of parents; craftsmanship in the local artist. Art education means having a serious encounter with the environment and expressing it visually. The environment provides the content of the visual product and supplies the equipment for creating it.

CHAPTER X

Evaluation in Art

Child art has a character of its own. Spontaneous self-expression through means of art materials is natural and fundamentally satisfying to all children. Children cannot approach art activities in the same way that adults do and should never have adult forms imposed on them. . . . The real test of whether a child's art is "good" is not how much the tree he has drawn represents the natural appearance of the tree, but how fully the child, when working, has entered into a personal reaction of his own to the tree and its environment. . . .

MAUD ELLSWORTH and MICHAEL ANDREWS[1]

What do you look for when you view a piece of art? What pleases you? Do you have specific "tastes"? For instance, do you say, "I don't like modern art" or "These old classics are stuffy"? Can you trace the development of your own tastes? Can anyone say of any other person that he has good taste? How can children's art best be evaluated—by grading or by testing? Knowing that all of us differ in our tastes, does not the grading or evaluation of children's art simply reflect our own tastes? This chapter pulls together concepts dealing with the problem of evaluation of children's art. The authors suggest that the reader review the material on p. 42 before reading this chapter.

1. Reprinted with permission of Random House, Inc. from Maud Ellsworth and Michael Andrews, *Growing with Art: A Teacher's Book* (Syracuse, N.Y.: The L. W. Singer Co., 1960). Copyright 1960 by the L. W. Singer Co.

One of the most frequently asked questions is "How do we evaluate children's artwork?" This is not only a problem for the elementary teacher; it is a problem for all who involve themselves in the more subjective aspects of human endeavors.

Why are some paintings considered to be priceless works of art, whereas others have no value? Why are some things considered to be beautiful? What is it about an individual that makes us perceive him as having good taste? When the child's intent is to produce a piece of visual art merely for the pleasure of doing so, how do we evaluate the result and, perhaps more importantly, should we? If so, by what standards?

Posing these questions makes it obvious that the answer requires an understanding not only of the field of art, but of aesthetics, philosophy, psychology, and the humanities. The answer must come from a wide background of experiences.

Before we can make any evaluation of children's work, we must be aware of the way in which their art expression develops. This is discussed in Chapter 3. If we can perceive that their development is lagging or that their symbols have become fixed and do not reflect emotional, intellectual, and perceptual growth, then we have a point from which to begin.

In order to make any assessment in these terms it is also necessary to be acutely aware of the total child. His artwork is an expression of the totality of the individual in ways that no other medium is. It is necessary that we see the child clearly on a particular day and in a particular set of circumstances. What we are looking at is not only a product, but a stage in the process of the child's perceptual development. Sometimes it may be the end result of the process.

When we talk about the necessity of the teacher's accepting the child's work, we do not mean that there is no contribution that the teacher can make to his development. On the other hand, her contribution must be one that dovetails very closely with his developing concepts and abilities; it must not have the effect of cutting him off from his own line of development.

This is one of the great evils of coloring books; they often present the child with a set of sentimentalized concepts about such subjects as animals or transportation. There is an imposition of adult concepts that the child dutifully accepts. These concepts are often strong enough to make it difficult for the child to form and internalize his own concepts and experiences.

Children's art is not the same as adult art, and we cannot bring the same criteria to bear in its evaluation. However, there are ways in which the teacher can help the child to make his own evaluation and in most circumstances this will be very valuable.

GRADING, TESTING, AND EVALUATING

The ultimate goal of any type of evaluation in art is to help the student to grow, to improve his own ability to express himself through art media, and to recognize and appreciate what he has produced.   Inasmuch as the aim of evaluation is to help the child grow within himself, there can be no possible reason for evaluating a child's work in comparison to others.

Eisner advocates the comparison of a student's work to his previous work as a means of evaluation for individual growth.[2] This technique improves instruction, because it permits student and teacher to diagnose strengths and weaknesses in art performance.   The individual evaluation provided by this technique also allows for considerable individual attention to the student and personal planning for his own art program.

One idea that will not be new to most teachers is that they keep samples of children's work for this purpose.   Conferences that supply the teacher with a description of the student's interests, feelings, and satisfactions in art also provide the teacher with material for the guidance of each individual child (see p. 348).

Inasmuch as there are still some schools using report card systems where grades are given for art, let us take a look at grading, testing, and evaluating.   There is a definite distinction to be made among the terms grading, testing, and evaluating.

Grading

Grading is the process of assigning a symbol to a product.   The symbol stands for a judgment based on a specific set of criteria.

The important question is: Should children's art products be graded?   Grading serves no purpose in art.   A teacher who feels that she has been endowed with a set of mystical

2. Elliot Eisner, "Evaluating Children's Art" in George Pappas, ed., *Concepts in Art and Education* (New York: Macmillan Publishing Co., Inc., 1970), pp. 386–390.

criteria that enables her at any given time to be able to grade the creativity of any human being, be he child or adult, is indeed assuming a God-like attitude and a responsibility of gigantic proportions.

There is no logical reason why art products should be graded. Grades, at best, are based on a curricular hierarchy where everyone does the same thing and then is compared to everyone else. The goal in art teaching and in creative development is to help each individual become himself—different from everyone else. In any graded system, failure is automatically built in. We have already said that creative teaching is success-oriented.

Testing

Testing is one technique used to evaluate mastery of human performance. It is generally most effective with cognitive and performance learnings, for it is a way of finding out what cognitive learnings or performance skills a person has assimilated. It is one of several vehicles for gathering information in order to make some of the judgments necessary for a complete evaluation. It has little valid use in art education in the elementary school. Art *knowledge* can be tested, but the *evaluation* of children's art and the evaluation of children through their art is another matter.

Evaluating

Evaluating is collecting relevant evidence of various kinds to be used in forming value judgments at a given point in a person's growth. It is important that evidence be gathered during the course of growth as well as at the point chosen for evaluation. Evaluation is part of the growth process itself and helps child and teacher to find new directions for continued growth.

Some educators describe evaluation as the judgment of the adequacy of behavior in comparison to a set of educational or behavioral objectives. This definition is sound, but it does not always apply to creative growth or to growth in art education, which cannot be predicted and which often comes into being as the result of a willingness to experiment, to explore, and to take risks.

METHODS OF EVALUATION

Lansing made a study of the stages of development as outlined by Piaget and the implications of these stages to art.[3] He concluded that no good comes from criticizing the drawings or other visual forms of a youngster's work. If it is important to change the shape of the child's work, then we must first change his concepts.

Art expression belongs in the affective domain, and matters of feeling and emotion are changed more often by experiences than by facts. How, then, can artwork itself be evaluated? By the way it looks? By its texture or form? By its color or lines? By its shape or arrangement on a page? By all of these and even more criteria?

Evaluations by such criteria are generally no more than an indication of how near a child has come to hitting the tastes and values of the teacher (or evaluator). Much of the evaluation in art education is subjective and dependent upon the teacher's values and tastes. This once again points out the responsibility of the teacher to know how *not* to impose her values and tastes on children.

Evidence for evaluation in the art program is best gathered through: (1) listening to (and recording) children's comments and reactions; (2) studying children's behavior while they are engaged in processes (and perhaps writing notes on cards); (3) seeking specific behavior changes in children; and (4) studying children's art products.

Evaluation through Comments—The Interview Technique

Listening to what the child has to say is one way to evaluate change. Some teachers write notes of children's comments and put them in anecdotal files as a record of growth. Some teachers tape discussions periodically and identify growth in specific children by listening to the tapes and contrasting the comments.

The interview technique described below affords the children an excellent opportunity to talk and an equally excellent opportunity for the teacher to listen. Lessons such as those

3. Kenneth Lansing, *Art, Artists and Art Education* (New York: McGraw-Hill Book Co., 1969).

described on p. 193 tell how a teacher can help a child grow in art vocabulary. Comparing children's comments from week to week will help the teacher to note changes in their ability to handle the nomenclature of art, to use techniques, and to apply art knowledge. Only through listening to children's comments will the teacher be able to determine their growth in aesthetics or in "taste."

Ken has just completed a large painting. Much of what he started with he has painted out, and his intentions are by no means clear. He has, however, spent a considerable amount of time on it, and since he has just started first grade this represents the full utilization of his attention span. In the picture there are what appear to be several suns, and in the bottom corner what might be a moon. At one stage in the proceedings there was a great deal more detail, but Ken seemed to grow tired of the struggle to come to grips with the representation of symbols closer to his growing perceptions, so he scribbled over them with black. As a result, the whole thing is a trifle messy and has a nasty tendency to drip all over the newly carpeted area of the room. The total impact on the overworked teacher is apt to be one of horror. The evaluation in that moment is made. The unthinking response might well be, "Ken, look at the mess you are making; put it over there to dry."

A carefully conducted interview with the Kenneths of this world can turn up some incredible insights into children's work, and a few well-chosen questions may be the means of helping the child discover ways in which he might better have achieved his purpose.

"Tell me about it, Ken. It looks very interesting."

"It is going to get dark and all these people want to get home in a hurry because their mother says when the street lights come on it is time to be home. The sun goes down and down and pretty soon you can't see the people who are bad and don't come in when the lights come on. And pretty soon the sun has gone and then there is only the moon, but that is not very bright and you can't see anything." There is probably as much to this story as you have patience to listen to. It also becomes obvious that the child is beginning to perceive ideas that he had not considered while he was painting and that these are now being woven into the tale. What was a confused and messy mass now appears as a well-expressed concept of the passing of day and the setting of the sun. To express spreading darkness it was necessary to paint out detail in the same way that it faded with the light. The painting was not dealing with one moment in time but with a progression of events.

The questions that need to be asked are the ones that will help him to refine the concept and perhaps find different ways of expressing difficult aspects of the same experience.

"It is fun to stand outside on a dark night and see just how much you can see. Have you noticed that it never really gets black dark? There is always a little light coming from somewhere."

The intent of the question is to have Ken consider the indiscriminate use of black to suggest night. It may well be that he is capable of refining this symbol and that he can begin to form concepts about the way in which he sees things. Some things are sharp and clear, and other things are mere shadows. It may be a long time before he can deal with art concepts as difficult as this, but he can be considering the possibilities.

"It would be fun to make a picture of the morning with the sun coming up; maybe you could do that next time." He may not, but he is then confronted with the problem of reversal which we know to be a characteristic ability of creative people.

Never once in the interview does the teacher attempt to impose her standards or point of view on the child. The child is placed in a secure position from which he can make his own evaluation on the basis of ideas that have been generated by the questions.

The technique works equally well with older children. If third graders are still representing the human figure in stereotyped ways with little or no differentiation between sexes or conditions, the types of questions used in the following incident may help the children to evaluate their efforts.

Mr. Grange had been talking about the diversity of human activities with his fourth-grade class. He had suggested that they show some of these activities in paintings which would then form a little exhibition. As the paintings progressed he was disappointed to find that many of the figures were stereotypes. He hoped that by the use of open-ended questions he could help the class perceive the need for differentiation.

"Jim, I see you have chosen skiing. That's a good active sport. What kind of people go skiing?"

Jim thought just of men and then grudging allowed that girls did it too.

"Do you ski, Jim? I suppose you have proper boots and clothes?" (Jim's painting shows no real evidence of clothing at all.) "It must be pretty cold whipping down those slopes with the snow flying. Don't the sun and snow worry your eyes?"

Slowly Jim is helped to recall and relate an experience with which he is familiar. He has the information that allows him to differentiate between a skier and a football player. Mr. Grange's questions helped to bring it into focus, so that without once mentioning the deficiencies of the painting he arranged the outcome.

Jill had painted figures raking leaves that were as rigid as toy soldiers.

"Do you have any good tricks for making the leaves shoot along in front of the rake?"

Jill told of quick flicks using the rake like a broom.

"Doesn't all that bending of your arms and back make you stiff? That would be a good exercise for fat people. Do you think old people could do it? Are you going to put the idea in your painting?"

In coming to grips with questions about young, old, fat, and bending, Jill was helped to see the interesting things that her figures lacked.

The indirect approach through open-ended questions and statements leaves the child free to adjust his concepts at his own level. His artwork is still what he wants it to be and not what the teacher says that it should be.

It is fair to say that the only person who can truly evaluate his artistic works is the artist, for only he knows the full extent of his intent and whether, in fact, he achieved what he set out to accomplish. We may not like what he has produced; it may not be to our taste.

Let us now suppose that a child has produced a painting. He has done his part and now it is up to you to make some pertinent comments. You are not too sure what you think about it, but you have a feeling that there is room for improvement.

So play for time, saying anything that is kind and helps the child to feel he has achieved a degree of success. There must be at least one thing that you find attractive; say so. "I like the way you have used more than one kind of green. How did you mix them?"

Chances are the child will be quite prepared to spend the next hour describing the complexities of mixing greens. This you may have difficulty in following. Sidestep the problem by having him tell about his painting. As the telling unfolds you recognize a garden seat in which you think you see the child's favorite dog.   So, let's deal with the dog.   Since we are not concerned with being able to produce facsimile reproductions of neighborhood dogs, what are we to suggest?   Let's ask the child. "He looks like a friendly dog; what is he doing?"

The child jumps in with both feet and recites a variety of canine activities, all involving violent movement.

"Show me how.   Does he have a long tail?   It must wag a lot."

It may well be at this point that the child recognizes that his dog lacks a tail.   If you can help him realize that his dog also lacks movement and does not really express dog-type activity, then you and the child are well on the way to evaluating his work.

In every area of education it is necessary at times to stop and ask oneself whether there is any justification for what you are doing.   Can there be any justification for teaching the child to draw a better dog?   The answer, of course, depends upon what we mean by a better dog.   If we mean a more accurate physical description, then the value is doubtful.   If by a better dog we mean one that expresses a personal feeling about the dog and one that shows developing perception not only about dogs but about the total environment that the child shares with them, then this is valuable.

The questions of relevance and importance become very clear when you teach art.   Immersion in subject matter and facts sometimes blunts the ability to decide whether or not one's teaching can be justified.

In conducting the interview it now becomes necessary to put your own perception to the test.   The child realizes that he set out to express dog antics and ended with limbo.   The chances are that you are going to have to help him decide what to do about it.   You could quickly make sketches of dogs running, jumping, and doing whatever it is dogs do.   This is a bad idea even if you are great at sketching dogs in motion.   It is bad because you are telling him what his concepts and feelings about the neighborhood dog should be.

Showing him pictures in the encyclopedia would be equally futile.   A picture of a dog is a picture of a dog in the same way that a painting of a tree, no matter how well done, remains paint and canvas.

The adventures of Lassie on television are one set of experiences.   Involvement with the neighborhood dog is something else again.

The ideal solution is to find the dog in question and to

allow the child to take fresh stock of the situation: to reexamine his concepts about the dog and his relationship to it. If he could do this fully and adequately he would become a philosopher and a sage. It is possible to suggest ways in which all valuable knowledge can be arrived at from just such a starting point.

It is possible that the desire to reexamine his ideas and feelings is the most important educational happening of his week. It is also possible, schools being what they are, that schedules and rules do not permit playing with dogs between 8:30 A.M. and 3 P.M. unless one happens to stop by during lunch hour.

The next best solution is to provide time, materials, and encouragement for the child to put his new thoughts into a painting so that when 3 P.M. rolls around he can seek out his world with a new eye.

If all goes well, you have engineered a very successful and valuable art lesson (even if you still cannot draw a straight line). The values in drawing or painting are legion, but at the elementary level very few of them have to do with artistic ability.

It would be naive to believe that all interviews are going to be as successful. Let's do an instant replay and see what disasters wait around to spoil the whole endeavor.

Everything is set up—the child has space, paints, and time, and you have the urge and good will to have a great interview. The child presents his paper to you—nothing. "I can't think of anything to paint."

You could tell him what to do; you could make all sorts of enthusiastic suggestions. Or you could tell him to forget it and to go and do something else. Both of these solutions should leave you with an uncomfortable feeling that something is wrong.

What is wrong, of course, is the fact that neither of the solutions takes into account some of the fundamental reasons why children create. Ideally, before brush touches paper the following things should have taken place: (1) there should have been an experience (good or bad) that impressed the child enough for him to carry the memory with him to the time when he could reexamine it, probably the art period; (2) he should have related that experience in some meaningful way to his life in general so that he at least partly understands the experience; and (3) he must then have developed the desire to express what he feels about that experience.

One always marvels that children do as well as they do in school when time is used in such an arbitrary fashion. At 8:30 A.M. the entire class is expected to be bursting out with creative and artistic expression; at 11:20 A.M. everyone is supposed to desire nothing more than forty minutes of calisthenics.

If the child says, "I can't think of anything to paint," there are several options open.   One is to provide him with an experience.   This may be nothing more earthshaking than going down to the kindergarten to look at their goldfish.   The second possibility is to provide him with an alternative time when the muse is not inhibited—when he is not being asked to perform on a full stomach, an empty stomach, or drenched in post-gym sweat.   Thirdly, it is possible to make the art material provide the experience.   In the section on art projects there are several designed to do just that.   (See p. 289.)   The general idea is to suggest ways in which materials can be used so that there is always the element of the unexpected built in.

He might paint on the bottom of a tray or plastic-topped table in broad strokes with a few simple colors, blotting the result with drawing paper.   The effects can be varied by lifting the paper off in different directions.   The result is nearly always pleasing and should be accepted much as one accepts any pleasing found object.

The exercise becomes even more valuable when the student is asked to look at the print from all sides and project his imagination onto the page.   This is the old and wonderful pastime of lying on one's back and finding dragons in the passing clouds; it is now known as loafing.   The great value in this and related pastimes is the development of the power to visualize. Given one set of facts, can you visualize a second?   Given a cloud, can you see a dog, a blueprint, a house?   Radio used to develop this ability.   From voices and sounds the power of visualization allowed us to construct new worlds.   Television, on the other hand, does just the reverse.   It demands nothing but our passive acceptance and our valuable time.   Violence on television is probably not as damaging as time lost in viewing.

We have overcome the first hurdle; the child is now productive and the interview can begin.   It starts by the child saying that he hates his work.

"Why, it has such happy colors," you say.

"It doesn't look like anything."

At this point examine your own reactions to nonobjective art, art in which there is no recognizable subject.   Obviously one has to bring to bear a somewhat different set of values in evaluating it.   Again there has to be something about the picture you like.   Start there.

"How did you make all those little marks?   They look like trees far away."

This may be enough to encourage the child to reexamine the print and to find all kinds of things within the movements of colors and textures.   It may be that you both come to the conclusion that it is satisfying the way it is.   Untouched it will allow the possibility of an unhampered view tomorrow and a fresh experience.

It may be that the decision is made to tie it down to one experience by clarifying the images with paint, pencil, or crayon.

There are pitfalls in this type of situation.   Printing as a physical activity can be a lot of fun.   The end result can and often is a race to see how many can be made.   It takes a certain maturity to place quality above quantity.   Learning to discriminate between what is worth printing and what is not has repercussions outside the field of art.

There is another aspect of this situation that needs consideration.   After the enthusiasm of the first exposure is safely behind you, it is necessary to repeat the experience and reevaluate it.   Too often children make remarks such as, "Oh, we did that in first grade."   This invariably means that the experiences were poorly understood.   Often the child who comes to art in this way achieves very little.   It is as though he views the whole affair as a midway at the fair grounds.   It is fun to try everything once, but who cares to come back tomorrow?   There is no development, growth, or new discovery in his work.   It is possible that the damage was done at the time when the technique was first presented.   The child needs to see his materials and techniques merely as a means of achieving something else.   The answer to "I done it in kindergarten" might well be a flat statement, such as "Great.   You have had some practice, so you will be able to do something special."   It is a wise precaution to presume that the child has no information and little motivation.

After motivation has been provided, using a medium and a technique or some other method, the teacher proceeds to the second of the three ideal stages of art activity.   (The first was motivation, the gentle art of making a child produce in such a way that he is convinced that it was his idea in the first place.)   The second is the activity period where the teacher steps back and is as inobtrusive as possible.   It is a sound notion to refrain from the desire to teach while stage two is in progress.   Quiet observation of what is happening can be an invaluable guide in understanding the child.   Stage three, evaluation, is by far the most difficult. Our lives are filled with activities, very few of which we question or evaluate. Most of us are not very good at evaluating.

In a school with an organizational plan such as the open-school concept the classroom is full of exciting experiences; phases one and two are met in the regular activities as the child experiences and expresses himself in all subject areas. In these situations the evaluation becomes highly individual and very personal to the child.

When evaluation is made by the interview technique described above, the principle of deferred judgment is being put into effect.

Evaluation through Behavior

The behavior of children appears to be closely related to the types of pictures they paint and the manner in which they paint them. The evaluation of art products and behavior can provide clues to the child's problems and his progress in achieving the kind of personal integration needed for aesthetic expression.

Some behavior patterns that show a lack of integration on the part of the child are:[4]

1. The child appears tense or assumes a rigid posture while working.
2. He consistently requests help or seeks approval.
3. He frequently starts over.
4. The child exhibits uncontrollable movement, laughter, or anger.
5. He enjoys destructive play with materials: pounds clay with fists, throws paint on paper, tears paper excessively, etc.
6. He uses attention-getting devices such as talking loudly, pretending innocence, teasing, being exceptionally noisy, or being silly.
7. He wanders about the classroom and cannot seem to get to work.
8. He overpraises or ridicules the work of others.
9. He destroys his own products emphatically or throws them away.
10. He appears to lack imagination.
11. He will not take risks; he has little sense of adventure and appears to fear failure.

4. Adapted from material by Dr. Michael Andrews distributed at a conference at Syracuse University and used with special permission of Dr. Andrews.

12. He starts ideas in several media within a short period and does not finish any of them.
13. He actually seeks escape from the art experience (asks to be excused to go to the toilet or for other reasons, hides in closets).
14. He erases all the lines he draws.

Conversely, the teacher may look for the following clues that frequently indicate growing integration in the child.

An adjusted child exhibits the following characteristics:

1. He finds ideas easily.
2. He acts and talks purposefully.
3. He respects the different expressions of others; he seems interested but not concerned.
4. He has flexible ideas which can easily be altered to suit the medium.
5. He is mildly or not at all disturbed by mistakes. Instead he looks for a way of using the accidental.
6. He is not likely to discard unsuccessful attempts. If he does, his attitude is not destructive.
7. He is relaxed when working, or reveals in bodily movements or facial expression the action or feeling he is expressing in the art medium.
8. He weighs suggestions of others and accepts or rejects them.
9. He knows when he is finished.
10. He is absorbed in his work, and not easily disturbed.
11. He knows what he wants to do next or finds out for himself.
12. He enjoys trying something new.
13. He experiments freely without feeling that he has to finish with a product that others will admire.

Evaluation through Products

Eisner lists criteria for the teacher to use in a general evaluation of a child's products.[5] The authors suggest that these observations be used by the teacher as clues in developing the interview technique to be used with each child-artist.

1. *Technical skill displayed in the art product:* to what extent has the student displayed ability to handle with skill the technical characteristics of the material with which he is working?

2. *The aesthetic and expressive aspects of the work:* to

5. Eisner, *op. cit.*

what extent has the student attended to the organization of form in the work?   How do the forms function?

3. *The creative imagination used in the work:* to what extent does the work display ingenuity?   Has the student used the materials in a fresh way?   Does the work provide a sense of insight?

The art products of problem children appear to have many common qualities that offer clues to the teacher that a child needs particular help in personality integration.   The art products have the following characteristics:[6]

1. Symmetrical balance out of context.
2. Neatness out of context.
3. Lack of spacial organization.
4. Monotony.
5. Lack of experimentation.
6. Lack of evidence of feeling.
7. Imitation of natural forms without organization or personal vision.
8. Imitation of learned symbols and of cartoon characters.
9. Use of subject matter unrelated to experience, lack of identification.
10. Repetition of an idea over a long period of time without change.

The art products of the integrated child also reveal his creativity and his own personal adjustment.

In the art products of such a child we find:

1. Increasing evidence that he is able to integrate media, technique, feeling, spacial organization, and ideas into a unified product.   For instance, when he paints a rough sea he uses rough strokes of the brush.   His style helps to convey the feeling of the painting.   Almost intuitively he seems to be working for perfect integration.
2. A deliberate distortion of such elements as texture, color, line shape, size, or fact to express the feeling or idea of the product effectively.
3. Uniqueness of perception and expression.
4. Personal, emotional identification of the child with the subject matter of his picture.
5. Experimentation and spontaneity in the use of media.
6. Many ideas, both representational and abstract.

6. Andrews, *op. cit.*

Children's art products cannot be evaluated by totalling aesthetic or nonaesthetic elements, but by evaluating their total effect.[7] Some of the contrasts a teacher can look for are overuse of symmetrical balance instead of informal balance and monotonous use of color or line instead of interesting contrast in color and line. However, there is danger in suggesting these guidelines because special effects may be obtained very effectively by the deliberate use of one line. One eleven-year-old painted a picture called *Loneliness,* which was very dramatic because all lines but one were repeated in one monotonous rhythm.

Evaluation through Behavior Changes

The teacher can look for evidence of the following:

1. *The child's perceptions are deepening.* He is becoming increasingly aware of his environment and is reacting to it more fully with all his senses. This can be noted in a multitude of ways, one of which is in his creative products. His paintings, sculpture, craft work, and other art products are a reflection of what he sees and feels about his environment. By comparing these products from month to month the teacher may become aware of the kinds of sensory experiences that she should be offering to each child.

Studying his art products is only one way she can tell about his deepening perceptions. She must listen to him talk and read what he writes. One of the best arguments for making art an integral part of the total curriculum is that the art teacher who comes to the classroom for art periods does not generally have the opportunity to talk about the subjects of the child's painting during the day. A classroom teacher can encourage children to write about their paintings if they wish and can help each child find new words to express himself. She is affording him a verbal as well as a visual way to express his sensitivity.

She can find out, through conversation, the answers to such perceptual questions as, "What do you feel about your painting? Does it make you feel hot or cold or some other way?"

She can find out through observation the answers to such important questions as "Has he learned things about his environment since his last art piece? Has he sensory reactions to his work? What is he thinking while he is working and painting?"

7. *Ibid.*

2. *The child is better able to see relationships.* Helping a child to relate to his environment makes possible his general growth and enhances his ability to express himself through art media. In evaluating the behavior of children, the teacher will be guided by noting how well any particular child relates to his environment.

One of the special techniques mentioned previously in this book for developing creativity is that of forcing relationships: finding a relationship between two seemingly unrelated objects.

A teacher can note how children relate to their other school experiences and their classmates. This is not to say that the most popular children are the most artistic. Often the contrary is true—a child who is very quiet and not very active can be the most artistic in the class.

Observing the depth of a child's perceptions will enable a teacher to determine whether or not the child sees relationships.

3. *The child grows in his ability to conceptualize.* The child's ability to conceptualize is best studied by listening to him talk and by observing his art products. Children who cannot conceptualize are those who do not generalize; that is, they cannot select the common elements from many dissimilar or similar experiences. Lack of the ability to conceptualize can be detected in discussions of words and ideas (the child gives a word such as "hot" limited meanings), in observations of processes (the child repeatedly asks how to make a new color even though he has created colors several times before), and in studying children's paintings and art products (imitation of learned symbols without introduction of new ones, overuse of stereotypes, imitation of natural forms without organization or personal vision, use of subject matter unrelated to experience, excessive repetition of ideas, inability to symbolize).

4. *The child shows growth in his organizational skills.* Organizational skills can be checked (and developed) in areas other than art. How well can a child organize his working materials, his games on the playground, and his free time? The child's paintings show his ability to fill or use space, to balance and contrast, and to get his ideas across.

Saving sample paintings in a folder as suggested on p. 346 will prove to be a help in noting growth over a period of time in all these areas.

TEACHING EVALUATION:
THE DEVELOPMENT OF GOOD TASTE

Aesthetics were discussed on p. 192. How can we evaluate the development of taste, the critical aspect of art production that helps children respond aesthetically to visual art forms? Helping children to develop critical ability means helping them to find words to express their feelings and reactions. We read of one such classroom experience on p. 193. Developing the critical realm of art education means developing a descriptive, effective mode of verbal communication.

Good taste today is by no means the same thing it was in years past. Taste and fashion seem to run hand in hand to extremes. In spite of this, interspersed all through history there are artifacts, customs, and manners that have appealed to all ages regardless of the dictates of fashion.

Art provides the means for the child to examine and develop his aesthetic sensibility. This is not to be construed as a polite nicety; it has much to do with the way the child regards himself and his total environment.

It may be important to dress within the bounds of good taste, but it is even more important to relate to the world around us with sensitivity and good taste. Good taste, it would seem, has its origins in the perceived needs of a society. Good manners are essential to a crowded population, as are good table manners to those who eat close together. Manners have a nasty habit of becoming rigidified. This may mean stagnation in the arts and the dominance of academic traditions, or it may mean a period of revolutionary activity until new standards can be agreed upon.

Good taste far too often means conformity, which is reflected in a decrease in creative potential. The existence of art for art's sake has always contributed to a lively perception of the nature of good taste. In the best sense, the artist is trying to establish a personal identity and yet remain within the bounds of his society. Perceptions of universal values are often made concrete in the arts so that all are able to understand and accept them.

The child is little concerned that his art be in good taste; he is much more concerned with insights and sensitivity. Ultimately these qualities determine the question of taste.

In order to encourage students to judge the art of others, teachers can follow lessons such as the one on p. 193 by discussions of great paintings. This will enable the teacher to determine whether or not children are building a set of values and a set of criteria they can logically rely on when assessing the work of others.

SUMMARY

Evaluation in children's art cannot effectively utilize those forms of evaluation often used to measure children's cognitive learnings, nor can evaluations of art be expressed by a grade. Evaluation in art serves purposes other than those served by evaluation of growth in cognitive areas.

Evaluation in art, like in all creative growth, is best deferred until after the child has finished his work. The total purpose of the evaluation is to help the child to continue to improve in his art expression. Therefore, to be effective, it must be highly personal. It must be done in such a way that the child discovers insights and perceptions in his work and is inspired with ideas for his next work. The interview technique described in this chapter is a strategy for accomplishing this purpose.

Before useful evaluation can take place, a teacher must be aware of the direction of growth in children as described in Chapter 3, so deviations, as well as natural maturational patterns, can be recognized. The teacher needs to know the common growth patterns of children and the unique growth patterns of each individual child in order to evaluate growth in art expression.

Evaluation in art is made by observing the process and the product. A child's lack of integration of the art experience with his total experience will create in him certain behavior patterns that differ from those of children who have well-integrated personalities. A study of the child's art products helps the teacher in identifying children who need particular help in personality integration. Among those qualities that contribute to art development are the child's ability to perceive, his ability to see relationships, his ability to conceptualize, his ability to organize, and his ability to express his reactions to his artwork and the artwork of others.

Evaluation in art is a two-pronged affair. Besides evaluating children's art activity, there is the matter of developing the visual sensibilities of children to the degree that they build aesthetic "tastes." This aspect of evaluation requires the development of descriptive modes of communication and an understanding on the part of the teacher that developing good taste does not mean changing children so that they all like and appreciate the things that she values. It calls for highly objective feelings on the part of the teacher. Tastes change from generation to generation.

Evaluation in terms of behavioral objectives is not always possible in art or creativity because one facet of art is its unpredictability. Passing judgment on any child's art process or his art product is a ticklish affair at best. It must be done with the utmost care and with clear objectives in mind, the prime one being to help the child to grow in his ability to express himself through art.

ACTIVITIES

1. Collect artwork from pre-kindergarten through sixth-grade students and try to determine in which of Lowenfeld's six stages of development the works fall.
2. Identify commonly used stereotypes.
3. Show children some prints, ceramics, found objects, and jewelry. Ask them to rank their choices while pretending to be (a) blind, (b) very rich, (c) artists, (d) very poor, etc. Have them discuss the reasons for their choices.
4. Have children list things that they think of as valuable. Check off the items on this list that they think of as beautiful.
5. Take a common object and evaluate it in terms of form and function. For example, does the shape make for easy handling and pouring?
6. How many things can you think of that have decoration or material added to make them seem more valuable or to give status to the owner?
7. List all the open questions that could be asked of a student who has not been able to come to grips with
   a. spacial concepts
   b. tone
   c. texture
8. List ways in which perception is an integral part of evaluation.
9. Make a collection of art tests. What do they really measure? Also collect some tests of children's creativity (see the Torrance Tests of Creative Thinking). Compare the tests.

What do the creativity tests measure?   Could the creativity tests be used to measure art ability?   Try both tests out on a group of children and plot the correlation in scores.

10. Discussion questions:
   a. In the British open-classroom situation, is it realistic for a teacher to write behavioral objectives in any of the subject areas? Why or why not?
   b. What is behavior?   What does the word behavior mean to the educator, the psychologist, the doctor, the nurse, and the parent?   Could one aspect of the confusion about behavioral objectives be that so many people have so many different definitions of behavior?

SELECTED BIBLIOGRAPHY

Eisner, Elliot. "Evaluating Children's Art." *Concepts in Art and Education.*   George Pappas, ed.   New York: Macmillan Publishing Co., Inc., 1970, pp. 386–390.

Gaitskell, Charles D., and Al Hurwitz.   "Appraising Children's Progress in Art." *Children and Their Art,* 2nd ed.   Charles D. Gaitskell and Al Hurwitz, eds.   New York: Harcourt Brace Jovanovich, Inc., 1970, chap. 18.

INDEX